KU-656-425

Quentin Bell

Virginia Woolf

A Biography

Volume One
Virginia Stephen
1882 – 1912

Triad
Paladin

Published in 1976 by Triad/Paladin
Frogmore, St Albans, Herts AL2 2NF

Triad Paperbacks Ltd is an imprint of
Chatto, Bodley Head and Jonathan Cape Ltd
and its associated companies

First published in Great Britain by The Hogarth Press Ltd 1972
Copyright © 1972 Quentin Bell
Made and printed in Great Britain by Richard Clay (The Chaucer Press) Ltd
Bungay, Suffolk
Set in Monotype Bembo

This book is sold subject to the condition that it shall not, by way of trade
or otherwise, be lent, re-sold, hired out or otherwise circulated without
the publisher's prior consent in any form of binding or cover other than
that in which it is published and without a similar condition including this
condition being imposed on the subsequent purchaser.
This book is published at a net price and is supplied subject to the
Publishers Association Standard Conditions of Sale registered under the
Restrictive Trade Practices Act, 1956

FOR OLIVIER

2086
£1·50

Quentin Bell has been Professor of the History and Theory of Art, Sussex University, since 1967. He is a painter, sculptor, potter, author and art critic. He has held various academic posts such as Lecturer in Art Education, King's College, Newcastle; Professor of Fine Art, University of Leeds; Slade Professor of Fine Art, Oxford University, and Ferens Professor of Fine Art, University of Hull. His works include: *On Human Finery*; *Those Impossible English* (with Helmut Gernsheim); *Roger Montané*; *The Schools of Design*; *Ruskin*; *Victorian Artists*; and *Bloomsbury*.

Also by Quentin Bell

On Human Finery
The Schools of Design
Ruskin
Victorian Artists
Bloomsbury

CONTENTS

ILLUSTRATIONS

FOREWORD

The purpose of the present volume is purely historical; and although I hope that I may assist those who attempt to explain and to assess the writing of Virginia Woolf, I can do so only by presenting facts which hitherto have not been generally known and by providing what will, I hope, be a clear and truthful account of the character and personal development of my subject. In no other way can I contribute to literary criticism. Even if I had the equipment for such a task I should not have the inclination; I have found the work of the biographer sufficiently difficult without adventuring in other directions and indeed the business of gathering and presenting the facts would hardly have been completed without help.

In my next volume I hope to thank all my benefactors, but at the outset there are a few who must be mentioned.

The late Leonard Woolf persuaded me to attempt this work and helped me greatly when I was preparing the first draft of the present volume. The University of Leeds was willing to give me a sabbatical year in which to start my research, the University of Sussex actually gave it. A Leverhulme Research Award enabled me to use my time profitably. Mrs Ian Parsons has been most helpful and kind in every way; my wife has undertaken the arduous task of research assistant and the thankless role of critic. I wish that this book were worthy of their generosity.

O   O   O

In writing this volume I have drawn to a very large extent upon unpublished material. I list here the most important collections, giving an indication of their content and of the abbreviations I have used. I have provided footnotes only when they seem to be of general interest; detailed references to sources will be given in Volume II together with a selective bibliography.

BERG COLLECTION. The New York Public Library, Astor, Lenox and Tilden Foundations; the Henry W. and Albert A. Berg Collection of English and American Literature.

In 1957 Leonard Woolf made an arrangement whereby the 27 manuscript volumes of Virginia Woolf's diaries (1915–1941) would become the property of the Berg Collection after his death. (These diaries are referred to as *AWD(Berg)*; the selection from them published by Leonard Woolf in 1953 as *A Writer's Diary* is abbreviated to *AWD*). The Berg Collection was thus able to become the nucleus of a Virginia Woolf archive and could acquire, both from Leonard Woolf and from other sources, a very considerable quantity of material of biographical and of literary interest. It includes eight early notebook diaries (which are referred to by short descriptive titles followed by (*Berg*)); and, among its collection of autograph letters, four important series from Virginia Stephen/Woolf: to her sister Vanessa Bell, to Violet Dickinson, to Vita Sackville-West, and to Ethel Smyth. For reference purposes I have abbreviated these names to initials, using always the married surnames of Virginia and Vanessa Stephen, viz: *VW* and *VB*.

The building of the Virginia Woolf archive in the Berg Collection was the particular care of the late Dr John Gordan, to whom I owe a debt of gratitude; my correspondence and my meetings with his successor Mrs Lola Szladits has been the most agreeable of necessities.

CHARLESTON PAPERS. King's College, Cambridge.

Letters and other papers of Clive Bell, Vanessa Bell and Duncan Grant, on deposit in the College Library, including the correspondence between Vanessa Bell and Roger Fry. I have used the initials *CB*, *VB*, *DG* and *RF* and the abbreviation *CH* (Charleston Papers) where appropriate.

The care of these documents has I fear added to the heavy burdens carried with such enviable competence, wisdom and good humour by Dr A. N. L. Munby, the Librarian.

MONK'S HOUSE PAPERS. The Estate of the late Leonard Woolf.

The papers which Leonard Woolf made available to me for the purposes of this biography comprise not only a great number of letters to and from his wife and himself, but also a considerable quantity of manuscripts. These I have loosely divided into manuscripts with a biographical interest (MH/A) and manuscripts of mainly literary interest (MH/B), and numbered.

I have also been able, through the kindness of his executrix, to make use of Leonard Woolf's own laconic but trustworthy diaries.

FOREWORD

There remain in the possession of the heirs and descendants of Sir Leslie Stephen the following sources of information which relate to Virginia Woolf and her family:

The 'Mausoleum Book' (*MBk*), written by Leslie Stephen after the death of his wife Julia in 1895.

Old family letters chiefly to or from Mrs Leslie Stephen and her children.

Two binders containing copies of the *Hyde Park Gate News* (*HPGN*) for 1891, 1892 and 1895.

Six manuscript memoirs by Vanessa Bell (*VB/MS I–VI*).

Letters from Virginia Woolf to Clive, Julian and Quentin Bell.

Minutes of the Play Reading Society, 1908–9 and 1914–15.

I am grateful to my sister Mrs David Garnett and my cousins Mrs Richard Synge and Mrs Nigel Henderson for their willingness to allow me to quote from these documents.

In addition I have consulted material in the possession of Mr Mark Arnold-Forster, Mrs Barbara Bagenal, the Marquess of Bath, the British Broadcasting Corporation, Mr Duncan Grant, Harvard University (the Houghton Library), Lord Kennet, Mr Nigel Nicolson, Mrs James Strachey, Professor John Waterlow and Mr David Garnett, whose copy of Adrian Stephen's diary I have been able to use; I cannot trace the original. To all these I am indebted for their help and consideration and for permission to quote where I have wished to do so.

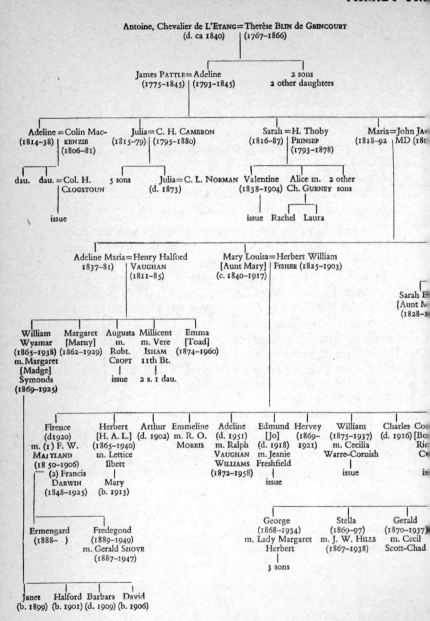

Antoine, Chevalier de L'ETANG = Thérèse BLIN de GRINCOURT
(d. ca 1840) | (1767–1866)

James PATTLE = Adeline   2 sons
(1775–1845) | (1793–1845)   2 other daughters

Adeline = Colin Mac-   Julia = C. H. CAMERON   Sarah = H. Thoby   Maria = John Ja
(1814–38) | KENZIE   (1815–79) | (1795–1880)   (1816–87) | PRINSEP   (1818–92 | MD (18
    (1806–81)   (1793–1878)

dau.   dau. = Col. H.   5 sons   Julia = C. L. NORMAN   Valentine   Alice m.   2 other
      CLOGSTOUN   (d. 1873)   (1838–1904)   Ch. GURNEY   sons

issue   issue   Rachel   Laura

Adeline Maria = Henry Halford   Mary Louisa = Herbert William
1837–81) | VAUGHAN   [Aunt Mary] | FISHER (1825–1903)
      (1811–85)   (c. 1840–1917)

Sarah E
[Aunt M
(1828–

William   Margaret   Augusta   Millicent   Emma
Wyamar   [Marny]   m.   m. Vere   [Toad]
(1865–1938) (1862–1929) Robt.   ISHAM   (1874–1960)
m. Margaret   CROFT   11th Bt.
[Madge]
Symonds   issue   2 s. 1 dau.
(1869–1925)

Flrence   Herbert   Arthur   Emmeline   Adeline   Edmund   Hervey   William   Charles Co
(d1920)   [H. A. L.]   (d. 1902)   m. R. O.   (d. 1951)   [Jo]   (1869–   (1875–1937)   (d. 1916) [Bo
m. (1) F. W.   (1865–1940)   MORRIS   m. Ralph   (d. 1918)   1921)   m. Cecilia   Ri
MAITLAND   m. Lettice   VAUGHAN   m. Jeanie   Warre-Cornish   C
(18 50–1906)   Ilbert   WILLIAMS   Freshfield
   (2) Francis   (1872–1958)   issue   is
     DARWIN   Mary   issue
     (1848–1925)   (b. 1913)

                                  George   Stella   Gerald
                                  (1868–1934)   (1869–97)   (1870–1937
Ermengard   Fredegond   m. Lady Margaret   m. J. W. HILLS   m. Cecil
(1888–)   (1889–1949)   Herbert   (1867–1938)   Scott-Chad
       m. Gerald SHOVE
       (1887–1947)   3 sons

Janet   Halford   Barbara   David
(b. 1899) (b. 1901) (d. 1909) (b. 1906)

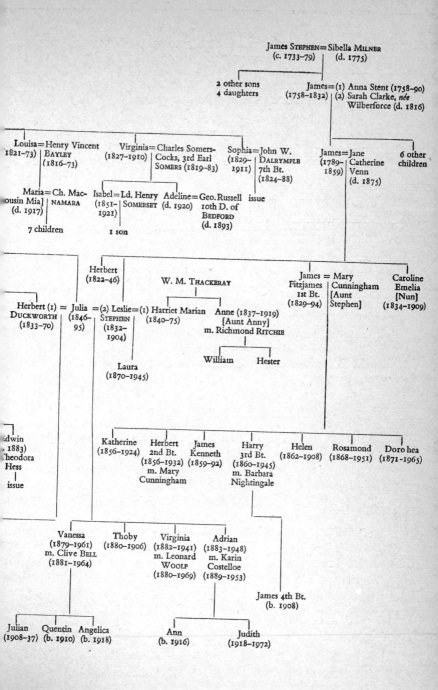

Chapter One

1882

VIRGINIA Woolf was a Miss Stephen. The Stephens emerge from obscurity in the middle of the eighteenth century. They were farmers, merchants and receivers of contraband goods in Aberdeenshire. Of James Stephen of Ardenbraught practically nothing is known save that he died about 1750, leaving seven sons and two daughters. Following the tradition of their race most of the sons wandered abroad to seek their fortunes. One, William Stephen, settled in the West Indies and prospered in the unpleasant trade of buying sickly slaves and then curing them sufficiently to make them fit for the market. Another, James, trained as a lawyer, became a merchant and was shipwrecked on the Dorset coast. A man of Herculean stature, he saved himself and four companions by the aid of his own exertions and a keg of brandy. It was dark, a tempest was raging; but they scaled a seemingly impossible precipice where "a cat could hardly have been expected to get up" and found themselves upon the Isle of Purbeck. Here James was first succoured and then entertained by Mr Milner, the Collector of Customs; he managed matters so well that he was able to secure not only much of the cargo of the vessel, but also the heart of Miss Sibella Milner, whom he secretly married.

The married life of Mr and Mrs James Stephen was not fortunate. He failed in business, fell into debt and presently found himself in the King's Bench Prison. In this predicament James Stephen reacted in a manner which was to set an example to his descendants. He took up his pen and argued his case. He was (so far as I know) the first of the Stephens to write a book and from that time on there was scarcely a one who did not publish and never, certainly, a generation which did not add something to the literary achievements of the family.

James Stephen also started a family tradition by carrying his argument to the courts. In fact, he went further and organised an agitation in the prison which nearly ended in an insurrection.

Imprisonment for debt was, he declared, a barbarous thing and moreover a thing repugnant to the spirit of the common law, to

Magna Carta, to statute law, justice, humanity and policy. These were things worth saying, but so far as he was concerned they had no practical effect and, in the end, he owed his release to his creditor. Stephen's legal and political battles had convinced him that his talents lay in the direction of advocacy rather than of commerce. He entered the Middle Temple, but the British Themis, who was to welcome so many of his descendants, rejected him. His protests had made him too many enemies and he was debarred by reason of his "want of birth, want of fortune, want of education and want of temper."

But there was a back door to the legal profession and by this Stephen made his entry. He became the partner of a solicitor under whose name he could carry on his business. It was not, however, a business which could bring him much credit. His clients were of a dubious kind. His work was done in public houses; it brought him little reputation and less money. His poor wife. who believed that these misfortunes were sent by the Almighty to punish her for having consented to a secret marriage, died in 1775. He followed her four years later. He was only forty-six; he left six children and about enough money to pay his debts.

James, the second of these six children, whom we may for convenience call "Master James," is the one who most concerns us. Brought up in an atmosphere of penury and litigation, he proved very much his father's son. He too was a writer of pamphlets and a pleader of causes; but whereas his father had been concerned with his own affairs, Master James used his argumentative talents for greater purposes. In the interests of patriotism and humanity he was to champion the cause of freedom and to start a war between two great nations.

His first campaign, however, was very much in the parental tradition. With little formal education James made his way to, entered, and despite ill-health pursued his studies at the Marischal College, Aberdeen. He read what was then called Natural Philosophy (i.e. science) and not without success; but he then found his way barred by an examination which was conducted in Latin. In this he knew that he would inevitably be failed and, what was even worse, be made to look ridiculous (he was a very sensitive man).

What then was to be done? It may be thought an extraordinary thing that a youth of seventeen should have the boldness to conceive, and the dexterity to accomplish, a plan for covering his own defects, and saving his credit, by innovating on the established practice of an antient University. Yet this I conceived and effected.

In other words he had the regulations changed to suit his needs.

The passage here quoted is from the *Memoirs of James Stephen* written by himself for the use of his children. It is an interesting document made more entertaining by a certain vein of complacency in the author. Stephen felt able to congratulate himself on this and other triumphs, on the exertions which enabled him to surmount very serious disabilities and yet become a Member of Parliament, a Master in Chancery and a very respected member of society, because he could ascribe the glory of the business to a Higher Power.

God answered his prayers, God watched over his interests, God guided his footsteps. There are moments when the relationship between James Stephen and his Maker seems almost conspiratorial. He put his trust in Providence with such perfect simplicity that, while paying his addresses to one young woman, he got another with child. Nor was this confidence misplaced. Between them they managed matters in the most satisfactory way. He married the one and the other found a husband. Their bastard son became a most respectable clergyman.

As a public man Master James became identified with two great causes. Both resulted from a sojourn in the West Indies. Here there was already a family connection begun by his uncle William; here Stephen practised as a lawyer and here he saw how easily the British blockade was being broken by French and American traders. He who, in his youth, had been a zealous partisan of George Washington, was indignant. He was moved to write a pamphlet entitled *War in Disguise*, a pamphlet which resulted in the Orders in Council, the Continental Blockade and, much to Stephen's chagrin and astonishment, the War of 1812.

But, from his first arrival in the Western Hemisphere, James had been dedicated to another and nobler cause. He first realised the infamy of slavery when he saw how monstrously a Negro might be treated by the West Indian Courts. Having once perceived the iniquity of the thing he made himself a restless and consistent friend of the oppressed. On his return to England he became the trusted ally of Wilberforce, whose widowed sister he married after his first wife's death. In the House of Commons, when he was not defending the Orders in Council, he was attacking slavery; it was the refusal of the Government to act on this question which led to his withdrawal from Parliament.

There was, in the neighbourhood of Clapham, a group of friends: prosperous and worthy men marked by a certain decent godliness, a fair degree of wealth, an ardent concern for the enlightenment of the heathen and the liberation of the slave. Amongst them were Charles Grant and Zachary Macaulay, John and Henry Thornton, John Shore (later Lord Teignmouth), Granville Sharp, William Wilberforce, John and Henry Venn—respectively rector and curate of Clapham; these were the so-called 'saints' of the Clapham Sect. James was drawn to this evangelical society not so much by his religious views—although he certainly took the spiritual colour of his surroundings—as by his political opinions. But in general the Clapham Sect was concerned with works rather than with faith, with policies rather than with parties. The abolition, first of the slave trade, and then of slavery itself, was its grand motive. It was therefore compelled to fight for its beliefs at the hustings and in the House of Commons. Its leaders were not divines but politically conscious members of the middle classes, men therefore who knew that, to attain their ends, they must collaborate with persons whose humanitarianism had a different origin than theirs. Tories and Anglicans, they found themselves allied to Radicals, to Quakers and to the followers of Bentham—men who in other connections were their antagonists—while Pitt, the intimate friend and political ally of Wilberforce, had sometimes to be their enemy. In the great work of committee-making, pamphlet-writing and public agitation these sincere, eloquent and influential men had, therefore, to learn the political lessons of tolerance and compromise. Thus the Christianity of Stephen and his Clapham friends, ardent though it was, never attained the dogmatic certainty, the super-mundane, persecuting passion of some other sects.

The Clapham Evangelicals must have felt themselves to be, as indeed they were, the conscience of the British middle classes and therefore an enormous political power. For this reason, if for no other, they were concerned above all with moral questions and when, in later generations, the eschatological superstructure of their faith collapsed, the moral fabric remained. This persistence of the moral, as opposed to the theological, element in the beliefs of their great grand-parents was to have a very important effect upon a later generation.

Master James died in 1832, just before the final abolition of slavery in the British Empire. His legitimate sons all became lawyers; it was indeed a decidedly forensic family. The third son, yet another James, must have shown considerable talent at the Bar (they all did), for he was soon earning £3,000 a year—a very handsome income in those days. He moved, sacrificing much of his income, to a permanent position in the Colonial Office. His reason for doing this was clear enough. It was as an administrator that he could best carry on the great family campaign against slavery. He was known in Whitehall as 'Mr Over-Secretary Stephen,' for he was not simply one of those civil servants who gently but firmly override the wishes of those ministers who, nominally, are set above them. He was a civil servant with a policy; in fact it was more than a policy, it was a mission, which had to be imposed, willy-nilly, upon the Colonial Office, the Colonies themselves and whatever Government happened to be in power.

That policy was, of course, the policy of Emancipation, for although other matters, such as the grant of self-government to Canada, occupied some of his time, the protection of the Negro was the grand business of his administration. To oppose, to delay, to nullify and to thwart that policy was the aim of the Colonies themselves, by which, of course, I mean the ruling white minority in the Colonies. The colonists, as always, were ably assisted by influential friends in London. These had to be outwitted, argued down, browbeaten, and Mr Over-Secretary Stephen was the man to do it.

Sir James Stephen, as he eventually became, was a courageous, intelligent and capable administrator. He was also, as he himself admitted, anything but a simple man. He inherited all the boldness of his father and his grandfather; he was formidable and implacable, driving others almost as hard as he drove himself, working long hours in the Colonial Office and making others work equally hard, still finding time for numerous contributions to the *Edinburgh Review*, dictating 3,000 words before breakfast. A monster of industry and learning, he was also a vulnerable and an unhappy man. His achievement fell far short of his ideals. He was blamed for measures that he had opposed as well as for those which he had favoured; he felt such criticism deeply, all the more so because, as a civil servant, he could not reply to it. He was desperately shy, he was intensely pessimistic. He was so convinced of his own personal ugliness that he would not have a mirror in his room. He would shut his eyes rather than face an interlocutor. He wished he had been a clergyman, a recluse, anything but what he was. He was terrified of being comfortable and although he would not deny pleasure to others he was anxious to deny himself. Once he tasted a cigar and liked it so much that he resolved never to taste another. It occurred to him that he liked taking snuff–immediately he emptied his snuff box out of the window.

"Did you ever know your father do a thing because it was pleasant?" asked Lady Stephen of her son Fitzjames. "Yes, once, when he married you" was the prompt reply of yet another brilliantly argumentative Stephen.

But James Stephen's marriage was not simply pleasant—it was in the highest degree prudent. In marrying Jane Catherine Venn, Stephen allied himself completely with Clapham, for the Venns were, so to speak, at the very heart of the Sect. The Venns had always been clergymen; they receded in an unbroken succession of pastors to that time at which it first became respectable to have a priest as an ancestor; their connection with Clapham Rectory was a long one, and it was Jane Venn's grandfather's *Compleat Duty of Man* which provided the Clapham doctrine, if one may here speak of a doctrine.

It might be supposed that the daughter of an evangelical parsonage would hardly be the person to discourage Stephen's natural inclination to gloom and to self-mortification. But the Saints of Clapham were not in favour of immoderate austerities and the Venns, in particular, were a cheerful commonsensical race who loved to crack a joke and saw no harm in innocent pleasures. There was something a little mad in Stephen's self-mortification; Jane Catherine Venn was as sane a woman as ever breathed. She was also a handsome, amiable person with a strong disposition to look always on the happiest side of any matter. She provided her husband with a home in which he could forget the agonies of public life. It was, by modern standards, rigidly puritanical; their children were to go neither to balls nor to theatres—but neither might they condemn those who enjoyed such amusements; it was for them a sober but a happy place, lightened by the benevolence of their father and by their mother's laughter.

One thing more must be said about the household of Sir James Stephen. It respected art, by which I mean literary art (painting and music were, I surmise, neglected). Lady Stephen admired Cowper and Wordsworth, Scott and Campbell. Sir James turned to more serious and more edifying writers, but he could also appreciate Voltaire and Montaigne; his friends, who were not numerous, included J. S. Mill, the Venns, the Diceys, the Garratts, a serious and enlightened company.

Sir James had five children—one died in infancy, one in early manhood; but the other three survived and were to be of importance to the children of the next generation. They were: James Fitzjames, Caroline Emelia and Leslie, the father of Virginia.

Caroline Emelia will reappear in this story; she was an intelligent woman who fell, nevertheless, into the role of the imbecile Victorian female. She fell in love with a student and had some reason to suppose that her affection was returned; but the young man never declared his feelings. He went to India and nothing more was heard of him. Her heart was broken and her health was ruined; at the age of twenty-three she settled down to become an invalid and an old maid. She lost her faith and set herself with great diligence to find another; after a number of experiments she discovered a congenial spiritual home in the Society of Friends.

Fitzjames, one may guess, smiled grimly at his sister's life of passive suffering and equable gentleness; but he would probably have allowed that a life devoted to religion and philanthropy was not unsuitable for a woman. He himself was, most emphatically, a man. His life had therefore to be more positive, more aggressive, more brutal. When he and Leslie went as day boys to Eton they were horribly bullied. He was ashamed of this always, for he felt that he had not resisted persecution stoutly enough. However, this humiliating acknowledgement of the superior strength of others came to an end at last. Fitzjames grew to be a big broad-shouldered fellow known to his playmates as 'Giant Grim' and well able to give blow for blow with anyone. He had, he said, learnt that "to be weak is to be wretched, that the state of nature is a state of War and *Vae Victis* the great law of Nature."

His younger brother, Leslie, was a nervous, delicate boy, his mother's darling, fond of and over-excited by poetry, too sensitive to be able to endure an unhappy ending to a story. At school he needed all the protection that Fitzjames could give him and thus I see them: the tough, self-reliant, no-nonsense Fitzjames, shouldering his way through the horrors of a British public school with a frightened, delicate junior in tow. At Cambridge too, it was Fitzjames who led the way, who became known in the Union as the 'British Lion,' a roaring, crushing, rampageous debater, packing a cruel punch in argument, chosen for the brightness of his intellect and his manifest intellectual integrity as a member of that arch-intellectual society, 'The Apostles,' while Leslie, altogether gentler, more diffident, less brilliant, was never an Apostle and never emerged from the main rank of undergraduates.

It must have been clear to everyone that the elder brother would make a name for himself, would be called to the Bar, would become a judge and a baronet – as indeed he did; while Leslie would become a clergyman and sink gently into decent obscurity – as he might have done. All his life Leslie was, I think, matching himself against his all too admirable sibling. Fitzjames was physically strong; he too would make himself strong. Like Fitzjames he would walk for miles; but he would do more, he would run, he would row, he would scale mountains, and in fact he became, as he, in his self-deprecating way, put it 'wiry.' He was in fact a famous walker, an oarsman, a coach of oarsmen, one of the great mountaineers of the nineteenth century. In the same way he adopted, I think, some of Fitzjames's robust habits of thought. He became half a philistine, almost anti-intellectual. He followed Bentham and J. S. Mill; he was "Broad Church," unsentimental and manly.

His nephews and nieces remembered Fitzjames in his later years as a powerful, bulky figure sternly buttoned into a frock coat conducting Lady Stephen to church every Sunday morning, there to pay his respects to a being in whom he had ceased to believe.

"He has lost all hope of Paradise," declared the irreverent young, "but he clings to the wider hope of eternal damnation."

This was unjust; but it was true that, to him, evil seems to have been a much more real thing than goodness. His constant pre-occupation was with the vices that menaced society; he had no use for optimism, cant, gush, enthusiasm or—as it sometimes appears—for compassion. The engines of repression were to be ruthlessly employed; justice, though it must be administered with scrupulous fairness, demanded that punishments should be inflicted in a spirit of righteous vengeance. For all his scepticism he accepted the morality of his age with few reservations. He is as far from the genial libertinism of the eighteenth century as he is from its frivolity.

The same could be said of Leslie; the younger brother had the milder temper and the warmer heart; but this did not prevent him from sharing the same inhibitions and the same indignations or, it should be added, from displaying the same courageous intellectual integrity.

While Fitzjames went to London, the Bar and journalism, Leslie gained a Fellowship at Trinity Hall. At that time it was still necessary for a Fellow of Oxford or Cambridge to take Holy Orders. Leslie was ordained in 1859 and thereby committed to a set of propositions in which he did not really believe. It is indeed hard, in this sort of context, to know what we are to understand by the word 'belief.' It is difficult to imagine Leslie, at any period of his adult life, praying for rain in a drought or for fine weather during a wet spell, solemnly uttering the words:

> O Almighty Lord God, who for the sin of man didst once drown all the world, except eight persons, and afterwards of thy great mercy didst promise never to destroy it so again. . . .

It was in fact at this point that Leslie stuck. The year was 1862, he was thirty, he had become convinced that 'Noah's Flood was a fiction' and that it was wrong for him to read the story as if it were sacred truth.

He had never been a zealot; he had preached the gospels as they were understood by F. D. Maurice and the Broad Church party, that is, in a spirit of reverential scepticism, and it would have been easy for him, as for so many others, to have paddled around Noah's Flood and never to have taken the plunge. Leslie had the courage to act resolutely in accordance with his convictions. He had a comfortable job at Cambridge but it involved telling what he now saw to be lies and this he refused to do.

At the same time it is possible that his loss of faith may have had unconscious motives. He had originally become a university teacher in order not to be a burden on his father; this involved, not only a profession of faith, but–for some years at all events–a celibate existence. After his father's death in 1859 he slowly realised, firstly that he was the most irreligious, then that he was the most uxorious of men. Gradually he discovered how much he longed for the outer world, how little he really had believed and how glad he was, now that his father could no longer be hurt by the avowal, to make his disbeliefs public.

To leave the security of Cambridge was a hazardous thing and he was, as he himself said, of a rather anxious temperament (this was an understatement); but he took the risk with an untroubled gaiety which in later life astonished him, and came to London without money or prospects.*

In London, however, Fitzjames was ready to help him. Leslie was soon making a small but reputable name for himself in the Republic of Letters. He began as a journalist and an apologist for the Federal Cause in America, a cause which had few friends in this country. His sympathy for the Union led to a visit to the United States, to an interview with Lincoln and, more importantly, to a life-long friendship with James Russell Lowell, Charles Eliot Norton and Oliver Wendell Holmes. His politics were radical, very much inspired by his friend Fawcett; they were not, however, his main interest. He tended more and more towards philosophical speculation and literary criticism.

* *MBk*, p. 4. There is a passage in this work which can be construed in such a way as to suggest that an adventure of the heart altered the course of his life and diverted him from the celibacy and religion of Cambridge, to London, matrimony and agnosticism. But this is guesswork.

VIRGINIA WOOLF

In 1882 he began, at the invitation of George Smith the publisher, to make one of the world's greatest instruments of scholarship: the *Dictionary of National Biography*; it is as the editor of that dictionary, as a literary critic and as an historian, that he is most gratefully remembered. He himself would rather have been remembered as a philosopher. His views were, to some extent, distorted by a morality which, though not as fierce as that of Fitzjames, was as narrow and as intolerant. It did not prevent him, however, from saying true, wise and amusing things about books and writers, or from taking a view of the world which is essentially honest, responsible and sane. Leslie Stephen's reputation has endured. Like Fitzjames he knew how to write a good forceful English, but there is more of intimacy, of delicacy, of humour and even of fantasy in the work of Leslie. In short he was more of an artist.

In the twenty years that followed Leslie's loss of faith he found himself as a writer and a thinker; he also found himself in another way. As we have seen, the escape from Cambridge was also an escape from the cloister; and although it took him some years to find a wife, when he at length did so he discovered that he was, in truth, a very domestic character. The wife whom he found was Harriet Marian, the younger daughter of Thackeray. She and Leslie fell in love and, after a rather awkward moment of hesitation and hanging back on his part, they were married.

We do not know much about the first Mrs Leslie Stephen. Her husband describes her as being neither very beautiful nor very clever; her nature was one of "quiet love"; she was amiable, gentle, simple with the simplicity of a child. Almost, one might guess from his account, a little dull, or at all events too childlike. And yet some of her letters have been preserved and from these it is evident that she had a sense of fun and was by no means deficient either in character or in intellectual curiosity. She seems, in fact, to have been a very proper wife for a highly intelligent man.

Certainly they were happy together, although their marriage encountered difficulties of a rather unusual kind. Until she found a husband the person whom Minny Thackeray loved best in the world was her sister Anny. In marrying the one sister Leslie discovered that he had, in a sense, married them both.

Now Anny was a more formidable, a more arresting personality than Minny. She was a novelist; her novels were tenuous, charming productions in which the narrative tended to get lost and in which something of her own vague, erratic, engaging personality is preserved. Minny considered that her sister was a genius; in this I suspect that she was mistaken, but she was a very talented person and one of her talents was for teasing. When Samuel Butler was at work upon *Shakespeare's Sonnets Rediscovered*, Anny bewildered him by remarking: "Oh Mr Butler, do you know my theory about the Sonnets – that they were written by Anne Hathaway?" Butler never realised that the joke was at his expense; he used to tell the story sadly shaking his head and exclaiming: "Poor lady, poor lady, that *was* a silly thing to say."*

At the age of seventy Aunt Anny, as she was called by all Leslie's children, could impress a child by her extraordinarily youthful, vigorous and resilient optimism; when she was young, not only in spirit but in years, her ebullience must have been overwhelming. It is not hard to believe that such cheerful impetuosity could sometimes be exasperating. Leslie found it so; he loved silence and she was for ever talking; he loved order, and she rejoiced in chaos; he prided himself on his realism, she was unashamedly sentimental; he worried about money, she was recklessly extravagant; he prized facts, she was hardly aware of them.†

> She and I had our little contentions. I had a perhaps rather pedantic mania for correcting her flights of imagination and checking her exuberant impulses. A[nny] and M[inny] used to call me the cold bath from my habit of drenching Anny's little schemes and fancies with chilling criticism.

But they were more seriously divided by the fact that between them there was a kind of undeclared war for possession of Minny. War is perhaps too strong a word, for the three were bound by strong ties of affection, and yet it was a sort of contest, a contest which lasted for several years until it began to turn decisively in Leslie's favour. For in time Minny came to the conclusion that her husband meant more to her than even her beloved sister. Perhaps she felt, as other women were to feel, how greatly Leslie depended upon her. At all events the marriage was eminently successful; it had been enriched by a daughter, Laura, born in 1870, and presently Minny was again pregnant. On the evening of 27 November 1875 she went to bed feeling slightly unwell. During the night Leslie was called to her.

* Samuel Butler published *The Authoress of the Odyssey* in 1897. The story is recalled in *Night and Day* (p. 322); Mrs Hilbery in this novel is a pretty straight portrait of Aunt Anny. See also: Mary MacCarthy, *A Nineteenth-Century Childhood*, 1924, p. 89, and Hester Thackeray Fuller and Violet Hammersley, *Thackeray's Daughter*, Dublin, 1951, p. 7.

† "There are 40,000,000 unmarried women in London alone!" she once informed him. "Oh Anny, Anny!" See VW, *Collected Essays*, vol. IV, p. 77 (*Leslie Stephen*).

I got up and found my darling in a convulsion. I fetched the doctor. I remember only too clearly the details of what followed; but I will not set them down. My darling never regained consciousness. She died about the middle of the day, 28 November, my 43ᵈ birthday.

Leslie was shattered, heartbroken, and desolated. Anny, it is true, remained to take care of him and his daughter, but here a further blow was preparing. Laura was no longer a baby and it had already been evident to her mother that she was a backward child. In this period of bereavement it became increasingly obvious that she was not simply backward; there was something seriously wrong. Leslie began to suspect that Mrs Thackeray's madness had been inherited by her granddaughter. How bad her case might be it was too soon to tell; but clearly she would require special treatment. This domestic agony served to increase the tension between Leslie and Anny; Louise, the nurse, set herself against Anny's authority and Leslie took her side. The scenes which, while Minny was alive, had been held in check became more frequent and more painful.

And then, rather surprisingly, Anny fell in love with young Richmond Ritchie, her cousin, her godson and her junior by seventeen years. He returned her affection and the flirtation, which had been treated as nonsense, suddenly became the real thing. Leslie found Anny and Richmond kissing each other in the drawing room and insisted that they should either marry or part. Although the marriage turned out well, Leslie hated the whole business; he was, as he realised, jealous; the quasi-maternal situation of the bride also aroused feelings in him the nature of which he may not have understood, and of course he lost his housekeeper.

Anny's place was for a time taken by Leslie's sister; but if Anny had been too resilient a companion, Caroline Emelia was altogether too flaccid.

Now Milly has loved me all her life; she has been much more like a twin than a younger sister; . . . Yet, as I found myself saying at this time, she was too like me to be helpful. If I put an argument in order to have it contradicted, she took it so seriously that I thought there must be something in it; if I was in doubt, she fell into utter perplexity; if I was sad, she began to weep–a performance which always came too easily to her. Consequently though a most affectionate she was a most depressing companion. And then, the society which suited me would have struck her as worldly; while her friends, though very worthy & some of them very clever people, struck me as intolerably dull.

The plan was tried and needless to say it failed. Milly's health broke down almost at once and Leslie began to look for a professional housekeeper. The Huxleys recommended a Fraülein Klappert who had been a governess in their household. But there was another solution, one that Leslie had had in mind for some time and which was considerably more to his taste.

On the evening of 27 November, 1875, a few hours before Minny fell into those convulsions which were the prelude to her death, the Stephens had been visited by a close friend of the Thackeray sisters, Mrs Herbert Duckworth, a young widow. Feeling her own chronic grief as a kind of intrusion upon their happiness – for they still had a few hours of happiness – she had soon withdrawn to her own sad home. For her, after her husband's death in 1870, "all life seemed a shipwreck." Though left with three children, George, Stella and Gerald (a posthumous son), her despair was complete. But if she could no longer be happy she could at least be useful: she might comfort the afflicted and nurse the sick (in the 1870s her own relations seemed to sicken and to die in rather large numbers). She had, one might say, renounced the world, or at least she had renounced the happiness of the world, although this renunciation could hardly be called mystical, one of the consequences of her bereavement being a permanent loss of faith. It was this perhaps which enabled her to moderate her awe of Leslie Stephen the intellectual with a sympathetic interest in him as a man. After Minny's death it was almost a matter of course that she should comfort him, mediate between him and her own friend Anny, reproach him when he was unreasonable, and listen to his grievances with the affectionate patience of a sister. Between them there grew up a close friendship, but it was at once understood that it was to remain fraternal; each had a requiem candle to burn before the altar of the dead.

It is unnecessary to describe the process which led to Leslie's sudden *éclaircissement*, a revelation vouchsafed to him just outside Knightsbridge Barracks when he said to himself "I am in love with Julia!" and knew that he might again be happy, nor yet his gradual passage from the consciousness to the declaration of passion and hers from a kind, sad, but completely unqualified rejection, not so much of him, as of marriage, love, and happiness itself, to the faint adumbration of a tentative surrender. For at last, after much debate, she did find herself in a situation in which she was at least ready to contemplate the proposition that life might yet offer certain possibilities of felicity.

In the end it was Fraülein Klappert who settled the business. Both Leslie and Julia felt that her installation would bring about a definitive arrangement, setting the seal, as it were, upon their separation. There was, at all events, enough finality in the proposal to make Julia Duckworth aware of her own feelings; she realised that she could not break with Leslie. They were married on 26 March 1878.

O O O

I must now attempt to say something about Virginia's mother's family. Here there is a good deal of uncertainty, of legend, and of scandal.

According to Virginia's cousin H. A. L. Fisher, the historian, there was at the Court of Versailles during the last years of the old régime a certain Chevalier Antoine de l'Etang; his person was pleasing, his manners courtly, his tastes extravagant and his horsemanship admirable. He was attached to the household of Marie Antoinette—too much attached it is said, and for this he was exiled to Pondicherry where, in 1788, he married a Mlle Blin de Grincourt.

M de l'Etang entered and died in the service of the Nawab of Oudh; he left three daughters. Adeline, the one with whom we are concerned, married a James Pattle who was, we are told, a quite extravagantly wicked man. He was known as the greatest liar in India; he drank himself to death; he was packed off home in a cask of spirits, which cask, exploding, ejected his unbottled corpse before his widow's eyes, drove her out of her wits, set the ship on fire and left it stranded in the Hooghly.

The story has been told many times. Some parts of it may be true. It is certainly true that Mrs Pattle came to London in 1840 with a bevy of daughters and that these ladies had a reputation for beauty. Four of them should be mentioned in these pages: Virginia, Sarah, Julia and Maria.

Virginia Pattle, the most beautiful of the sisters, married Charles Somers-Cocks and became Countess Somers; she was a dashing, wordly woman, impulsive, rather eccentric, who lived in great style. Of her daughters, one became Duchess of Bedford; the other, Isabel, married Lord Henry Somerset. This alliance, though grand, was by no means happy. Lord Henry, a charming man it seems, delighted Victorian drawing rooms with his ballads. He was, I believe, the author of *One More Passionate Kiss;* this embrace was reserved however, not for his beautiful wife but for the second footman. Lady Henry endured his infidelities for a time but presently she could stand no more. She confided in her mother who, allowing her indignation to master her prudence, made a public scandal. The sequel is interesting in as much as it gives a notion of the ethos of the Victorian age and of a system of morality which Virginia Woolf and her contemporaries were to encounter and to oppose.

Lord Henry fled to Italy and there, in that land of Michelangelesque young men, lived happily ever after. His wife discovered that she had been guilty of an unformulated, but very heinous, crime: her name was connected with a scandal. Good society would have nothing more to do with her. She was obliged to retire from the world and decided to devote herself to the reclamation of inebriate women, a task which she undertook with so much good sense and good humour that she won the affection and admiration, not only of men of charity and good will, but even of the women she assisted.

Sarah Pattle made her empire in a less fashionable but more interesting part of the world. She married Thoby Prinsep, an Anglo-Indian administrator of some eminence who was, until its dissolution, a member of the Council of the East India Company. The Prinseps settled outside London in an old farm-house, Little Holland House, in what is now Melbury Road, Kensington; it was a pretty, rambling, comfortable sort of place and here, while her sister collected the aristocracy of birth, she entertained the aristocracy of intellect. Tennyson, Sir Henry Taylor, Thackeray and his daughters, William Allingham, Tom Hughes, Mr Gladstone, and Disraeli were *habitués*. They were able, at Little Holland House, to enjoy a respite from the formality, the regularity and the stuffiness of mid-Victorian society. Their hostess was both charming and eccentric. Meals were oddly timed and oddly disposed. There was something outlandishly charming, something free and easy about Little Holland House and to this ambience the painters must have made an important contribution. Chief amongst them was G. F. Watts; he was, for many years, a resident, Mrs Prinsep having 'taken him up' and established him in a studio. Holman Hunt, Burne-Jones and Woolner were very frequent visitors and so it would seem was Ruskin.*

But perhaps the most remarkable of the artists who frequented Little Holland House was Julia Margaret Cameron, the second of the Pattle sisters, the least beautiful but the most gifted. Like Sarah,

---

* Ruskin refers to Mrs Prinsep and her sister (probably Lady Somers) as "two, certainly, of the most beautiful women in a grand sense – (Elgin marbles with dark eyes) – that you could find in modern life . . ." The former he regarded as an old friend. See *The Winnington Letters of John Ruskin*, ed. Van Akin Burd, London, 1969, p. 149 (Ruskin to Margaret Bell, 3–4 April 1859; this letter contains a lively picture of an evening at Little Holland House).

Julia had married an Indian Civilian, like her she had a passion for artists and men of letters. It has been said of her that "she doubled the generosity of the most generous of her sisters, and the impulsiveness of the most impulsive. If they were enthusiastic, she was so twice over; if they were persuasive, she was invincible."

The inhabitants of Putney saw her—and we may justly envy them—talking and walking in flowing red velvet towards the Railway Station; in one hand a cup of tea, in the other a teaspoon, by her side an embarrassed friend who attempts, vainly, to decline the gift of a priceless Cashmere shawl. They saw in her an eccentric; we see in her an immortal, not one of the great immortals, but still an artist who has survived and will survive.

Not that she would ever have achieved immortality if, when she was fifty, her daughter had not given her a camera. She began at once to take photographs. It became her passion, her vocation. Beautiful women and distinguished men were obliged, for she was of an imperious nature, to sit for the long poses that were then necessary. Her friends and servants were disguised as angels and Arthurian heroes, they were draped, garlanded, muffled and photographed. A family legend persisted according to which Tennyson and Mr Gladstone were posed under a tree and forbidden to move while she sought some necessary implement of her mystery. While searching she was distracted by some other project and left the poet and the statesman immobile for two hours beneath a shower of rain.

Vague, silly and sentimental, Mrs Cameron had, nevertheless, a streak of pure genius. She needed a curb or a brake, something that would restrain her sentimentality. In her letters and, no doubt, in her unfinished novel she was unbridled—it was Sir Henry Taylor's nightmare that he would one day have to read that novel. But the nature of her art, an art which after all deals with facts, supplied a check; there were indeed occasions when she could find her way past fact to fancy with disastrous results but, when called upon to give the likeness of a sitter her disposition of forms, her choice of pose, her Venetian understanding of chiaroscuro, are miraculously subtle and strong and she does the kind of thing that Watts might have done had he been a greater artist. She is the best of the Victorian portraitists and has given us a worthy monument of the society in which she lived—a milieu, to quote Ellen Terry, "where only beautiful things were allowed to come."

Hither Maria Jackson, the fourth of the Pattle sisters, brought her three daughters, Adeline, Mary and Julia. Maria had married yet another Anglo-Indian, Dr Jackson; he had a flourishing practice in

Calcutta but he does not seem to have been a person of any distinction. In his wife's letters, at all events, he cuts practically no figure at all. It was her daughters who interested her; she loved them all, but principally, I think, Julia; or at least Julia, because she was so unhappy and because she devoted herself so much to her mother, became in the end her mother's dearest child. To her she wrote, once, twice, sometimes three times a day and often there would be an additional telegram for her "dear heart, her lamb." Her grand topic was health, or rather maladies; she was not a doctor's wife for nothing. When, after her first husband's death, Julia became a kind of unofficial nurse, she reported symptoms to her mother who, with great assurance, diagnosed and recommended treatment. When there was not a sister, a niece, a cousin, a grandchild to fill her page with medical details, she had an unfailing store of her own afflictions: she suffered from headaches, rheumatism, giddiness and indigestion, which she treated with morphia and chloral. Second only to the question of how to preserve health was the question of beauty, and here too she was full of excellent advice. Only very rarely is one reminded, in all the voluminous correspondence between Mrs Jackson and her daughter, of the aesthetic and intellectual interests of Little Holland House. Reading her one feels as though one were struggling through a wilderness of treacle. Mrs Jackson was as good as gold; but there is not one original thought, very little common-sense and not the slightest dexterity in the use of language in all her hundreds and hundreds of letters.

Mrs Jackson's letters display the dull side of the Pattles; their silliness, their gush, their cloying sweetness, their continual demands for affection and with it a mawkish vein, a kind of tender gloating over disease and death. Of the recipient I have already said a little. Julia was perhaps the most beautiful of Mrs Jackson's daughters, the one most intimately connected with the Little Holland House circle. Her effect upon the Pre-Raphaelites was notable; it was said that she could have married either Holman Hunt or Woolner; in an age of crinoline she was 'aesthetically' draped; Burne-Jones used her as a model and I think that the 'Burne-Jones type' owes something to her profile.

Mrs Jackson used to say that every man who met her fell in love with her. Mrs Jackson was a goose; but there may be a certain measure of truth in this and it is perhaps because everyone was in love with her that she is so elusive a subject. Both her husband and her daughter attempted to describe her. Leslie Stephen has drawn the portrait of a saint and because she is a saint one cannot quite believe in her. He speaks of her beauty and here his accuracy is attested by her aunt Cameron's many photographs; he speaks of her goodness and certainly she was a good woman; he admits that some people found her stern and noticed that sorrow had left something of gravity in her which time could not eradicate; but it is from other sources that we know that although she could be playful and gay with her children she could also be severe and that, although she looked like a saint, her wit could be almost shocking. Mrs Ramsay in *To the Lighthouse*, although she is drawn only from a child's memories, seems to me more real and more convincing than Leslie's portrait. All the loveliness, the tenderness is there; but Mrs Ramsay is not perfect; neither she, nor the woman in the Cameron photographs, was so 'pure' as the lady whom Leslie imagined to be unaware of her own beauty. Mrs Ramsay's relationship with her husband is not entirely saintly; she is ever so slightly critical; she is capable of mockery. She is, as Leslie himself noticed, a matchmaker but, as he did not notice, not always a wise one; there is a trace of self-assurance, a little blindness in her management of other people's affairs. In short Virginia's portrait of her mother is more human, more fallible, perhaps more likeable than that painted by Leslie.

Julia certainly did not lack courage. When she married Leslie he was a middle-aged widower without much money; between them they had four children and one of the children was insane. To this family they added a fifth in 1879, a girl, whom, since she had a half-sister named Stella, they called Vanessa.* In the following year a son was born who was named after his great-uncle Thoby. Here they decided to bring their family to a halt.

But contraception was a very imperfect art in the nineteenth century; less than eighteen months later, another daughter was born. She was named Adeline Virginia.

◯   ◯   ◯

As soon as she was able to consider such things, Virginia believed that she was the heiress to two very different and in fact opposed traditions; indeed she went further and held that these two rival streams dashed together and flowed confused but not harmonised in her blood. The Stephens she saw as a very definable race. In the nursery it was believed that all Stephens were born with little tails seven inches long, but discounting this tradition (which was, I

* Leslie's study of Swift was published in 1882; he may already have been at work on it when he gave what was then a very unusual name to his daughter.

believe, invented to annoy Virginia's Stephen cousins) it will I hope be clear that they had a very marked pattern of behaviour. They were all writers; they all had some gift, some pleasure in the use of the English language. But they wrote like men who are used to presenting an argument, who want to make that argument plain but forcible; seeing in literature a means rather than an end.

Their minds are formed to receive facts and when once they have a fact so clearly stated that they can take it in their hands, turn it this way and that, and scrutinise it, they are content; with facts, facts of this kind, they can make useful constructions, political, juridical or theological. But for intuitions, for the melody of a song, the mood of a picture, they have little use. There is therefore a whole part of human experience of which they fight shy, in which they confess themselves frankly at a loss, as Leslie did at Little Holland House, or which they dismiss as sentimental humbug.

The Stephens were bold, as advocates have to be bold. They had plenty of moral, physical and mental audacity. James the debtor insulting Lord Mansfield or scaling the rocks of the Dorset coast in a tempest, James the Master remaking the regulations of an ancient university, Sir James browbeating ministers, Leslie defying God upon the escarpments of the Matterhorn, are bold figures and, like most bold figures, they are capable of brutality; but they were not insensitive–no, certainly they were not insensitive. James the Master in Chancery was a troubled and compassionate man deeply worried by his inability to speak Latin; Sir James, his son, was very obviously neurotic; Leslie, like Fitzjames, built a façade of stern commonsensicality and behind it sheltered a quivering bundle of vulnerable feelings. The very strength of the Stephens was rooted in weakness; the prodigious capacity for hard work, the ability to take risks, the athletic feats were but the sorties of a garrison that has no walls.

The Pattles were an altogether less intellectual race than the Stephens; they had no aptitude for words, they are chiefly remembered for their faces. So far as the records go–and we can now look at five generations–it seems that a certain kind of beauty appears and reappears, sometimes vaguely, sometimes strikingly reincarnated from avatar to avatar. This type lies dormant in the men of the family to re-emerge in their daughters, those daughters who have delighted successive generations of artists. It is the painters who have most admired these women. It is hard to look at their features without admiration; they were magnificently formed, grave, noble, majestic, but neither vivacious nor very approachable. Their beauty suggests, and is sometimes associated with, a certain moral grandeur, a certain monumentality of character. They were not bluestockings; we shall not find amongst them the great pioneers of female emancipation, and in this they differ from families which in other respects were close to them, as for instance the Stracheys and the Darwins.

But even the vague benevolence, the woolly-minded silliness, the poetic gush, the cloying, infuriating sentimentality that one finds in Maria Jackson can somehow be lifted out of folly into poetry and to something like genius in the case of Mrs Cameron.

Here then were the two sides of Virginia's inheritance, an inheritance which was, at all events, real enough in her imagination. It is not hard to find labels for the paternal and maternal sides: sense and sensibility, prose and poetry, literature and art, or, more simply, masculine and feminine. All such labels are unsatisfactory but they suggest something that is true.

To this it is necessary to add a further distinction. Julia and her family were, socially, a little better than the Stephens. Both Julia and Leslie belonged to the upper middle classes but within those classes there were many fine shades of difference. Julia's first husband was certainly a much better *parti* than Leslie; he came from a family in Somerset so long established that, despite its commercial origin, it counted as landed gentry; their children were given the name de l'Etang; Julia herself had aristocratic connections which were sufficiently impressive; the Duchess of Bedford was her first cousin. Among her sisters, cousins, uncles, and aunts family feeling was strong; they relied, in a very aristocratic fashion, upon influence and patronage. When one of Julia's relations did make a really disastrous *mésalliance* the young couple were firmly but kindly removed to the colonies.

The Stephens on the other hand had but recently escaped from the lower middle class. James the debtor was an unsuccessful foreign adventurer, his son although not a political hack had done political hackwork and was socially insecure. Sir James was the first to establish them securely in the professional classes; but his children had neither the money nor the influence of the Prinseps, the Camerons or the Duckworths. Their achievements had been founded upon intellect and initiative, their dignities had been won in courts of law and their family pride was the pride of the *noblesse de robe*.

Considered collectively Mr and Mrs Leslie Stephen belonged to what one might call the lower division of the upper middle class. (Speaking academically I should place them on the margin between an upper and a lower second.) They kept seven maid-servants but no man-servant. They might sometimes travel in a cab but kept no carriage; when they went by rail they travelled third class. The ladies had their clothes made by a reasonably good dressmaker. Leslie was a member of the Athenaeum and of course of the Alpine Club. Despite their grand relations they did not venture into what was called 'high society;' in fact they lived very quietly, although Julia had her 'Sunday Afternoons' when a visitor might encounter a part of the intellectual society of London. Their house was in a respectable part of town.

It was taken for granted that the boys would go to public schools and then to Cambridge. As for the girls, they would, in a decorous way, become accomplished and then marry.

Chapter Two

1882–1895

VIRGINIA was born on 25 January 1882, at No 22 Hyde Park
Gate. The house still stands and bears her father's name. It had
five storeys and to these the Stephens added two further storeys
of atrocious design. It is a tall dark house with a fairly large back
garden.

At the top of this house were two nurseries inhabited by the children of Leslie's second marriage. Laura, Minny's child, lived apart
until she was sent to a "Home" and eventually to an asylum in York.*
George, Gerald and Stella were well past the nursery stage when
Virginia first knew them; thus the nursery was a unit of four
members: Vanessa, Thoby and Virginia being joined by Adrian,
who was born in 1883, and they were not divided by any great
difference in age.

In one respect Virginia was an unusual child; it took her a very
long time to learn to talk properly; she did not do so until she was
three years old. Her sister, and no doubt her parents, were very
worried. In appearance she was, like Vanessa, remarkably pretty;
a plump, round-faced child with the eyelids and the mouth of a
Buddhist carving, deeply sculpted but exquisitely smooth. She had
rosy cheeks and green eyes–thus her sister remembered her, im-
patiently drumming on the nursery table for a breakfast that she
had not yet learnt to call for in words.

Words, when they came, were to be then, and for the rest of her
life, her chosen weapons. I say weapons, for in that nursery there
was both love and conflict. Vanessa, although but a year older than
Thoby, was almost maternal in her care of him, shielding him from
harm, sacrificing herself for his benefit and loving him tenderly.
He, from the first, learnt to take such ministrations for granted and
to be, if not spoiled, outrageously favoured. Already, when he was
quite small, he was described as a stalwart, determined, masterful
little boy; he would be yet another Stephen, not a delicate nervous
Stephen like his father but a jolly rumbustious extrovert like his
uncle Fitzjames, while Vanessa it seemed would be a thorough

* Where she died in 1945

Pattle. Thus these two made an excellent pair in the nursery; the girl delighted to give, the boy to receive.

Virginia, inevitably, turned this symmetrical pattern of reciprocal affection into a triangle. The arrival of Adrian did not result in a re-formation of the original pattern; for Virginia tended to cling to the older children and was in fact as much devoted to Thoby as was Vanessa. Thoby was so much more obviously admirable, whereas Adrian was delicate and doleful and tiny. Thus the two girls must in some measure have competed for Thoby's favour.

Despite this latent and, it would appear, unconscious rivalry, the two sisters were from the first, and for as long as they lived, passionately fond of each other. But their mutual admiration was felt, or at least expressed, in rather different and very characteristic ways. Vanessa, while perceiving Virginia's precocious brilliance, her cleverness and her command of language, was bowled over, above all, by her sheer beauty. "She reminded me always of a sweet pea of a special flame colour." Virginia, while conscious of Vanessa's loveliness, valued above all her sister's calm honesty, her grave assumption of responsibility for the younger ones, her quiet unceasing benevolence, her practicality and her good sense. Also, from a very early age, she understood something of the magic of friendship, the peculiar intimacy which comes to those who have had private languages and private jokes, who have played in the twilight amidst the grown-up legs and skirts under the table. She not only loved her sister but, it would seem, loved the affectionate relationship between them. Thus, for the elder, appearances were always the most fascinating things in the world, or at least, when she loved, love presented itself to her in a visible form. For the younger, the charm of sisterly love lay simply in the intimate communication with another being, the enjoyment of character. From the first it was settled between them that Vanessa was to be a painter and Virginia a writer.

There was of course a good deal of skirmishing in the nursery; it is of interest, not so much because it happened–no nursery, surely, is complete without it–but because of the manner in which hostilities were conducted. Vanessa and Thoby were unoriginal in their tactics; they yelled and hurled abuse and on occasion, no doubt, came to blows; sometimes, when the provocation was gross enough, they would 'tell tales.' Virginia used her nails* and, at a very early

---

* "Miss Virginia, aged 2½, scratches her brother, aged 4. I insist upon and ultimately obtain an apology or kiss. She looks very thoughtful for some time and then says, Papa, why have we got nails? There is a bit of infantile teleology

age, discovered that she could torment her sister by scratching a distempered wall—a thing which set poor Vanessa's teeth dreadfully on edge; but later on she learnt to use her tongue and this was far worse; she called Vanessa 'The Saint'; it was the *mot injuste*, it stuck and even the grown-ups smiled and joined in the sarcasm, to which no adequate retort seemed possible.

But it was not by words alone that Virginia could vent her displeasure. Then, as always, she knew how to "create an atmosphere," an atmosphere of thunderous and oppressive gloom, a winter of discontent. It was done without words; somehow her brothers and sisters were made to feel that she had raised a cloud above their heads from which, at any moment, the fires of heaven might burst, and here again it was hard to find any reply.

And yet, there was a reply. Those who can thrust a rapier into their adversary's psyche know how it is done because they themselves are vulnerable. This at all events was true of Virginia. There was some technique for making her turn 'purple with rage.' What it was we do not know; but Thoby and Vanessa knew and there were terrible occasions when she did turn a colour which her sister described as "the most lovely flaming red." It would be interesting to know how this was done, still more interesting to know whether, as Vanessa surmised, these paroxysms were not wholly painful to Virginia herself.

From the first she was felt to be incalculable, eccentric and prone to accidents. She could say things that made the grown-ups laugh with her; she did things which made the nursery laugh at her. Is it to this, or to a rather later period, that we can ascribe an incident in Kensington Gardens when, not for the last time by any means, she lost, or at least lost control of, her knickers? She retired into a bush and there, in order to divert public attention, she sang *The Last Rose of Summer* at the top of her voice. It was this and similar misadventures which earned her, in the nursery, the title of "The Goat" or more simply "Goat," a name which stuck to her for many years.

None of the children were baptised. Leslie would have considered such a performance ridiculous and indeed profane, but they had godparents of a kind: "persons in a quasi-sponsorial relationship." Vanessa, Thoby and Adrian appear to have been provided with prosaic and unrewarding sponsors. But Virginia's godfather was James Russell Lowell, who celebrated her birth with the gift of a

---

for you. I replied: To scratch Froudes (not exactly in those terms)." Leslie Stephen to C. E. Norton, 23 December 1884. (I am indebted to Professor John Bicknell for calling my attention to this letter.)

silver cup and some indifferent verses and to whom she wrote a
letter when she was six years old. It is the earliest document in her
hand.

MY DEAR GODPAPA HAVE YOU BEEN TO THE ADIRONDACKS
AND HAVE YOU SEEN LOTS OF WILD BEASTS AND A LOT OF
BIRDS IN THEIR NESTS   YOU ARE A NAUGHTY MAN NOT TO
COME HERE   GOOD BYE YOUR AFFECT[B] VIRGINIA.

Naturally amiable and, as the children later came to believe, more
than half in love with their mother, Lowell was open to such
persuasions. When he was Ambassador to the Court of St James he
frequently visited 22 Hyde Park Gate and, when he was replaced
by President Cleveland's nominee, he continued to pay summer
visits to England. From a ring chain purse he would produce
threepenny bits for each child; but for Virginia there was always
a sixpence. This was distinction enough, but nursery jealousy
knew no bounds when he gave her a real live bird in a cage. Undoubtedly, in the competition for godparents, Virginia had won
hands down.

The children slept in the night nursery at the top of the house and
there, from quite an early age, Virginia became the family story-
teller. When the lights had been extinguished, all save that which
came from the dying coal fire, she would begin her tale. There was one
involving the Dilke family next door which continued from night
to night beginning always with Vanessa's invocation: "Clementé,
dear child . . ." - this said in a very affected drawl - and then Virginia
becoming Clementé would begin: gold would be discovered beneath
the nursery floor and this treasure trove would purchase enormous
meals of bacon and eggs, the favourite diet of the young at 22 Hyde
Park Gate; and so it went on, a mounting fantasy becoming grander
and vaguer, until Clementé slept and her audience had to wait until
the following night for her next adventure.

In this cosy propinquity, not only stories but diseases were shared
by all. In the Spring of 1888 the children were attacked by whooping
cough. They were very ill, lost a lot of weight and were sent off to
Bath to convalesce. Soon they all made a complete recovery-all
save Virginia. When they returned she was no longer so round and
so rosy as she had been. She was marked, very gently but still
perceptibly, by that thin, fine, angular elegance which she kept
all her life. Nor was this all; at the age of six she had become a
rather different kind of person, more thoughtful and more specu-
lative.

One evening, jumping about naked in the bathroom, she shocked and startled her elder sister by asking her which of her parents she liked best. Vanessa was appalled that such a question could be put; but she replied at once, for she was a very honest and forthright girl, that she thought she loved her mother best. Virginia, after much delay and deliberation, decided that she preferred her father. This odd little exchange seemed, to Vanessa, to mark the transformation in her. From now on conversations between the sisters became more thoughtful and more serious.

Whether this intellectual revolution resulted from her illness it is impossible to say. But one may fairly guess that it had nothing to do with Virginia's formal education. Leslie and Julia had decided, whether from motives of economy or from a belief in their own pedagogic attainments, to educate their children themselves. That is to say that the boys would have their elementary teaching and the girls the main part of their schooling at home. There were indeed governesses, both Swiss and French (including one who was thrown under a table by Vanessa and Thoby), but the main part of the teaching seems to have been done by Julia and Leslie.

Before Virginia was seven, Julia was trying to teach her Latin, history and French, while Leslie took the children in mathematics; he had previously taught George and Gerald and certainly believed that he had some gift for instruction; he had even attempted, pathetically enough, to make an intelligence for his poor mad Laura. But, a wrangler himself, he was quite unable to perceive the difficulties that a small child encounters when faced by a simple calculation; naturally he lost his temper. The only one of his children who had aptitude enough to learn any mathematics from him was Thoby. Vanessa's arithmetic was always rudimentary and Virginia continued throughout her life to count on her fingers. Neither was Julia a good teacher. In dealing with her own children she had a hasty temper. Virginia may have learnt some Latin from her, but she was never fluent in any modern language and her history, like her sister's spoken French, was learnt later in life. The foreign nurses and governesses invariably learnt English from the children and gave no language in return.

The best lessons were probably given out of school hours. When he was not teaching, Leslie could be an enchanting father; he had a talent for drawing with which he delighted his children; he could cover sheets with pencilled animals or cut creatures out of paper with magical precision. He could tell stories of dizzy alpine adventures, sometimes he would recite poetry and in the evenings he might read aloud, often from the novels of Sir Walter Scott, and call on his children to discuss what they had heard.*

There were other sources of enlightenment. Thoby returned home from his first school – Evelyns – and in an odd shy way – walking up and down stairs as he talked – told Virginia about the Greeks, about Troy and Hector and a whole new world which captured her imagination. Perhaps it was then that she decided that one day, like Thoby, she would learn Greek; and perhaps it was then that she realised that the Greeks belonged to Thoby in a way that they didn't belong to her, that they formed a part of the great male province of education – this I think was how she saw it – from which she and Vanessa were to be excluded.

The acquisition of female accomplishments was not much compensation. Drawing, dancing, music and graceful deportment had to be learnt – or at least they had to be taught. Drawing was a success: Mr Ebenezer Cook, who taught Vanessa, was a remarkable man; but the other teachers were unsympathetic. Neither of the girls was musical, neither loved the music teacher who expected her pupils to attain such deftness that they could play a scale with a sixpence on their knuckles – the sixpence would be a reward for this feat and was once contemptuously, humiliatingly, given to Vanessa when she had failed.†

Singing was better; but here Virginia disgraced herself. She discovered that the music mistress, Miss Mills, a well-known practitioner of the tonic sol-fa system, was intensely religious; in answer to a question about the meaning of Christmas, Virginia replied that it was to celebrate the Crucifixion, and then exploded in such peals of laughter that she had to be removed from the room. They were taught riding and 'graceful deportment' and there were dancing classes; these were conducted by the then celebrated Mrs Wordsworth. She wore black satin and a glass eye and she carried a stick. At her command all the little girls jumped up and down, as though in a frenzy; the Miss Stephens voted the thing a bore and retired whenever they dared to long sessions in the lavatory. But the piano lessons were the worst, they were a torment second only to that final horror, the visits to the dentist, on which occasions the

* "At the end of a volume my father always gravely asked our opinion as to its merits, and we were required to say which of the characters we liked best and why. I can remember his indignation when one of us preferred the hero to the far more life-like villain." VW in F. W. Maitland, *The Life and Letters of Leslie Stephen*, 1906, p. 474.

† The incident is remembered in *The Waves*, p. 47.

girls tossed up to decide which should go in first; the loser would have a further hour of dreadful anticipation in the waiting-room.

But, when their interests were engaged, the sisters were ready to undertake their own education. Vanessa, having obtained a copy of *The Elements of Drawing*, set herself painfully to perform the tasks which Ruskin enjoins, and Virginia remembered her slowly and carefully filling rectangles with perfectly regular hatching in the manner prescribed in *Exercise Number Seven*. Virginia produced a newspaper. It was not, at first, a single-handed venture, for Thoby was a partner in the enterprise; but much of the time he was at a boarding school, and gradually the thing fell into her hands almost entirely. It is perhaps significant that the paper carried very few illustrations; they would have been Vanessa's concern; but she was too shy to exhibit her work. Virginia also had her diffidence, but it was weaker than her longing for publication. The *Hyde Park Gate News* started in 1891* and, so far as we can tell, it appeared weekly until April 1895. Thus, when the first number appeared Virginia was just nine years old. Like other children she enjoyed playing at being grown up, but whereas they usually do so with the aid of hats, skirts, trousers and umbrellas, she played the game with words and phrases; half giggling at her own audacity, half seriously, she apes the grandest journalistic style. When a son returns home and meets his brother she celebrates the occasion thus:

> How sweet it was to see him bend down with eyes expressing worlds of joy! (O how much can eyes express!) and kiss the rosy frontispiece turned up to him.

Or again, the Stephen children adopted a stray dog which, having fouled the carpets beyond bearing, was sent to the Lost Dogs' Home and there refused admittance:

> So the boy turned him lose to wander at his own sweet will "Like a drop searching for it's fellow traveller in the vast ocean". Nothing more has as yet been heard of him.

The *Hyde Park Gate News* was read by the grown-ups, certainly by Leslie and Julia and perhaps by others; Mrs Jackson took an interest in it. Virginia was able to watch her public reacting to her prose. This was made possible by the position of a cheerful little room at the back of the house at Hyde Park Gate; this room was made almost

* The first number that we have is dated 6 April 1891, and as this is the 9th in a weekly series we may assume that the first issue was on 9 February 1891. The series continues with gaps until 19 December 1892 after which no more files exist until 7 January 1895.

entirely of glass, it had a skylight and big glass windows facing the garden. Here the sisters would sit together and Virginia would read aloud from Charlotte M. Yonge–they kept a score of the number of deaths in those very necrological novels–and later, Thackeray, George Eliot, and indeed most of the Victorian novelists. And from this room the girls could see into the large double drawing-room. Vanessa would put the latest number of the *News* on her mother's sofa while her parents were at dinner. Then there was an interval of suspense.

Virginia was always enormously sensitive to criticism and, when her parents came into the drawing-room, her excitement became almost unbearable. For a time the paper would lie unnoticed; then at last Julia would pick it up and begin to read. Would there be any spoken comment? That was the awful question; and when, calmly but distinctly, Julia observed to Leslie: "Rather clever, I think," the authoress was, for a time, in heaven.

With such a public it is not surprising that the policy of the journal was, from a parental point of view, impeccable. *An Article on Chekiness* roundly declares that:

Young children should be nipped in the bud of cheekiness otherwise impertinance which when the child increases in years it grows into audacity. It is then indeed a great hinderance to mankind. . . .

But this, I suspect, was written by Thoby. Virginia's devotion to the cause of discipline was qualified. It does not prevent her from being, in her own way, audacious.

Miss Millicent Vaughan [Virginia's cousin] has honoured the family of Stephen with her company. Miss Vaughan has like a dutiful sister been to Canada to see her long absent sister who is residing there. We hope that no pangs of jealousy crossed her mind when she saw her sister so comfortably settled with a husband when she herself is searching the wide world in quest of matrimony. But we are wandering from our point like so many old people. She came on Monday and is still at 22 Hyde Park Gate.

Did *she*, one would like to know, read the family newspaper?

Then there was General Beadle, 'the prince of talkers.' Enough is preserved of his sovereign talk to show that, at the age of nine, Virginia knew a bore when she met one.

The *Hyde Park Gate News* also contains some first efforts at fiction; but they are not as amusing as the news items. *The Midnight Ride* (signed A. V. S.) is her first extant story. In 1927 she noted that she could make up situations but, she adds: "I cannot make up plots." This is certainly true of *The Midnight Ride*. Here she contrives a situation in which a boy will have to ride at midnight through a dangerous North American bog to see his brother, who lies ill at school. Having sent him off she loses interest in the adventure and the story folds up in the tamest fashion. A series of letters from imaginary people is more successful. They are love letters written in the belief that all adult love-making is, in itself, funny. ". . . you have jilted me most shamefully," writes Mr John Harley to Miss Clara Dimsdale; who replies: "As I never kept your love-letters you can't have them back. I therefore return the stamps which you sent."

There is also some fun in *A Cockney's Farming Experiences*, a serial inspired by the adventures of Mr Briggs in *Punch*; *Punch* was a strong influence on these early productions.

One returns to the news and tries to deduce a picture of the Stephen family. The first thing that strikes the modern reader is the great number of people who made up a household in those days. In addition to the eight children there were seven servants, of whom the chief was always Sophy, the cook and the family treasure. Dogs play an important part in their lives and seem to have been far more ferocious then than now; there are also rats, bugs and relations, in particular the Fishers, the Duckworths, the Vaughans, the Stephens, Mrs Jackson, Lady Somers, the Duchess of Bedford. There are a few distinguished names: Meredith, Burne-Jones, Walter Headlam–but these are rather distant figures.

The usual joys and calamities of family life are recorded: lamps flare, pipes burst, children fall ill, brothers go off to school, there are visits to the circus and the zoo; but the grand event of the year is the summer exodus to Cornwall. It was in 1881, the year before Virginia's birth, that Leslie, on one of his many walking tours, discovered St Ives, "at the very toenail", as he put it, "of England." In the following year he took a house, Talland House, on the high ground above the bay, and thither the family went every summer. St Ives must, therefore, have been one of Virginia's earliest memories.

That day [Wednesday, 11 May 1892] is stamped deeply in the minds of the juveniles for two things. The first was ices and the second was that Madame Mao who we may as well inform our readers is the Stephens' instructress in the art of music was to come twice a week!!! But this blow was very much softened by the fact that the Stephens were going to St Ives very much earlier than usual. This is a heavenly prospect to the minds of the juveniles who adore St Ives and revel in its numerous delights. . . .

The annual promise and recollection of St Ives made London, by comparison, a poor place and the excursions to Brighton to see Mrs Jackson (she died in April 1892) or the Vaughans and the Fisher cousins (who were not popular) were no substitute. It was better to wander in Kensington Gardens, which had then a certain wildness; here Vanessa and Virginia would lie in the grass and consume three-pennyworth of Fry's chocolate and a copy of *Tit-Bits*, their favourite journal, to which Virginia sent an early effort at fiction which, needless to say, was not published. At some earlier period, wandering in the long grass which lay between the Round Pond and the Flower Walk, the children were delighted to discover the abandoned corpse of a small black dog. But even this was small compensation for seeing the Spring and the Summer go by in London streets. St Ives was the only real country and the children longed for it.

I have a lively image, although it is based upon very slender evidence, of that family exodus: Mr and Mrs Stephen, the girls, Adrian (Thoby might come later from school), Stella and perhaps her brothers, Sophy the cook, Ellen the parlour maid, a Swiss governess and all their luggage in surely not less than two four-wheelers, the children bubbling with excitement as they made their way to Paddington Station to catch, let us say, the 10.15 (the 9 o'clock train was impossibly bad, stopping at every conceivable little station). And then the long journey, starting in high spirits as the *Cornish Express* bustled from Paddington to Bristol, reaching Temple Meads at 12.45; here there was an opportunity to get a luncheon basket unless, of course, they had their own sandwiches; then followed the long, hot, sticky and increasingly quarrelsome journey, nature relieved into a chamber pot, papers, books, the *Strand Magazine* crumpled and discarded on seats, an interminable hot afternoon. It was nearly 4 o'clock when the train drew into Plymouth and thereafter its conduct was hesitant and dilatory. They went by way of Truro, arriving at St Erth at a quarter to seven, which gave the travellers exactly six minutes to get themselves and their belongings onto the little branch-line train to St Ives. By now, however, lassitude would have been replaced by excitement; the children had seen the ocean at Hayle, after which the train travels along the coast, skirting Carbis Bay until it reaches the terminus at St Ives just after seven.

It was a summer evening, and there were still hours of daylight. Talland House was not far from the Station; one might almost run there. There stood the hedge of escallonia by the gate and beyond it was the garden, all up and down the slope with a galaxy of little lawns and shrubberies and private places; there was the cricket pitch, where 'small cricket' was played all through the afternoon and so late into the evening that the ball had to be covered with luminous paint that they might continue, and beyond it the sea. And that first night of the holiday, they would hear the sound of the waves breaking on the shore and know that for weeks and weeks it would be theirs.

On Saturday morning Master Hilary Hunt and Master Basil Smith came up to Talland House and asked Master Thoby and Miss Virginia Stephen to accompany them to the light-house as Freeman the boatman said that there was a perfect tide and wind for going there. Master Adrian Stephen was much disappointed at not being allowed to go.

Thus the *Hyde Park Gate News* for 12 September 1892, and the literary historian may, if he so wishes, find in this report what Henry James calls the *donné* of one of Virginia's most celebrated works. The point is not one that can be proved; but certainly St Ives provided a treasury of reminiscent gold from which Virginia drew again and again; we find it not only in *To the Lighthouse*, but in *Jacob's Room* and, I think, in *The Waves*. For her, Cornwall was the Eden of her youth, an unforgettable paradise, and she was always grateful to her parents for having fixed on that spot. She was to love other places, but for Cornish people and Cornish things she had a kind of patriotic emotion; they seemed to be made of some particularly fine matter which made them more romantic and more distinguished than the products of any other soil.

Family life at St Ives was rather shabby and casual; Talland House was untidy and overrun with people. For in addition to the family there were guests: cousins, uncles, nephews and nieces in great quantities; Meredith, who used to sit under a tree reading his poetry to Julia and Mrs Jackson, Lowell, Henry James, and a number of obscurer characters who had failed or had yet to make a name for themselves, as, for instance, Mr Wolstenholme, known to the children as 'The Woolly One.' He had been a brilliant mathematician but his opinions and his life had made Cambridge impossible; he had married disastrously and came to Talland House to get away from his wife; he spiced his mathematics with opium.*

And there were younger people, those whom Virginia described as the tyrants and demi-gods of their childish world: their half-brothers Gerald and George who went to Eton and Cambridge; their

* It seems probable that Virginia had him in mind when she described Mr Carmichael in *To the Lighthouse*.

half-sister Stella, who grew up to a world where one 'came out'; Jack Hills, a young solicitor who came in pursuit of Stella, Kitty Lushington, an old friend and the daughter of an old friend – it was under the jackmanii in the garden of Talland House that she agreed to marry another of the younger guests, Leo Maxse. All of these were to play an important part in Virginia's life; more important, perhaps, than the friends of her own age, for although they met a good many other children – there were tea-parties and picnics and such like junketings – in retrospect it seemed to Virginia that "us four," as they called themselves, formed a rather isolated group. We may suppose that their more private and more juvenile amusements, as for instance their funeral ceremonies for birds and mice, were family affairs. Cricket, on the other hand, was more adult, more public and more social. Indeed it was on the cricket ground during the summer of 1893 that Virginia first knew a boy who was later to become interesting to her – though he was then only six – for Dick and Rupert Brooke were zealous participants in the daily games at Talland House. Cricket was played with enthusiasm, and Virginia was considered a formidable bowler.* Leslie's favourite exercise was walking; he would sometimes go for what he called "a potter," covering thirty miles or so. His children were also expected to be pedestrians and their father encouraged them to botanise as they walked; but botany never went very far; they preferred what they called "bug hunting." This was an occupation that was begun unofficially and then, with the help of Jack Hills, put on a regular footing with all the proper apparatus of nets, collecting boxes, setting boards, killing bottles, cabinets and works of reference. The Stephen children collected butterflies and moths for many years, in fact until they were quite grown up.

As blood sports go, the killing of lepidoptera has a good deal to recommend it: it can offend only the most squeamish of humanitarians; it involves all the passion and skill of the naturalist, the charm of summer excursions and sudden exhilarating pursuits, the satisfaction of filling gaps in the collection, the careful study of text books, and, above all, the mysterious pleasure of staying up late, and walking softly through the night to where a rag, soaked in rum and treacle, has attracted dozens of slugs, crawly-bobs and, perhaps, some great lamp-eyed, tipsy, extravagantly gaudy moth. This again was

* "Gin can bowl a good deal better than some of the chaps who came this term." Thoby to Adrian and Virginia c. 1891. ". . . the demon bowler as she was called by her brothers in the nursery . . ." George Rylands in *Portrait of Virginia Woolf*, BBC Home Service, 29 August 1956.

something that Virginia never forgot and to which she returns affectionately in her writings.

But it was the sea that made the splendour of their holidays. The sea invited them to sailing, to fishing and to bathing. Bathing indeed was something in which the whole family was involved. William Fisher, their cousin, who taught the children to make a paddle boat and was known as 'The Admiral'—which indeed he was in all seriousness to become, remembered his aunt Julia bobbing about in the water in a large black hat. The most dramatic sport and the grandest event that the sea could offer was the taking of the pilchards; but this was something for which the children and indeed a great part of the population of St Ives longed in vain. Day after day the Huer waited in his little white watch house on the cliff for that darkening of the ocean that would bring out boats to draw the fish, not by the thousand but by the million, from the silver commotion of the waves. One year they were sighted and the Huer's horn was sounded; but the shoal passed out of the bay and was lost. And so the pilchards became a kind of dream, a Cornish myth that was anticipated but never realised from summer to summer.*

But there was much else that the sea could give: the annual regatta, the sands, the rock pools with sea anemones blooming below the darting fishes, the great bay with its sails and its steamers hull down on their way up to Bristol, or to Cardiff or perhaps to Brazil. And there was Cornish cream and the Town Crier with his muffin bell—not that these came directly from the sea—and the general richness and happiness of life.

This was the season of the year when a basket lowered from the window on a string might, if Sophy were in a good mood, come up again heavy with fine things from the grown-up dinner table. If she were in a bad mood, nothing came up but a severed string. This was the time when Virginia could walk out with her father to the Loggan rock of Tren Crom and the fairyland of great ferns which stood high above a child's head, or to Halestown Bog where the osmunda grew; when Mrs Latham brought live blue lobsters in a bucket into the kitchen and the great storms of autumn sent

* There is a mystery here: "It was only in 1905, when, after Father's death, us four took a little lodging house at Carbis Bay that the pilchards came ... All the years that we were at St Ives the pilchards never came; and the pilchard boats drowsed in the bay ..." MH/A 5c. See also *Cornwall Diary*.

But: "How nice it is that you have seen the great event of the St Ives Year the taking of pilchards. How pretty of Adrian it was to say it was a fleet " of light" I am so glad for all your sakes ..." Mrs Jackson to Mrs Leslie Stephen, 12 October 1889.

waves and sea birds screaming towards the Gurnard's Head.

It was the happiest time of a happy childhood. For certainly they were fortunate, and would have been so if they had only had one week at Margate. Julia could have created what Virginia called "The felicious family of Stephen" in most situations. But in St Ives, feeling the beatitudes of life as keenly as she did, Virginia was allowed a taste of paradise.

Like any other earthly paradise it was menaced. From the outset, Virginia's life was threatened by madness, death and disaster. Whether there was, in those early years, any seed of madness within her, if those "purple rages" were the symptom of some psychic malady, we do not know; neither probably did she; but madness walked the streets. I write advisedly; the scene in *The Years* where the child Rose sees a man exposing himself by a lamp-post is based on experience; there was such a man who hung around Hyde Park Gate and was seen by both Vanessa and Virginia. And of course there was madness in the home; Laura, 'Her Ladyship of the Lake,' was still with the Stephens in 1891 and was a considerable burden upon poor Julia. So far as I can make out she was regarded as a joke by her half-sisters. They wrote her letters, they treated her, I suppose, more or less as an equal; but she could do disconcerting things–calmly throw a pair of scissors into the fire–and there must, as they grew up, have been something disquieting about her. Something much more disquieting was to follow.

Fate struck Fitzjames. He had achieved a great deal, he was a judge, a baronet; he had finished his great work on the history of the criminal law. Then in 1889 his handling of the Maybrick case led to attacks in the press; in 1891 he was advised to retire and did so. Meanwhile his second son, J. K. Stephen, had met disaster.

J. K. Stephen* stands with a red flower in his buttonhole, gazing serenely at the dons of King's in their Combination Room, a massive, powerful, genial figure. Having made a tremendous success at Eton as a scholar and an athlete he became a Fellow of his College; he was the author of light ingenious verses which, in their day, took the town by storm and *Lapsus Calami* is not quite forgotten even now; Fitzjames must have been enormously proud of him.

In 1886, while paying a visit to Felixstowe, the young man had an accident†; he damaged his head, and although the hurt did not appear to be serious it was, in fact, fatal and he began to go mad.

---

* Painted by Charles Furse.

† The nature of the accident is not certainly known; in the Stephen family it was said that he was struck by some projection from a moving train.

VIRGINIA WOOLF

One day he rushed upstairs to the nursery at 22 Hyde Park Gate, drew the blade from a sword stick and plunged it into the bread. On another occasion he carried Virginia and her mother off to his room in De Vere Gardens; Virginia was to pose for him. He had decided that he was a painter–a painter of genius. He was in a state of high euphoria and painted away like a man possessed, as indeed he was. He would drive up in a hansom cab to Hyde Park Gate–a hansom in which he had been driving about all day in a state of insane excitement. On another occasion he appeared at breakfast and announced, as though it were an amusing incident, that the doctors had told him that he would either die or go completely mad.

But the most difficult and painful thing about his insanity was that it led him to desire Stella and violently to pursue her. The children were told to say that Stella was away, staying with relations in the country, whenever their cousin appeared. Fitzjames refused to admit that his son was mad; if he were troublesome then no allowances were to be made for him and Leslie should refuse to receive him.

"I cannot shut my door upon Jem", answered Julia.* She had the power to command him, even in his wildest moods, and she did all that she could for him until his death in February 1892. His father died two years later, broken-hearted.

Stella, the object of this unhappy passion, was a most important figure in the lives of her half-sisters. She was her mother's lieutenant, though by no means her favourite. Not very clever, but with a certain feminine wisdom, kind, gentle, quiet and beautiful; less strictly beautiful than her mother but with a more approachable loveliness than Julia's.† She had a number of eligible suitors, of whom the most determined was Jack Hills, a clever, bright, self-reliant young man. He proposed at St Ives during the summer of 1894 and, for one reason or another, she rejected him. It was, as events were to prove, an unwise decision and perhaps she felt a little of its unwisdom, for that night the children heard her crying in the next room. It must have been a rather disturbing incident and that summer they had other things to disturb them.

*Thus, Leslie Stephen (*MBk*, p. 60). But, through the kindness of Lady Hills, I have been able to see letters from Julia to Stella which show that this was precisely what she had to do, on one occasion at least.

† She was noticed by Holman Hunt, who had an eye for a pretty girl, and sat to him for the head of the Lady of Shalott (Manchester City Art Gallery). A study exists (Coll. Mrs Elizabeth Burt) but it was not used in the final picture. *See* Mary Bennett, *William Holman Hunt* (Exhibition Catalogue), 1969, p. 57, and W. Holman Hunt, *Pre-Raphaelitism and the Pre-Raphaelite Brotherhood*, 1913, II, p. 310.

Somebody had bought the land in front of Talland House and now a big oatmeal-coloured hotel rose up and turned its back on them, blotting out the view of the sea. Was it worth staying on? It was cumbersome and expensive having a house so far from London; expense always worried Leslie and expenses were growing. Thoby was going to Clifton and Adrian had also to be educated. A notice announcing that Talland House was to let made its appearance; there were no takers, but this was only a reprieve. The doors of paradise were closing.

That was in 1894; in January 1895, after an interval of three years, we are able to consult the *Hyde Park Gate News* and discover that Virginia, now about to celebrate her 13th birthday, has ceased to be a child. The hand in which these pages are written is much more adult, though not always easy to read.* Her spelling is orthodox, her language is on the whole correct. Her essays and her attempts at fiction are serious exercises based upon approved models.†

As might be expected, the charm and fun of the earlier numbers has evaporated. Occasionally a phrase, a joke, a turn of speech anticipates her adult style; but the general impression is rather flat. She is still writing for an adult audience; but now she has reached a self-conscious age and plays for safety. She attempts a novel of manners; she writes an article describing a dream in which she was God. These are both in their way interesting, but they are also very clearly the work of a girl making a deadly serious study of English literature.

The news is also of a more adult kind than in the previous series. There is an account of a performance at the Lyceum and a report of the wedding of Virginia's cousin Millicent Vaughan, whose search through "the wide world in quest of matrimony" was now safely concluded by an excellent match. There are many references to the exceptionally severe weather, and a long and competent report of a meeting held at the Mansion House with the object of rescuing Carlyle's house in Chelsea "from the tooth of time."

"For the last fortnight Mrs Leslie Stephen has been in bed with

---

* Some fluent and regular pages are clearly in Vanessa's hand; since she always denied making any contribution to the text of the paper, presumably she acted as an amanuensis.

† The following quotation from a letter written to his mother by Adrian in February 1894 gives a notion of what Virginia was reading, or at least of what she thought that he ought to be reading when he was eleven and she was twelve. ". . . tell Ginia that I have not taken any books by Tenyson or Wordsworth or any of the authors she mentioned but I've taken a book called The World of Adventure. . ."

the influenza"—this was on March 4th. On the 18th we are told that she continues to improve, and on April 8th that George, Gerald and Stella are to go abroad in three days' time. This, almost certainly, was the last number of the *Hyde Park Gate News*.

Five years earlier, Mrs Jackson had written to her grandchildren begging them not to cause their mother any anxiety. It was a wise appeal for, even in that age of cheap domestic labour, a family of ten posed fearful problems for a very devoted mother. And there were so many other burdens upon her. Everyone who wanted help turned to her knowing that it would not be denied. After her death Virginia found in her mother's travelling desk all the letters received one morning at Talland House and brought to London to be answered. There was a letter from a woman whose daughter had been betrayed, a letter from her son George, one from her sister Mary Fisher, one from a nurse who was out of work; there were begging letters, there were many pages from a girl who had quarrelled with her parents. Everyone demanded some kind of help or sympathy, everyone knew that, from her, they would get it. Somehow she would find the time and the means to give aid and comfort. "Ah, thank Heaven, there is no post tonight!" she would exclaim on Saturday evening, and Leslie would protest: "There must be an end of this, Julia." But, as he knew too well, such protests were futile and, worse still, he himself was the heaviest of her burdens.

Essentially the happiness of the Stephen home derived from the fact that the children knew their parents to be deeply and happily in love. This, surely, was the genial fire from which they all drew comfort.But it was also the means whereby the whole edifice might be reduced to ashes. Despite her charities and her maternal commitments, Julia lived chiefly for her husband; everyone needed her but he needed her most. With his temperament and his necessities this was too great a task for even the most heroic of wives; his health and his happiness had to be secured; she had to listen to and to partake in his worries about money, about his work and his reputation, about the management of the household; he had to be fortified and protected from the world. He was, as he himself said, a skinless man, so nothing was to touch him save her soothing and healing hand.

His health was, necessarily, linked to hers and in the seventeen years of their marriage it had not been very good. The labours involved in the making of the *Dictionary of National Biography* were arduous; Virginia believed that she and Adrian had been crushed and cramped in the womb by those important volumes. In 1888 Leslie suddenly collapsed; there was another attack in 1890 and again he was ill in 1891. He suffered from insomnia and what he called "fits of the horrors"; Julia had to wake him up and comfort him. In 1891 she persuaded him to give up his work on the *Dictionary*; it was ruining his life. But still there was this incessant, and often quite fantastic worry about finance,* and here too Julia had to comfort, to reassure, and indeed to administer for him.

Beautiful still, but increasingly worn and harassed, Julia became more and more obsessed by time. She was always in a hurry, ever more anxious to save time by doing things herself, ever more anxious that others should be spared. And so she exhausted herself. Still young in years, she had raced through a lifetime in altruistic work and at length her physical resistance burnt out.

The attack of influenza mentioned in the *Hyde Park Gate News* was at length shaken off, but the *sequelae* were not. Towards the end of April Stella hastened back from the Continent, for clearly her mother's condition had taken a drastic turn for the worse. The doctor said something ominous about rheumatic fever; the relations gathered. On 5 May 1895 Julia died.

* It is said that Leslie told Edmund Gosse that he was completely ruined; there was only £1,000 left. Gosse and other men of letters decided that something must be done; but first it was necessary to know more about the financial situation of the Stephen family. Further enquiries revealed that what Leslie meant was that his favourable balance at the bank was reduced to £1,000; his income and his capital were unchanged.

Chapter Three

1895–1897

"HER death," said Virginia, "was the greatest disaster that could happen."

And yet, if Virginia's loss had simply been a shattering bereavement the situation would not have been so bad as to be unendurable. The real horror of Julia's death came in the mourning of her. Naturally, inevitably, the chief mourner was Leslie; he, a man of sixty-three, had every expectation of being nursed out of the world by a wife almost fifteen years his junior (and she would have done it so well). He had done his stint of widowerhood and had endured it with as much fortitude as any man could reasonably display. How then could fate do this to him? For a long time he abandoned himself to grief; his life, like his writing paper, was confined within a deep black border. His working hours he gave up to a panegyric on 'My Julia.' He wrote sentimentally and without restraint and yet he was, as he himself said, so much a professional author that he could not help making the thing readable and even amusing; it was, I suspect, his only consolation at this time.

But, outside the study, the sedative of work was gone. He resolved to teach those lessons which Julia had previously taken with the girls and gave up half the morning to this purpose. It was a large sacrifice and a sacrifice made with the very best intentions; but it did not make him a more cheerful or a less irascible teacher. In fact, it was an arrangement which brought no comfort to anyone.

At meals he sat miserable and bewildered, too unhappy and too deaf to know what was being said, until at length, in one scene after another all through that dreadful summer, he broke down utterly and, while his embarrassed children sat in awkward silence, groaned, wept and wished that he were dead.

In the accounts that Vanessa and Virginia have left of this period in their lives the image that recurs is one of darkness; dark houses, dark walls, darkened rooms, 'Oriental gloom.' And by this I think that they meant, not only physical darkness, but a deliberate shutting out of spiritual light. It was, for the children, not only tragic but chaotic and unreal. They were called upon to feel, not simply their natural grief, but a false, a melodramatic, an impossibly histrionic emotion which they could not encompass.

Leslie now resembled one who, through long years of infirmity, has taught his body to move with the aid of a crutch and who then, suddenly, finds that his support has gone. In such an emergency stoicism, reserve, philosophy are all beside the point; you fall and, falling, clutch at whatever may save you from disaster. Leslie, snatching at the nearest support, found Stella.

Stella was, indeed, his legitimate prop. She accepted her position without question. She was ready to comfort, to console, to order dinner, to buy coal or underclothes, to chaperone the girls, to keep the house running without alarming expense, to make all social arrangements and in particular to marshal the long procession of sympathising females who came to be closeted with Leslie, to listen, to condole and then, emerging red-eyed and garrulous from his room, came with more comfort, more tears and more advice for Stella. All this was given to her as a duty and tacitly accepted; but in that household and at that season far more was required of her; she had to listen to her stepfather's confessions and to absolve him.

There had been differences between him and Julia–"trifles," but also "things that were not quite trifles"; he had not always been kind, not always considerate; and at the memory of such faults he groaned and cried aloud. If he had had a burden on his conscience like that which had tortured poor Carlyle he would be tempted to commit suicide, but that, he hoped, was not possible. Stella could bear witness; he had not, surely he had not, been as bad as Carlyle? And Stella, who didn't know much about the married life of Mr and Mrs Carlyle, bravely concurred, gallantly attempted to set his uneasy mind at rest.

All this was particularly hard on her because Leslie, after all, was not her father. They had never been very close, and indeed it is more than likely that she regarded him with a kind of resentment. Her passion had been all for her mother: to save *her* trouble and pain, to preserve *her* health, sometimes boldly to steal a part of her mother's load, these had been Stella's cares. And Julia, loving her less than she did the others, and loving Leslie more, had been willing to sacrifice her and the rest to his convenience, and–what was far worse from Stella's point of view–had sacrificed herself, so that at length, in the great campaign to save her mother from exhaustion, she had been defeated both by Leslie and by Julia.

In those last weeks when she was sent abroad, white, desperate, reluctant, knowing that Julia needed her, she was not recalled, but rather recalled herself, suspecting that her mother's letters concealed, as indeed they did conceal, the true gravity of her state. She arrived home so late that she seemed almost to have been cheated not only of her mother's life but of her very death.

Nevertheless, patient, reliable, uncomplaining, bowing to the inevitable yoke of her sex, she accepted her tasks. Pale as a plant that has been denied the sun, concealing the tears that often fell, she could nevertheless find the strength to help her mother's husband and his children; more particularly Adrian and Virginia. It was she who got Adrian off to school in the mornings and coped with his maddening habit of losing gloves, books and coats; it was she who had to look after Virginia, a care, which, as we shall see, now became urgent, heartbreaking and terrible.

Her half-brothers and sisters, who loved her, understood enough of all this to try as best they might to take something of her burden. Vanessa, at fifteen, had earned a reputation for good sense and practicality. She could be, no doubt she was, a comfort and Leslie himself made touching, heroic efforts at cheerfulness, and indeed not just at cheerfulness but at a real and emotionally genuine contact with his children, in which happiness could be regained without any unfaithfulness to his wife's memory and in which something constructive could be built out of their common sorrow. So there were moments when, with a supreme effort, he could again be a delightful parent. But such moments were brief and few. For most of the time the children had to live with a father who was in such a state of despairing, oppressive, guilt-ridden gloom that their own sharp, uncomplicated unhappiness seemed by contrast a relief.

Friends and relations observing the Stephen household at this time could discover two bright luminaries in what would otherwise have been a prospect of unrelieved gloom. Stella was, clearly, a model daughter. George Duckworth was the model brother. The eldest of the Duckworth children, he was now twenty-seven, very handsome, comfortably well-off, pleasant, urbane and generous. His devotion to his half-sisters was exemplary. He made them presents, he took endless trouble to arrange treats, parties, excursions; he would even go off butterfly-hunting with them, and this for a fashionable young man represents a considerable sacrifice.

After their mother's death his kindness knew no bounds; his was an emotional, a demonstrative nature; his shoulder was there for them to weep on; his arms were open for their relief.

At what point this comfortably fraternal embrace developed into something which to George no doubt seemed even more com-

fortable although not nearly so fraternal, it would be hard to say.
Vanessa came to believe that George himself was more than half
unaware of the fact that what had started with pure sympathy ended
by becoming a nasty erotic skirmish. There were fondlings and
fumblings in public when Virginia was at her lessons and these were
carried to greater lengths–indeed I know not to what lengths–
when, with the easy assurance of a fond and privileged brother,
George carried his affections from the schoolroom into the night
nursery.*

To the sisters it simply appeared that their loving brother was
transformed before their eyes into a monster, a tyrant against whom
they had no defence, for how could they speak out or take any action
against a treachery so covert that it was half unknown even to the
traitor? Trained as they were to preserve a condition of ignorant
purity they must at first have been unaware that affection was
turning to concupiscence, and were warned only by their growing
sense of disgust. To this, and to their intense shyness, we may
ascribe Vanessa's and Virginia's long reticence on the subject. George
was always demonstratively emotional, lavish and irresponsible in
his endearments and his embraces; it would have taken a very
knowing eye to perceive that his caresses went perhaps further than
was proper in even the most loving of brothers, and the bedtime
pettings may have seemed no more than a normal extension of his
daytime devotion. It would have been hard for his half-sisters to
know at what point to draw a line, to voice objections, to risk
evoking a painful and embarrassing scandal: harder still to find
someone to whom they could speak at all. Stella, Leslie, the aunts–
all would have been bewildered, horrified, indignant and incredu-
lous.

Their only course seemed to be one of silent evasion; but even this
was denied them; they must join in praising their persecutor, for his
advances were conducted to an accompaniment of enthusiastic
applause in which the girls could hear the repeated hope that 'dear
George' would not find them ungrateful.

* ". . . this led us to the revelation of all George's malefactions. To my surprise'
she [Janet Case] has always had an intense dislike of him; & used to say 'Whew–
you nasty creature,' when he came in & began fondling me over my Greek.
When I got to the bedroom scenes, she dropped her lace, & gasped like a benevolent gudgeon. By bedtime she said she was feeling quite sick, & did go to the
W. C. which, needless to say, had no water in it." VW to Vanessa Bell, [25th July]
1911. However, Virginia also recorded Jack Hill's assurance that George had
"lived in complete chastity until his marriage"; it depends on what one means by
complete chastity. (MH/A 15.)

In later years Virginia's and Vanessa's friends were a little astonished at the unkind mockery, the downright virulence with which the sisters referred to their half-brother. He seemed to be a slightly ridiculous but on the whole an inoffensive old buffer, and so, in a sense, he was. His public face was amiable. But to his half-sisters he stood for something horrible and obscene, the final element of foulness in what was already an appalling situation. More than that, he came to pollute the most sacred of springs, to defile their very dreams. A first experience of loving or being loved may be enchanting, desolating, embarrassing or even boring; but it should not be disgusting. Eros came with a commotion of leathern wings, a figure of mawkish incestuous sexuality. Virginia felt that George had spoilt her life before it had fairly begun. Naturally shy in sexual matters, she was from this time terrified back into a posture of frozen and defensive panic.

I do not know enough about Virginia's mental illnesses to say whether this adolescent trauma was in any way connected with them. It is probable that George made himself disagreeable to her in this way at a later date, when fate struck again at the Stephen family,* whereas the first 'breakdown' or whatever we are to call it, must have come very soon after her mother's death.

And here we come to a great interval of nothingness, a kind of positive death which cannot be described and of which Virginia herself probably knew little—that is to say could recall little—and yet which is vitally important to her story. From now on she knew that she had been mad and might be mad again.

To know that you have had cancer in your body and to know that it may return must be very horrible; but a cancer of the mind, a corruption of the spirit striking one at the age of thirteen and for the rest of one's life always working away somewhere, always in suspense, a Dionysian sword above one's head—this must be almost unendurable. So unendurable that in the end, when the voices of insanity spoke to her in 1941, she took the only remedy that remained, the cure of death. But her mind could make a scar that would serve,

* Statements by Leonard Woolf and the late Dr Noel Richards suggest that George's advances were made shortly after his mother's death; on the other hand unpublished memoirs (MH/A 14, 15 and 16) by Virginia make it almost certain that his activities began at, or were continued to, a much later date, i.e. 1903 or 1904. It was not only George's attentions which disturbed Virginia: "I still shiver with shame at the memory of my half-brother, standing me on a ledge, aged about 6 or so, exploring my private parts." (VW to Ethel Smyth, 12 January 1941). A document (MH/A 5a) which came to light after the first publication of this volume makes it clear that the half-brother here referred to was Gerald, not George.

in some measure, to heal and to conceal her lasting wound. She did not, could not, admit all the memories of her madness. What she did recall were the physical symptoms; in her memoir of this period she hardly mentions the commotions of her mind and although we know that she had already heard what she was later to call "those horrible voices," she speaks of other symptoms, usually physiological symptoms. Her pulse raced–it raced so fast as to be almost unbearable. She became painfully excitable and nervous and then intolerably depressed. She became terrified of people, blushed scarlet if spoken to and was unable to face a stranger in the street.

Dr Seton, the Stephens' family doctor,* put a stop to all lessons, ordered a simple life and prescribed outdoor exercise; she was to be out of doors four hours a day and it was one of Stella's self-imposed duties to take her for walks or for rides on the tops of buses.

The *Hyde Park Gate News* came to an end; for the first and only time Virginia lost the desire to write, although in 1896 she did keep a diary for a short time. But she read feverishly and continually. She went through a period of morbid self-criticism, blamed herself for being vain and egotistical, compared herself unfavourably to Vanessa and was at the same time intensely irritable.

St Ives was given up. Leslie could not bear the idea of going there without Julia and so, perhaps a month after her death, Gerald took a train to Cornwall, saw someone and settled the business. Each year now the Stephens looked for a summer residence. In 1895 they went to Freshwater in the Isle of Wight. That was almost their blackest period of mourning; in 1896 they took a house belonging to Mrs Tyndall, the scientist's widow, on the top of the North Downs at Hindhead, and this house became the setting for what should, in conventional terms, have been the last act in the romance of Stella Duckworth and Jack Hills.

John Waller Hills was an Etonian; he came of a very respectable family handsomely established in Cumberland but not, apparently, able to do much for Jack. His father had been a judge and something of a wit. His mother collected Chelsea enamel boxes and minor literary men. He himself was to be a solicitor; he had political ambitions and was an enthusiastic fisherman. He was an honest,

---

* Dr Seton–"my dear Dr Seton" as Virginia calls him in her diary for 1897– was much loved by all the children; he was a favourite also of the Woolf family in Lexham Gardens. Years later he met his two former patients Leonard and Virginia, now Mr and Mrs Woolf and his neighbours in Richmond, where he died in February 1917, aged ninety. (VW/VB, [11 February] 1917). "He was," said Leonard Woolf, "a doddering old man, but awfully nice."

tenacious fellow with a bad stutter; he had to wrestle with each sentence and yet in that conflict managed always to have his say in the end. He had refused to accept Stella's rejection of his suit and, in his refusal, he had a powerful ally in Julia. Julia was always a matchmaker and a friend to young lovers; she had been largely instrumental in carrying matters so far. After the first rupture, she had determined to mend matters and succeeded so well that, by the time of her death, the young man was again a frequent guest at Hyde Park Gate.

He proposed again and was again rejected. We can only guess at the reasons for this second refusal, but in view of what followed it is likely that Stella was deterred, not by her feelings for Jack but by a sense of duty to her step-father. She might not love Leslie or might love him only in a very tepid fashion; but he had laid a claim upon her conscience; he and his children were dependent upon her, he relied on her for the few scraps of comfort that he could now enjoy. To desert him would be inhuman. And so, following her conscience rather than her inclination, Stella refused Jack for a second time.

But he would no more accept the second refusal than the first, nor is it hard to see how the very situation which made Stella reject him could, from another point of view, be represented as the strongest argument in favour of marriage. That a girl of Stella's kindness and beauty, so obviously formed for matrimony and motherhood, should devote herself to a man who, after all, might live another twenty years, was monstrous. Stella, at twenty-seven, was neither so young nor yet so old that she could easily sacrifice her time.

If she heard such arguments, she must, howsoever strong her moral rectitude, have allowed some inward sigh of assent to contradict her overt resolve to continue in that tedious and heart-breaking course of duty to which she found herself committed. And then, as the young lawyer could not have failed to point out, there was a further consideration: Vanessa was now seventeen; she had already shown an admirable degree of calm, of judgment, of practicality. She alone of the household was not dependent upon Stella and she, far more than Stella, was bound by natural claims. As Leslie's daughter she would find it easier to minister to and to sympathise with him. That these arguments, or something like them, were debated between Jack Hills and Stella Duckworth is made probable by the circumstances of Jack's third proposal.

This event left a profound, though confused, impression upon Virginia. On 22 August 1896, Jack Hills bicycled to Hindhead and lingered all the afternoon with the Stephens. It was a warm summer day followed by a hot summer night. Jack and Stella went into the garden after dinner and did not return. The children had business in the garden too–they had moths to catch–but Jack and Stella evaded them. The place seemed full of the rustle of skirts and the whisper of voices. There was some little drama–a tramp or other trespasser suspected and hailed by Thoby. When they came in Leslie sent the children upstairs; clearly he was perturbed. Everyone felt uneasy, frightened; there was a sense of expectancy, of fatality almost, in the house; the children collected in Adrian's room and waited to see what would happen. And then at last Stella came in; she was radiant, blushing. She was, she said, very happy. . . .

Adrian, feeling perhaps that he was losing a mother once more, wept; Leslie rebuked him. They must all be happy, for Stella was happy and besides, his Julia had always wished it.

My Julia [he wrote] . . . would have been more delighted than any of us: the thought of her approval would have reconciled me if reconciliation had been needed. . . . I cannot imagine that I could contemplate Stella's marriage with more perfect confidence and satisfaction under any conceivable circumstances. If any thing could make me happier, this ought to: but [he adds ominously] my happiness is a matter of rapidly diminishing importance.

Yes, they ought to, they must, rejoice, Adrian must dry his eyes. But how could Leslie obey his own injunctions? It was an irreparable blow; only one thing could reconcile him to it–the fact that Stella would not leave his house.

How this proviso was reached we do not know–perhaps Stella exacted it from her lover, perhaps Leslie made it the condition of his blessing. At all events matters were fixed in this manner in August and, so far as Leslie was concerned, that was the end of it.

But, having gained his first point the young man went on to gain his second. How would they live? Where would they live? Who would be the master of the house? The difficulties grew ever more formidable; the arrangement began to look less and less realistic. In the end Stella went to see her step-father and told him that she must, after all, have a house of her own. We do not know what passed between them; certainly there was an explosion, but she got her way. Even so there had to be a compromise. Stella would not go far; there was another house available, No 24 Hyde Park Gate, just across the street. They would live there. It was no distance.

But from now on Leslie spoke in increasingly despondent tones about the whole business. He groaned and sighed, "he has picked my pocket"; how could Stella marry such a man? The name Jack was "like the smack of a whip."

A painful transaction was made more painful by the discretions of the dying century. Leslie could not altogether scrutinise his own emotions and realise the extent and character of his jealousy. Had he done so a man of his high moral character could surely have come to terms with the situation. But he had to see matters through his own distorting glass: he, a lonely old widower, a man broken and distracted by grief, had been betrayed. This was his version of the matter and it was a version which was accepted by the host of female supporters who had once seen in Stella the model daughter and now discovered her to be disgracefully selfish. But Stella was not greatly troubled; she had the strength of one who is happily in love and forms part of a strong alliance.

Virginia did not much care for Jack Hills and, in a way, she detested the marriage. The loss of a sister was for her almost as important as was the loss of a daughter to Leslie; and yet she rejoiced. Her slow recovery was assisted by a newly discovered source of happiness–the spectacle of Stella coming to life again. For Stella, who had been pale, numb and desolate, bloomed, smiled, and radiated joy. Virginia had never before been in the presence of such happiness; in later years she used her memory of Stella's love as a measuring rod. If a couple were said to be in love she would consider whether their affection would bear comparison with Stella's love for Jack or Jack's for Stella; *that* had been the real thing. She had not imagined that human beings could know such joy; she supposed that this was some special, some quite unusual manifestation of love. Shyly she confided this belief to Stella who, hardly less shy, laughed, thought that it was nothing out of the common but something that her sisters would also discover. Vanessa was beautiful; she would be 'coming out' now; she too would know love and so would Virginia.

Things were in this posture, half exquisitely happy, half painfully sad, at the beginning of 1897. On 1 January the children decided to start keeping diaries. Virginia's diary was kept, regularly for the first six months, intermittently for a year and a day; from it we can get a fairly exact picture of what was to be a momentous period.

Beginning in the middle of the Christmas holidays the diary begins also by recording a number of entertainments–visits to the theatre and the pantomime, to the zoo twice, to the National Portrait Gallery and the National Gallery, a first glimpse of those new curiosities of science the 'Animatograph' and 'Röntgens Rays,'

Decorations by Vanessa at the foot of a letter from
Virginia to Thoby Stephen, 1 February 1897.
(King's College Library, Charleston Papers, VWTS 23.)

IN VIRGINIA'S HAND:

A libel I protest—my skating is
particularly graceful, and I never
once have come to grief this
winter—Maria shall not
ornament *my* letters
again in a hurry.

IN VANESSA'S HAND:

V. Stephen fecit.

threepenny seats at the Albert Hall. There was also an entertainment of a different kind: *Clementina's Lovers*, written by Thoby and acted by all the children for the benefit of the maids. Such performances were always advertised by means of a handbill which began thus:

DENIZENS OF THE KITCHEN
COME IN YOUR THOUSANDS!!

The audience usually consisted of one housemaid but on this occasion there were two: Elizabeth and Florrie, together with the French maid, Pauline. They applauded loudly, but although Thoby killed every one of his characters in the last act, Pauline remained under the impression that it was a performance of *Aladdin*. In the evenings, Leslie continued to read aloud to his children; in January 1897 he was reading *Esmond*; sometimes he would recite poetry. Presently Thoby returned to Clifton, where he was a thoroughly successful schoolboy, playing games with forceful enthusiasm and construing Latin roughly but on the whole efficiently. It was at this time that the children were amused to hear Aunt Anny exclaim: "O Leslie, what a noble boy Thoby is!"

Adrian was following a less glorious and less happy career at Westminster, and Vanessa, while preparing for the Royal Academy at Mr Cope's School of Art, resumed lessons with her father.

Virginia, it would seem, had not had any lessons since November 1896. "I hope, though I still hope with trembling, that she is a bit better," wrote her father to her aunt Mary Fisher a year later. Clearly she was still in a very nervous condition. But in February Dr Seton allowed her to do some lessons; we find her on the 22nd learning history and German; in March she was studying Livy and records "I did some Greek."

Meanwhile she was reading a great deal. In her diary she keeps a careful record, noting the beginning and ending of each book. Between 1 January and 30 June 1897 she read the following: *Three Generations of English Women* (volumes 2 and 3); Froude's *Carlyle*—here she makes the following notes: "1st volume of Froude which is to be read slowly and then I'm to re-read all the books that he [Leslie] has lent me"; Creighton's *Queen Elizabeth*; Lockhart's *Life of Sir Walter Scott*; *The Newcomes*; Carlyle's *Reminiscences*; *The Old Curiosity Shop*; *Essays in Ecclesiastical Biography* by Sir James Stephen; *Felix Holt*; *John Halifax, Gentleman*; *Among My Books* and *My Study Windows* by J. R. Lowell; *A Tale of Two Cities*; *Silas Marner*; *The Life of Coleridge* by James Dykes Campbell; *The Heart of Princess Osra* by Anthony Hope; three volumes of Pepys; Macaulay's *History*;

Barchester Towers; a novel by Henry James; Carlyle's *French Revolution*, his *Cromwell* and his *Life of Sterling*; a work by Lady Barlow; *Shirley*; Thomas Arnold's *History of Rome*; *A Deplorable Affair* by W. E. Norris.

"Gracious child, how you gobble," Leslie would say as he got up from his seat to take down the sixth or seventh volume of Gibbon, or Spedding's *Bacon* or Cowper's *Letters*. "But my dear, if it's worth reading, it's worth reading twice," he would go on and, to himself: "Ginia is devouring books, almost faster than I like."

It was about this time, however, that the system of issuing books came to an end and Virginia was granted the freedom of her father's library. There were certain books on his shelves, he managed shyly to convey, which were not, in his opinion, entirely suitable for young ladies and amongst them, it would appear, was *Trilby*. But his daughter must decide for herself what she ought to read; clearly literature was her great passion and literature had to be accepted with all its risks. She must learn to read with discrimination, to make unaffected judgments, never admiring because the world admires or blaming at the orders of a critic. She must learn to express herself in as few words as possible. Such were his precepts and such was the educational opportunity that he gave. Leslie might be a disastrous teacher of mathematics; but he made up for it as a teacher of English literature.

Apart from the *Hyde Park Gate News* and one essay, I do not think that Leslie ever saw any of her early attempts at writing. But there was plenty to see. Before she was thirteen Virginia was trying to imitate the novels or at all events the style of Hawthorne. Then about the year 1897 Leslie brought her Hakluyt's *Voyages* from the London Library. Thereafter she modelled herself upon the Elizabethans, wrote a long essay entitled *Religio Laici* and another, seemingly a more characteristic effort, *A History of Women*. Of these early manuscripts nothing remains.

We may think of Virginia at this period as a rather tall, rather thin overgrown girl reading or writing in a back room at Hyde Park Gate. Until the time of Stella's marriage, she had no room of her own; her reading and writing were done either in the glazed room at the back of the house or in an armchair in the day nursery. But wherever she might settle, she made a fortress from which she was not easily driven. This reluctance to leave the sober, but to her important, comforts of her work place appears more than once in her diary.

In January Jack Hills had an operation – it was a very slight affair;

VIRGINIA WOOLF

but it led to the postponement of the wedding. After it he and Stella planned to go to Bognor for his convalescence and it was suggested that Virginia should go there too, presumably as a chaperone. This, she told her diary on 1 February, was "a terrible idea"; on 2 February she told her family the same thing. She would on no account go alone with Jack and Stella on such an expedition. She was pressed to change her mind; the pressure came, not from her father, but from her half-sister. Leslie in fact took a gloomy view of the proposed holiday. Bognor, he guessed, was "rather nasty, and somebody has told us that the drains are bad. . . . Perhaps I shall go for a night or two." In the end Virginia got Vanessa to come with her. It was a depressing excursion; they did not like the place and the weather was atrocious. Even Jack and Stella had to admit that it might lack charm for others. Leslie, when he arrived, observed with gloomy satisfaction that he never saw such ugly country or such bad weather in his life; the sea, he declared, was made chiefly of mud. Virginia had no doubt of the derivation of the name Bognor. Leslie's determination to hate the whole business is easily explicable, for he was in a mood to hate anything and to find fault with any plan that Jack and Stella might advance.* Virginia's reluctance to join the excursion is harder to explain. I will advert to it later. But in part her irritation was caused by the general bother and stress of a ceremonial wedding.

Sunday 28 March '97. In the morning we three [Vanessa, Virginia and Adrian] went to Church at St Mary Abbots! This was the last Sunday on which the banns were to be read, so that we had resolved to go. It began at 11.30, and finished at 1.15. We had rummaged the house for prayer books and hymn books; our search produced two hymn books (tonic sol fa) and one prayer book. This last however was left behind. A little black gentleman showed us into seats at the top of the church. Soon music and singing began, the row in front of us rose, and behind a wheezy old lady began to follow the choristers in a toothless, tuneless whistle—So on for the rest of the performance—At certain parts we stood, then sat, and finally knelt—this I refused to do—My neighbour looked so miserable and uncomfortable—In the middle the banns of John Waller Hills and Stella Duckworth along with several others were

* A letter from Leslie to Thoby written in January gives a clear enough indication of his state of mind: "It is a regular thaw, though Stella wants to take V[anessa] and V[irginia] to a skating place at the Botanical Gardens. I said that it was not safe as a lot of people fell into the round pond on friday and the thaw will have made the ice worse. *She* said that Jack said it was safe. I said that Jack was a —— no, I did not say that because I have been told that she is to marry him on the 1st of April: a very proper day, I think." (30 January 1897).

read, and no one pronounced any reason why etc. etc. Our prayers and psalms were rather guess work–but the hymns were splendid. We had a sermon from a new pastor–he said "we shall never hear the beloved voice again" alluding to the departed vicar. The old ladies snuffled and sobbed.

Then there were dresses to be made; for the first time in her life, Virginia found herself obliged to wear stays, things which she found herself unable to name in her diary. There was the question of Stella's wedding and going-away dresses, the "dreadful idea" that Vanessa and Virginia ought to be bridesmaids, Stella writing to Thoby at Clifton and sending him a cheque so that he might make a presentable appearance at the wedding, Leslie protesting that he need not buy new clothes–"Do you think that I . . . may be allowed to go in my ordinary costume? I don't see why I should not; but am half afraid that Gerald may bully me." Apparently he did. Then there was Stella's present from the Stephen children to be discussed, the money to be found, the thing to be purchased and so on. And there were other presents; soon the place was crammed with lace, engravings, plate etc.–"about as amusing to me," said Leslie, "as the dry plants at Kew."

Friday 9th April '97. We did nothing all day but arrange presents and write cards etc.–All the morning was spent like this. In the afternoon Stella and Father went to Highgate [to visit Julia's grave]–At last about 11 o'clock at night things were more or less finished, Mrs Jones arrived with a supply of underclothing. We went to bed–but Stella and Georgie & Gerald stayed up till 2 packing in her room. Jack stayed away all day long–Too much to do to be dismal, though the last evening was in danger of ending unhappily. Remembered however (Nessa and I) our resolve to be calm and collected.

Saturday 10th April '97.
Stella & Jack's Wedding Day.
The morning was still rather a hurly-burly–The finishing touches to everything had to be given–Eustace [Hills*] came often to arrange things with Stella–Huge boxes of flowers arrived throughout the morning and had to be arranged. . . Adrian did not go to school. At about 12 the Fishers came–and Stella went up to dress. M. Emile the hairdresser did her hair and also Nessa's–goodness knows how we got through it all–Certainly it was half a dream, or a nightmare. Stella was almost dreaming I think; but probably hers was a happy one. We went to the church at 2. Jack was there looking quite well and happy. Then at about 2.15 or 30, Stella and father came in–Stella walking in her sleep–

* Jack's brother and best man.

her eyes fixed straight in front of her—very white and beautiful—There was a long service—then it was all over—Stella and Jack were married— We went up and saw her change her dress—and said goodbye to her—So they went—Mr and Mrs Hills! These are some sentimental tokens of the day—white rose leaves from S's bouquet and red tulips from ours that Jack gave us.

After three days, largely spent in discussing the late festivities with Kitty Maxse and Margaret Massingberd, recognised authorities on all mundanities, the Stephen family left for Brighton. It was far from being their favourite resort; moreover the whole business of the wedding had left Virginia in a state of nervous exasperation. On 13 April she went to bed "very furious and tantrumical," on the 15th she regrets her "beloved armchair" at Hyde Park Gate; then she observes of their rented house in Hove that "truly such a dismal place was never seen." Brighton itself was full of "third rate actresses turned out in gorgeous clothes—tremendous hats, powder and rouge; and dreadful young men to escort them." And on 21 April:

> Father took Nessa and me for a walk along the Parade to the Steine or some place of that kind—near the Pagoda at the other end of Brighton— I regret to say that various circumstances conspiring to irritate me, I broke my umbrella in half . . .

But in retrospect it appeared to be a season of hope. Stella's letters from Florence seemed to promise a new kind of life in Hyde Park Gate; there had been much talk of loneliness and separation but, now that the thing was done, all this seemed nonsense. Stella would be so close to them, in a young household, a home which would almost be theirs but which would be uncurtained by the gloom of age and mourning. Better still, Leslie was making an effort to adapt himself to the new situation. The last seven or eight months of the engagement had, he admitted, brought him "a good many selfish pangs: but—well I should be a brute if I really complained." Vanessa was old enough now to take Stella's place at home; she would soon be 'coming out'; such an emergence could not fail to be momentous and might be salutary; and there was Virginia, clearly destined for his own profession. He set himself to know her better; he began telling her about the distinguished literary figures of the past whom he had known when he was young. It seemed to be the beginning of a new and happier epoch in all their lives.

On the afternoon of 28 April, the day of their return to London, they were met at Victoria by George; he told them that Jack and Stella had returned and that Stella was in bed with a gastric chill. At Hyde Park Gate they discovered that she was very bad indeed.

On the 29th Dr Seton decided that it was not a chill; he looked very grave and diagnosed peritonitis. By that evening they were all living in a nightmare.

Stella was worse in the afternoon – the pain was bad – After tea Nessa went back again [to relieve the nurse] & I sat again over those eternal old Graphics and my Macaulay which is the only calm and un-anxious thing in this most agitating time – Dr Seton came after dinner, and was rather frightening. It is Peritonitis – she is to be kept quite quiet – there is to be another nurse, & straw put down on the road. Poor Jack very unhappy. This is one of the most terrible nights so far. No getting rid of the thought – all these ghastly preparations add to it – The people jar at every possible occasion. I slept with Nessa, as I was unhappy. News that she is better at about 11 o'clock – what shall I write tomorrow?

That was written on the night of the 29th; on the next day Stella was much better; the improvement was maintained; by 2 May she was believed to be out of danger and by 17 May she was able to take carriage exercise. Much to her horror Virginia was told that she must accompany her half-sister on these expeditions. It seemed to her that the streets had become murderous. On 25 February she had been in a carriage accident; on 26 March she saw a lady cyclist run over by a cart; on 8 May she had witnessed two accidents in Piccadilly; on the 12th a cart horse fell down in front of her; on the 13th there was a collision between a runaway carriage horse and a waggon. Did these accidents really occur? Her state of health since the wedding and, even more, since Stella's illness had been deteriorating. On 9 May she was examined by Dr Seton and lessons were stopped, she was ordered to have milk, outdoor exercise, and medicine. She was certainly in a nervous condition and I think that she imagined or greatly exaggerated some of the accidents; but one of them – the accident with the lady cyclist, certainly did happen.*
It was a particularly agitating business because the lady, who ran straight into a cart in Gloucester Road, came from the direction and at an hour which Vanessa would have taken on her way back from her art school. Leslie, who was there, thought for a moment that it was indeed she.

At all events, it is clear from her diary that she really had become terrified of the simplest journey through the streets; she makes fun

* ' . . . Ginia saw the whole thing. . . . The poor old Goat was in a dreadful state as you may think and now she wants me to give up riding altogether, which of course I shan't do. Its very unlucky that it should always be the goat who sees accidents.' Vanessa to Thoby Stephen, 28 March [1897].

of her own terror but it was real enough. Thus, a part of her reluctance to go out with Stella can be explained by her reluctance to go out with anyone anywhere in the streets of London. But I think there is something else here, a strange ambivalence about Stella herself. Virginia was equally reluctant to go with her to Bognor in February and when, later, it was proposed that Stella should go to convalesce in the country:

> She . . . irritated me extremely by saying that I should have to go with her when she goes away, which I with great vehemence, declared to be *impossible*.

Why was it impossible? Virginia might reasonably anticipate that Bognor in February would be unrewarding; but in a very hot, sticky London summer the idea of a country holiday need not have distressed her, unless it was Stella herself whom she wished to avoid.

Certain diary entries make me think that this was the case. There can be no question of Virginia's distress when, in the last days of April, she feared that Stella would die; but a week later when Vanessa reported that their half-sister was looking fatter and decidedly better than after the wedding, Virginia notes that although this was most satisfactory, she was "unreasonable enough" to be irritated; and, five days later:

> This Sunday a most distinct improvement upon last–Then we were not out of the wood (as [Dr] Broadbent said) Vaguely unhappy. Cousin Mia a fixture–melancholy and large, in the drawing room, and sympathetic enquirers dropping in every now & then–Now that old cow is most ridiculously well & cheerful–hopping about out of bed etc: Thank goodness, nevertheless–

That "nevertheless" certainly gives one cause for speculation. Without attempting to probe very deeply we can, at least, note that between a good, kind, not very clever woman standing in a position of vague authority–half elder sister, half surrogate mother–and a very nervous, irritable, intelligent girl of fifteen, there can be plenty of causes for friction and some kind of friction there surely was. During that summer of 1897 Virginia's health and Stella's were in some way connected; they were bound, not only by feelings of affection on both sides, but, on Virginia's, by a sentiment of guilt.

In late May, however, tensions relaxed a little. It was known that Stella was going to have a baby; it was believed that she was cured and this belief persisted, despite a relapse at the beginning of June. It seemed possible to try to enjoy the events of the summer; they were of two kinds: public and private. The Queen celebrated her

Diamond Jubilee; Vanessa 'came out.' She went to various parties and Virginia thought that she looked exceedingly beautiful; but her account of the great world was not encouraging; it was, she declared, uncommonly dull. As for the Jubilee, they saw troops and horses and the old lady who had come to the throne when Leslie was a boy; but it aroused no deep emotion. There was no pleasure to be got out of anything that summer.

I growl at every thing – the effect of nerves doubtless! . . . hot, hot, hot.

It was indeed a summer of "relentless, thundery, sunless heat." At night she continued reading long after her light was supposed to have been put out; Hawthorne, Miss Mitford and Cowper's letters were her night books; she also read Macaulay and Henry James because she found that they soothed her nerves, and clearly her nerves needed a sedative.

Years later Vanessa was to describe that summer as "three months of . . . horrible suspense, muddle, mismanagement, hopeless fighting against the stupidity of those in power." From this it would appear that she knew more of what was going on than did Virginia. But Virginia must have become aware that, although the doctors continued to be reassuring, Stella was not getting well and as this gradually became more and more apparent Virginia's health deteriorated, her psychological illness was accompanied by physical symptoms. She complained of rheumatic pains and presently had a temperature.

On 13 July Virginia found herself so ill at Stella's house that Dr Seton sent her to bed there. The next night Virginia had what she called 'the fidgets,' and Stella sat by her stroking and soothing her until it was almost midnight. Three nights later Virginia was taken back to Number 22; George carried her wrapped in Stella's fur cape. The nurse told her that Stella was better and Stella herself called out "goodbye" as Virginia passed her door. But on the following evening Stella was operated on and at three in the morning of 19 July George and Vanessa came to Virginia's room and told her that Stella was dead.

Chapter Four

1897–1904

IT will have been noticed that the tragedies of the Stephen family were enacted with the assistance of a chorus composed mainly of female friends and relatives. When Stella died, this body proved itself fully equal to the occasion: there had never, they wailed, been so perfect a creature—except her mother—it was indeed a tragedy, nobody deserved happiness more. Sorrow and despair became a universal theme, almost a duty; Helen Holland, a Duckworth cousin, insisted upon praying in the room in which Stella had died; Cousin Mia, Aunt Minna and Aunt Mary were in constant, lachrymose attendance. The horror of the occasion, already in the childrens' view substantial enough, was by every means magnified and funereally enriched. Virginia suffered intensely from what she called "the ghastly mourners." She and Vanessa were glad enough to escape to Painswick, to the Vicarage which, although it overlooked a celebrated churchyard shaded by no fewer than ninety-nine yew trees, seemed to them decidedly more cheerful than the darkness and lamentation of Hyde Park Gate.

Before following them thither it may be helpful to look more closely at this tragic chorus, or at least at some of its constituents, and also at the younger generation in which Virginia was beginning to make some friends.

Cousin Mia was a grumpy, massive specimen of the Victorian age; she was Julia's first cousin and was celebrated as a model of the domestic virtues. She never let a birthday pass without making a suitable present and she expected others to be equally punctilious; if any child should forget her kindness Cousin Mia would be elaborately and pointedly hurt. Being hurt was one of her talents. She collected and disseminated bad news; she loved to report illness or death; she would enter lovingly into every circumstance of mortality; she loved to mourn, to weep, to prophesy disaster.

Aunt Minna Duckworth, Julia's sister-in-law, painted watercolours; she was a rich, fat old lady and entirely commonplace, and in all these respects very unlike Aunt Mary, Julia's elder sister, the wife of Herbert Fisher and the mother of seven sons and four daughters. "My mother was a saint," declared her eldest son, H. A. L. Fisher. "A more selfless, unworldly being never drew breath. Her life was a perpetual surrender of ease and comfort to the service of others." Her nieces would have agreed, but they would have made certain qualifications. Their mother also, they felt, was a kind of saint; but she was a little less emphatically saintly. In the same way, they would have agreed with their distinguished cousin that Aunt Mary had great beauty, a beauty equal but different to that of her sister. Julia's face is generous, intelligent and humorous; Mary has a Burne-Jones melancholy, her features are a little sharper, her cast of countenance is drooping, dyspeptic, almost bitter. Like Julia, Mary was heroic; Virginia noted the courage with which, exhausted and washed-out, she carried the weight of the family trials–and they were heavy–upon her back. But the warmth, the gaiety, the smiling philosophy of Julia's bravery is lacking. Moreover her feelings were a shade less pure; her magnanimity could be displayed in a way that punished the beneficiary.

> My dear Virginia *you* must have the last piece of cake; yes, I *am* particularly fond of it and there will be nothing left for tomorrow's tea; but it would give me particular pleasure to sacrifice it to you.

Such, according to Vanessa and Virginia, was the Fisher style, and, as Virginia said: "The Fishers would have made Eden un-inhabitable."

This overwhelming sweetness made their frequent family visits to Brighton, where the Fishers lived, a great trial and led the sisters to dislike that charming town for many years. And, of course, Aunt Mary was a constant visitor at Hyde Park Gate; she had to enquire, to observe, to interrogate; she had to know how her motherless nieces were behaving and if, in her opinion, they were behaving badly, she must exert the authority of a mother. Her curiosity was insatiable, her censure vigorous. Virginia felt that she was continually prying and making comments, continually extending long, soft, tough, elastic tentacles to try and bring her and Vanessa into the family embrace, to suck them in and assimilate them to the Fisher pattern of conduct, belief and manners.

The Stephen side of the family was hardly more popular with Virginia and Vanessa than were the Fishers. Aunt Caroline Emelia was kindly but dull; the family of Fitzjames Stephen was formidable but unsympathetic. Lady Stephen, his widow, was a distant though uncongenial figure; so too was Katherine, the eldest daughter– already Vice-Principal of Newnham. The sons Herbert and Harry, though generally censorious, were reasonably remote. But of the three other daughters they saw more than they liked. Dorothea, the youngest (who was rather a favourite with Leslie), was in particular a frequent and unwelcome visitor to Hyde Park Gate. She was an ardent and aggressive High Church Anglican, and lost no opportunity of asserting the dogmas of Christianity before her benighted cousins. "She talks" wrote Virginia, "every minute of the day, wants no encouragement but a yes or no, & will only be stopped by your going out of the room." These Stephen sisters were not stupid, but pompous, absurd, and opinionated; "the most ungainly creatures in the world," said Vanessa, "who insisted upon forgiving us however badly we behaved"; and to Virginia it seemed that they were ugly and sweated and were altogether hateful.

Virginia could get some entertainment but little else from her Fisher and Stephen cousins. Her relationship with the orphaned children of her mother's sister Adeline and Henry Halford Vaughan was altogether happier. Of these five, Emma, the youngest, who studied music, seems to have been Virginia's chief friend and correspondent. A good many of her letters to Emma have been preserved; they are lively productions full of private jokes and family gossip and certainly not dull, though they portray a fairly humdrum existence: Greek lessons, social encounters, bookbinding (a hobby pursued by both)–such were the topics that Virginia discussed with Emma. She wrote also to Emma's sister Margaret; but Margaret devoted her life to good work amongst the poor and was much less of an intimate. The only son in this family was William Wyamar; his importance lay in the fact that he was to marry Madge, a daughter of John Addington Symonds, who had once spent a winter at Hyde Park Gate when Virginia was seven years old and was known thereafter to the children as The Chief.

Madge must have seemed to Virginia a romantic figure. She had grown up among the Swiss mountains in an atmosphere of freedom, she was a writer, she was passionately interested in the arts–and there was something melancholy about her. Her father's death in 1893 had hit her very hard and she had an intense capacity for suffering. But there was also something childlike, wondering and fresh about her attitude to life. She was modern, adventurous, 'aesthetic'– very much a girl of the 'nineties, and this inevitably was attractive; and then she was herself attractive.

Virginia was in fact in love with her. She was the first woman– and in those early years Virginia fled altogether from anything male– the first to capture her heart, to make it beat faster, indeed to make it almost stand still as, her hand gripping the handle of the water-jug in the top room at Hyde Park Gate, she exclaimed to herself: "Madge is here; at this moment she is actually under this roof." Virginia once declared that she had never felt a more poignant emotion for anyone than she did at that moment for Madge.* Certainly it was a very pure and very intense passion – pure in almost every sense of the word; Virginia at sixteen, for all George's kissings and fumblings, was by modern standards almost unbelievably ignorant. It was pure also in its sincerity, in its lack of jealous feeling. It was the passion of a girl in a junior form for a dashing senior, not a passion based upon intimacy.

The friendship with Emma and the passion for Madge were valuable; they provided some measure of relief and refuge in the domestic storms of the period, those afflictions to which we must now return.

Stella's death did not produce a complete breakdown in Virginia's health; as will be seen she was more capable of meeting than of anticipating disaster. She seems in fact to have made a fairly good recovery, to have been well enough, at all events, to join in the business which occupied her and Vanessa very much at this time, that of comforting Jack. Virginia now beheld what was for her a new form of grief – the grief of a man whose future is entirely desolated and who suffers, along with everything else, the deprivation of physical love. He came to Painswick every week-end and when they left there they went, to please him, to spend a week at his parents' home, Corby Castle, near Carlisle. The house was splendid and gorgeously appointed, the river Eden where Jack fished for salmon was beautiful, the situation romantic, and, in her diary, Virginia noted:

Terrible long dinner. Everything grand & strange. Jack unhappy. Old Hills silly. Mrs Hills talkative & rather unpleasant, Susan [Lushington] talkative and very pleasant. VS and AVS silent & miserable... Everything is miserable and lonely. Why did we ever come?

The fact was that they didn't like Mrs Hills at all and she, evidently, didn't like them. There was an atmosphere of hard calculating snobbery which they found detestable. Worse still, their sacrifice, which was supposed to bring aid and comfort to Jack, was failing in its purpose and he seemed unaware of what they were doing for him. They returned to London with a sigh of relief. They could

* "V[irginia] told me the history of her early loves – Madge Symonds who is Sally in Mrs Dalloway." V. Sackville West, *Journal of Travel with VW*, 29 September 1928.

help him better there; and in fact he came to stay at 22 Hyde Park Gate that autumn while a new house was being prepared for him and was, indeed, a member of the family. As such he must have been a witness of the curious transactions which now took place.

It must be remembered, in considering what follows, that Leslie during these years of miserable bereavement was becoming more and more solitary. He was cut off from society by his deafness and by the loss of his friends.* He had good reasons for being sorry for himself. Nevertheless Jack was the chief mourner on this occasion and Leslie came very near the end of the funeral procession. He was of course afflicted, but his tread was elastic, his eyes were dry. Stella had been a nice, good, dear girl, but she had not actually been his daughter. She had been his prop; and already, before her death, she had ceased to serve him in that capacity. She had been snatched from him and he, like a sensible man, a philosopher, had reconciled himself to the situation. Stella's death was of course a very bad business; "poor boy," he muttered, blandly unconscious of the pain that he inflicted, "poor boy, he looks very bad," and Jack, hearing himself thus described, was miserably embarrassed and turned the conversation. But for himself, well, he could bear it, he had a new prop—his eldest daughter.

Virginia said that Leslie actually told Vanessa that, "when he was sad, she should be sad; when he was angry, as he was periodically when she asked him for a cheque, she should weep." But Leslie had bred a daughter who possessed just those qualities which he would have prized in a son: honesty, courage, firmness and tenacity; but in a girl, who, after all, should descend to some little sweet artifice in favour of the men she is appointed to serve, who should make a grace of weakness and display a certain charming, yielding timidity, these virtues became a wholly unwomanly boldness and obstinacy. One incident of those years which Virginia remembered tells us a good deal about the family and about Vanessa. One summer evening when she and Virginia and Adrian were walking in the garden enjoying themselves, their father called them in to play whist with him. They did not want to do so, nor did they join him until a long remorseful interval had elapsed. They found Leslie disconsolate and lonely. "Did you hear me call?" he asked. The younger ones remained silent but Vanessa admitted that she had. There was then,

* The final pages of the *Mausoleum Book* are largely a necrology: John Ormsby, James Dykes Campbell, Thomas Hughes, George du Maurier, Mrs Gurney, Mrs Brookfield, F. W. Gibbs, James Payn, Henry Sidgwick, George Smith, Herbert Fisher—one by one they die and Leslie is left increasingly lonely.

as there always was, a certain devastating frankness about her which Virginia found at times appalling and at times comic. Thus she came better armed than Stella to meet the demands and the assaults of her father.

'Assaults' is not, I think, too strong an expression. It is at all events hard to find any other word for the Wednesday afternoon interviews when the weekly accounts were examined. Vanessa was responsible for these reckonings, everything had to be made out in a very detailed and elaborate way and Vanessa, whose arithmetic was shaky, found the technical side of the business hard enough. But the real trouble came if the weekly books exceeded a certain sum; and this, Sophy being inflexible in her adherence to a tradition of decent extravagance, they nearly always did. Then Leslie would be overcome by a terrible feeling of financial insecurity. He felt hurt by the world, he felt terrified and aggrieved; he insisted that his misery should be appreciated and shared and so he made a scene.

The scene would begin with groans and sighs, then expressions of rage, then really terrible outbursts of bellowing fury in which Leslie would quite literally beat his breast, sob, and declare that he, a poor, broken, bereaved old man was being callously hounded to ruin. They were shooting Niagara; they would have to go to the house in Wimbledon. "And you stand there like a block of stone. Don't you pity me? Haven't you a word to say to me?" For all this was heard in silence by Vanessa. "What an aggravating young woman I must have been," she reflected in later years, "I simply waited till the cheque was signed." There were occasions when, with the connivance of Sophy, the accounts could be cooked so as to be made palatable to Leslie, but such occasions were very rare. The row was, almost, a weekly event. It ended when Leslie, with a piteously trembling hand, signed the cheque, all the time acting, and acting superbly, the part of the ruined and injured father.

Virginia, who witnessed it all, was consumed with silent indignation. How could her father behave with such brutality and why was it that he reserved these bellowings and screamings for his women? With men his conduct was invariably gentle, considerate and rational, so much so that, when Virginia and her aunt Caroline Emelia Stephen suggested to Maitland, his biographer, that Leslie was sometimes rather difficult, Maitland simply wouldn't believe it. Leslie, he objected, was the most modest, the most reasonable of men – and so he was with his own sex. But he needed and expected feminine sympathy. Vanessa's fault, which exacerbated the situation, making it far worse than it had been with Julia or with Stella, was that she would not sympathise. She would do her duty; but that was all, and her notion of her duty by no means corresponded with his. A complete and self-effacing devotion was what he demanded and this she was not ready to provide.

The uncomfortable fact was that Vanessa's childhood statement that she preferred her mother to her father had now hardened into something more positive. She, being the eldest, had observed the manner in which first Julia and then Stella had immolated themselves in order to make Leslie comfortable. She had seen them wear themselves out and die; she did not feel inclined to follow their example. Moreover Vanessa was not only more intelligent and more resolute than Stella, she was more selfish; she was fortified by the unyielding egotism of the artist. In the life-room, in that blessed peace which is broken only by the gentle scrape of charcoal upon paper, in that pleasant atmosphere of hard work and turpentine, she could for a time enjoy an existence which must have seemed utterly remote from Hyde Park Gate. For she could then inhabit a world in which certain questions of shape and colour, of tone and contour, of the behaviour of objects under different circumstances of illumination and disposition, were of supreme importance—matters which never bothered the heads of the other inhabitants of Hyde Park Gate. Leslie could certainly know nothing of such things. He, who had so often looked far over the plains of Lombardy from the summits of the High Alps, never once went down into Italy. Painting meant nothing to him at all. Virginia had a wider vision, but all her life she was intrigued, mystified and perplexed by her sister's art; it was something odd and alien, and because she was a writer she was in fact far closer to her father than was Vanessa. They had a common mystery, a common shop and, as she felt her vocation ever more loudly evident, there was a real bond of sympathy between them.

But Vanessa's art was her shield; she met adversity—and during these years her distresses were many—with the fortitude of a hard pressed but well-armed soldier. Moreover she had an ally. Jack Hills had no great reason to like his father-in-law, a father-in-law who had done all that he could to stop the match and had in the end only acquiesced with a groan. Now, so it must have appeared to him, Leslie, while remaining callously indifferent to Stella's death, was calmly setting out to exploit the next victim. At Painswick Jack Hills had confided equally in both sisters and both had been equally devoted to the task of comforting him; but he turned increasingly to Vanessa. She was only too ready to join with him in lamenting

Stella's death and, when it came to criticising Leslie, they had a common theme.

Virginia's diary tails away towards the end of 1897 and she finally makes an end of it in January 1898. Thereafter the evidence is scanty. The family went to Ringwood in the New Forest in the summer of 1898 but there are no substantial records of this holiday. In the following year they went to the Rectory at Warboys, within reach of Godmanchester and their Stephen cousins. Here Virginia decided again to keep a diary. It is in many ways an exasperating document. She had, at this time, taken to using a very fine pen and this led her to cultivate a minute, spidery, often virtually illegible hand, which she made more difficult to read by gluing her pages on to or between those of Dr Isaac Watts's *Right Use of Reason*.* The whole thing is now an admirable exercise in patience and decipherment.

This Warboys journal is very different from the diary of 1897. It is more grown-up, more reticent, more impersonal. The other occupants of the house, her father, Vanessa, Thoby, Adrian, and their guests, are barely mentioned. She describes people only when they are outside her immediate circle; as for instance the local curate or her Stephen cousins; an account of a perfectly horrible picnic with them is one of the best things in the diary. But her main purpose is to practise the art of writing.

> ... the edge of this ... [cloud] glistened with fire–vivid & glowing in the east like some sword of judgment or vengeance–& yet the intensity of its light melted & faded as it touched the gray sky behind so that there was no clearly defined outline. This is one observation that I have made from my observation of many sunsets–that no shape of cloud has one line that is the least sharp or hard–nowhere can you draw a straight line with your pencil & say "this line goes so" Everything is done by different shades and degrees of light–melting & mixing infinitely–Well may an Artist despair!
>
> This was the central point of the sunset but ... there was another glory, reflected indeed but no less glorious and perfect of its kind than the original. ... The afternoon had scattered gray clouds pall mall about the sky–some of these were now conglomerated into one vast cloud field in the east & south–others were sailing like solitary icebergs. All bore on them the imprint of the dying kiss of the sun. The icebergs

---

* *Logick/or/the right use of Reason/with a variety of rules to guard against error in the affairs of religion and human life as well as in the sciences/by Isaac Watts D.D. London/mdcclxxxvi.* Virginia bought this in St Ives for its binding and its format: "Any other book, almost, would have been too sacred to undergo the desecration that I planned."

VIRGINIA WOOLF

shone glowing pale crimson; the icefields [?] were broken up into exquisite blocks of crimson but a crimson which looked all the more delicate & exquisite that its background was soft cold gray.

This was all over in 10 minutes–When we got back home the east & west were rapidly taking on the darkness of night–No gleams of crimson lived to tell that the sun had sunk.

It is interesting to compare this Ruskinian exercise in descriptive writing with a letter written in the same spidery hand to her cousin Emma Vaughan.

12 August 1899
Warboys Rectory
Warboys
Huntingdonshire
(this is all the address necessary)

Dearly beloved Toad,

This morning we heard from Susan Lushington that she arrives on Monday at Huntingdon about 12.30. Some of us must, I expect meet her there, which means that we shall not be back here till 1.30–I do not know when you will arrive (if at all) but we *expect* you for luncheon; therefore to be brief and at the same time explicit; if we are not all here to greet you on your arrival shd. your arrival take place much before 1.30: we beg that you will in no way feel slighted, but that you will make yourself at Home–go on the Punt–feed the sea gull–visit the stables–examine the photographs–& take possession of our bedrooms & their appurtenances. I fear that Susan Lushington may in some way interrupt our afternoon, but she is sure to be unpacking, resting, & letter writing; besides she is a charming animal, & can play the Spinet to perfection. *Some* other people–toads I should say–nasty slimy crawling things–*think* they can play–ahem!

You see–my dear toad, that the terrible depression of this climate has not yet affected my spirits. I suspect you & Marny [Margaret Vaughan] of ulterior motives in thus blackening our minds. Or perhaps you are too unimaginative & soulless to feel the beauty of the place. Take my word for it Todkins, I have never been in a House, garden, or country that I liked half so well–leaving St Ives out of account. Yesterday we bicycled to Huntingdon–& paid a visit to our relatives [Lady Stephen and her family]. Coming back we forgot all our cares– (& they were many–Nessa & I each had a large string bag full of melons which bumped against our knees at every moment) in gazing –absorbing–sinking into–the Sky. You dont see the sky until you live here. We have ceased to be dwellers on the earth. We are really made of clouds. We are mystical & dreamy & perform Fugues on the Harmonium. Have you ever read your sister in law's Doges Farm?* Well

* *Days Spent on a Doge's Farm* by Margaret Symonds (Mrs W. W. Vaughan) 1893.

66

that describes much the same sort of country that this is; & you see how she, a person of true artistic soul, revels in the land. I shall think it a test of friends for the future whether they can appreciate the Fen country. I want to read books about it, & to write sonnets about it all day long. It is the only place for rest of mind & body, & for content-ment & creamy potatoes and all the joys of life. I am growing like a meditative Alderney cow. And there are people who think it dull & uninteresting!!!!

This all flowed from my lips without my desire or knowledge. I meant only to be short & businesslike. Poor Toad—when you come I shall say to you—Have you read my letter and you will confess that you did try a bit of it on the road, & you really do mean to have another shot on the way back. And you are only waiting for a rainy day to finish it altogether. Augusta* thinks it bad for your eyesight, & Marny has telegraphed "Forbid you to read Virginia's letters" I am a little cracky this afternoon. It is the hottest day I have yet lived thro'; I have read a whole long novel through; beginning at breakfast this morning & ending at 4 P.M.

It is now tea time. ([Two words illegible] Toadus inquit)

I am very sorry to have written such a long letter, but I will write a digest in very black ink so as to make up.

Love to dear Marny & all my Nieces and nephew.

Yrs always Goatus.

Do find some News to tell us. We long for some.

Oh October October

I wish you were *ober*

[in a large legible hand] This letter only to say that we have to meet Susan Lushington on Monday morning so that we may be late for you, but shall be in for luncheon 1.30 anyhow; & beg that you will Make Yourselves at Home—& not think yourselves slighted! The rest all the better for keeping.

News of a certain person & another *unknown* urgently required.

Do you see how much superior this paper is to yours?

This letter, with its pace, its mockery, its exaggeration, its flights of fancy, is already, despite some schoolgirlish remarks, not unlike the kind of letter that she was to write in later years. And those who remember her conversation will recognise certain turns of phrase, a certain impetuosity of address, which shows that at the age of seventeen she was already very like the person whom they knew. In a sense then she was precocious and old for her years, but in another way she was still very much a child and a very timid child at that. Peering out from the edge of the nest she observed the drop

* Emma's elder sister, Mrs Croft.

VIRGINIA WOOLF

below with terror, a terror that was increased by her sister's unlucky attempts to fly.

Vanessa was 'out' and the business of bringing her out was undertaken by George; Vanessa was not enjoying it at all and Virginia feared that she would enjoy it even less. It was an alarming prospect and she felt that she would be very much happier in the schoolroom. Here, with increasing health, she was fairly active learning both Greek and Latin. Greek was taught her by Miss Clara Pater,* the sister of Walter Pater–"very white and shrivelled" she called her–and then by Miss Case. Janet Case was 'thorough'; she observed that Virginia had a tendency to rush for the sense of a passage leaving grammar and accents to look after themselves, and that with Miss Pater she had got away with a very slovenly approach to the language. She had now to go back to the beginning and learn her grammar anew. But despite, or because of, these severities she knew how to hold Virginia's attention, and indeed her regard. She argued and took her pupil's arguments seriously; she herself was intensely interested not only in the language but in the ideas of the Greeks; she had a passion for Aeschylus and for Euripides and saw their relevance to her own time; so the lessons became discussions in which Virginia must have learnt a good deal. In July 1901, writing to Thoby, she says that she is reading the *Trachiniae* and has gone through the *Antigone* and *Oedipus Coloneus*. There was some sparring between her and her teacher; she tried, but did not succeed in making Miss Case lose her temper. But the lessons were the beginning of a lifelong friendship.

Thoby, now at Cambridge, was also to some extent her teacher, or at all events an intellectual sparring partner; and the following extract from a letter which Virginia wrote to him on 5 November 1901 gives some idea of their discussions:

My real object in writing is to make a confession–which is to take back a whole cartload of *goatisms* which I used at Fritham & elsewhere in speaking of a certain great English writer–the greatest– I have been reading Marlow, & I was so much more impressed by him than I thought I should be, that I read Cymbeline just to see if there mightn't be more in the great William than I supposed. And I was quite upset! Really & truly I am now let in to [the] company of worshippers–though I still feel a little oppressed by his–greatness I suppose. I shall want a lecture when I see you; to clear up some points about the Plays. I mean about the characters. Why aren't they more human? Imogen & Posthumous

* Miss Pater is probably the origin of Miss Craye in "Slater's Pins Have No Points" in *A Haunted House*, 1943.

- & Cymbeline - I find them beyond me. Is this my feminine weakness in the upper region? But really they might have been cut out with a pair of scissors - as far as mere humanity goes. Of course they talk divinely. I have spotted the best lines in the play - almost in any play I should think -

Imogen says - Think that you are upon a rock, & now throw me again! & Posthumous answers - Hang there like fruit, my soul, till the tree die! Now if that doesn't send a shiver down your spine, even if you are in the middle of cold grouse & coffee - you are no true Shakespearian! Oh dear oh dear - just as I feel in the mood to talk about these things, you go & plant yourself in Cambridge.

Tomorrow I go on to Ben Jonson, but I shant like him as much as Marlow. I read Dr Faustus, & Edward II - & I thought them very near the great man - with more humanity I should say - not all on such a grand tragic scale. Of course Shakespeares smaller characters are human; what I say is that superhuman ones *are* superhuman. Just explain this to me - & also why his plots are just cracky things - Marlow's are flimsier; the whole thing is flimsier, but there are some very "booming" (Strachey's word) lines & speeches & whole scenes - When Edward dies for instance - . . .

The Strachey to whom she refers was one of Thoby's new friends; he had, it appeared, met some tremendously interesting fellows at Trinity: Strachey was a wit, a man of undoubted genius; there was also Sydney-Turner, another genius, who slept all day and sat up reading all night, browsing through Menander as you or I might glance through a newspaper; Woolf, a strange wild man of powerful intellect; Bell, who wrote poetry and knew about pictures and had a capital seat on a horse. Thoby found Bell's horsemanship almost as interesting as Sydney-Turner's erudition, for he took a hearty commonsense view of the world; just as his father had been a muscular Christian, so he was a muscular atheist. The intellectuals liked him and he liked them; but between him and them there was a tenuous but perceptible frontier - his nickname 'The Goth' conveyed a shade of affectionate disapproval; he was a little more conventional, a little more conservative than they, and while for them Cambridge was exhilarating because it was a place buzzing with ideas, for him it was also a theatre for the traditional delights of privileged youth. And so, when the intellectuals considered whether to invite him to join that arch-intellectual semi-secret society - the 'Apostles' - they concluded, not without heart-searching and hesitation, that he was not really 'apostolic'; his sympathies placed him closer to Bell than to the 'Bretheren' - Bell, who had Edna May to lunch in his rooms at Trinity, rode out to Newmarket and studied the works, not only of G. E. Moore, but of Surtees.

That Cambridge was then a place reserved for men and one in which their sisters could hardly enter save as rare shy intruders was undeniable; but Cambridge as reported by so heartily masculine an observer as Thoby would have appeared quite aggressively and unbearably anti-feminist. In Virginia this must have provoked a great deal of serious reflection. She and her sister might spend the mornings studying Greek or drawing from the cast; but their afternoons and their evenings were given up to those occupations which the men of the family thought suitable: looking after the house, presiding at the teatable, making conversation, being agreeable to George and Gerald and to *their* friends, being polite to Aunt Minna, Aunt Mary, Aunt Anny, Cousin Mia, Lady Stephen and all Leslie's friends and admirers. The grand intellectual adventures and liberties were kept for Thoby and would, later on, be available to Adrian, and if this cost money, as it did, then they, the daughters, would be sacrificed for the benefit of the sons. Clearly it was the sons who were to have the lion's share of life.

> I dont get anybody to argue with me now, & feel the want. I have to delve from books, painfully & all alone, what you get every evening sitting over your fire & smoking your pipe with Strachey, etc. No wonder my knowledge is but scant. Theres nothing like talk as an educator I'm sure. Still I try my best with Shakespeare. I read Sidney Lee's Life . . .

But Sidney Lee's life of Shakespeare, as Virginia understood very well, was no substitute for Lytton Strachey's conversation. For the rest of her life she considered herself to be ill-educated and felt that this was an injury inflicted on her by reason of her sex. This radical inequity in the arrangement of the world was to be revealed in quite another fashion, and one which hit Virginia and Vanessa hard.

At the end of Thoby's first year at Cambridge the family had spent the summer at Fritham in the New Forest, and it was here that George, taking Virginia aside one evening in the garden, had a serious talk about Vanessa. Vanessa, he explained, was behaving unwisely. She was seeing altogether too much of Jack Hills. It was, of course, most imprudent and people were beginning to talk. Could not Virginia use her influence?

Virginia had been more or less unaware of what was happening. She had indeed noticed that Jack was more with her sister than with her. But she had not realised that Vanessa's feelings of sympathy had turned to something more passionate. She was in fact falling

seriously in love with Jack and he was, at all events, not unwilling
to be loved.

Did George perceive the irony of the situation? Probably not;
he must have been engrossed by a very understandable alarm, to
which no doubt was added a certain jealousy. Under the law as it
then stood—it was altered in 1907—a man was forbidden to marry
his deceased wife's sister. Numerous attempts had been made to
legalise such marriages. The Commons frequently passed bills which
would have had this effect, but the Lords, inspired by the bishops,
resisted the will of the elected House until 1896. A motion was then
set before their Lordships which was so drafted as to placate a large
section of the clergy, and was passed. But Lord Salisbury, the Prime
Minister, voted against it and it was no doubt through his agency
that it never reached the Commons. If it had, this story would have
been very different; also it would have been told by someone else.

A love affair between Vanessa Stephen and Jack Hills was therefore, of necessity, something guilty. The best issue that could be
hoped for was a foreign marriage such as that of the Holman Hunts—
not, perhaps, quite the marriage for a rising young solicitor with
political ambitions. The more probable outcome would be scandal-
ous. That an insufficiency of Parliamentary time or the political
calculations of a Prime Minister should be able to convert an
innocent affection into a sinful attachment seems a *reductio ad
absurdum* of official morality. The fact that Parliament could make
her an honest woman led Vanessa, who always had her doubts
about Parliament, to question whether, in this usage of the word,
'honesty' had very much meaning. She came by her own hard and
private road to conclusions very similar to those of Thoby's friends
who maintained that virtue lay, not in the mere fact of obedience
to rules or in a reverential attitude towards received traditions, but
in a state of mind; her own state of mind, she decided, had nothing
to do with the strength of the Unionist Party in Westminster.

None of this, one may imagine, ever occurred to George, nor,
if it had done so, would he have given it a moment's attention.
All that he knew, and all that he needed to know, was that "people
would talk." His interests would be touched, his career would be
jeopardised. The half-sister whom he had hoped to present as a
social asset—and with her looks she might have captured the younger
son of a duke—would become a disastrous social liability. But
George certainly went beyond self-interested calculations. An affair
of this kind was 'not the thing' and he most sincerely and ardently
worshipped 'the thing' without ever wondering what in fact it

might be. When he took Virginia aside that evening at Fritham he was, doubtless, convinced that he was acting in the interests of morality, the family, and, naturally, of Vanessa herself.

Virginia, taken unawares, hardly knew what to say, felt that it was very shocking, went guilelessly to her sister and, stammeringly, presented George's views. "So you take their side too," was Vanessa's reply: a reply so touching, so bitter, and at the same time so effective that Virginia at once discovered that she was, as always in all their struggles, at one with her sister.

The party against them was strong: George had many allies. But it must be noted that it had one signal weakness; Leslie, with a greatness of spirit which deserves to be remembered to his credit, refused, despite George's entreaties, to join the forces of public morality. In his view Vanessa had to decide this matter for herself. But, for the rest, the outlook was dark indeed. To Virginia, who may have been prejudiced, it seemed that Jack himself bore a heavy responsibility; he had encouraged Vanessa, drawn comfort from her kindness, without ever considering what price she might have to pay for it. He was thoughtless, he was selfish, he behaved with masculine egotism. But, of course, the chief tormentors belonged to George's faction and consisted largely of the usual regiment of female relations. Mary Fisher–again according to Virginia–was particularly vicious. So much so that Vanessa avoided her aunt and cut the Fishers when they met in the street. This conduct drew a reproof from Thoby. How much he understood of the business is unclear–in general he seems to have known very little of what was happening to his sisters–but at all events he knew what respect was due to his aunt and he announced with Olympian calm, but also with a hint of Olympian fire power, that he thought it not right that his aunt Mary should be treated so. Thoby was on the side of authority–masculine authority; if George wanted the girls to go to parties then they should go; if Leslie demanded sympathy, then the girls should be sympathetic. This attitude was made possible by the fact that there was never an explanation between Thoby and his sisters. Sex was taboo, the dead were taboo, half their most important emotions were taboo; they were all too shy to come out into the open. Vanessa, devoted as she was to her brother, and far too reserved to argue a point involving her own emotional life, must then have reached the nadir of her despair.

All this must be imagined against a background of small engagements and steady routine. During the years 1897–1904 life at 22 Hyde Park Gate must have been something like this: Vanessa would start the day with a ride up and down the Ladies' Mile on a horse given her by George. Breakfast at 8.30, first Vanessa and Gerald, then Leslie and Adrian, the latter usually late–half his gear forgotten– for school, the former groaning because there were no letters for him (Everyone has forgotten me) or growling over a bill from Barkers (We shall be ruined). Then Vanessa would descend to the basement, which was almost totally dark, interview Sophy and order the day's meals. Then she would bicycle off in a long dress and a large floppy hat to Mr Cope's School of Art or, later on, to the Academy Schools (she passed ahead of her friends from the Antique to the Life Room in 1902). Gerald might offer her a lift eastwards in his hansom–he had a regular hansom–on his way to the publishing business which he founded in 1898. George and Virginia would come down later, George completely armed for the gentilities of London life, shining, immaculate, impeccable; he would engage Virginia, if he could, with an account of his social triumphs of the previous night, before going off to his work as unpaid secretary to Charles Booth or Austen Chamberlain. Leslie would retire to his study and remain there all the morning. When George stopped chattering and left, Virginia too would go upstairs with Liddell and Scott to tackle Sophocles or Euripides or to write letters and essays. This she did in the old nursery at the top of the house. Here she accumulated a great many books and here she sometimes received friends or teachers–Janet Case or one of the Vaughan girls. The room had white walls and bright blue curtains. Her manner of working was unusual. She had a desk standing about 3 feet 6 inches high with a sloping top; it was so high that she had to stand to her work. For this peculiar method of operation she advanced various reasons but it would seem that her principal motive was the fact that Vanessa, like many painters, stood to work in order to be able to move away from and look at her canvas. This led Virginia to feel that her own pursuit might appear less arduous than that of her sister unless she set matters on a footing of equality, and so for many years she stood at this strange desk and, in a quite unnecessary way, tired herself.★

Like Vanessa, Virginia would be dressed with little regard for fashion and of the two Virginia would be the more untidy; from ten till one the great world could be ignored. After lunch–Leslie's lunch always consisted of a mutton chop–social claims might become more urgent and by 4.30 they were important, for there

★ "For the rest of her life," says Holroyd, *Lytton Strachey*, vol. I, p. 404; this is certainly an exaggeration–possibly until 1912.

was tea to be taken in the front room which at Hyde Park Gate was separated from the back by folding doors. In this room, the Stephen girls might entertain Mrs Humphry Ward, Mr C. B. Clarke, Mr F. W. Gibbs and, to represent the younger generation, Mrs Maxse and her sister Miss Susan Lushington, the Miss Massingberds, the Miss Stillmans, Mr Ronald Norman–all those whom Adrian was later to call the 'Hyde-Park-Gaters': Freshfields, Booths, Protheroes, Pollocks, Creightons, Ritchies. These families, socially and intellectually respectable representatives of the middle class, many of them eminent or connected with eminence, many of them neighbours of the Stephens in Kensington, had been friends of Leslie and Julia; it was assumed that, in their generation, the children would also be friends. There might also be aunts and cousins and they all had to be arranged socially. The right person had to be found to shout the right things into Leslie's ear trumpet and the young ladies, who now had to appear as such, had to make the right kind of small talk. This art they learnt and never entirely lost–the art of being agreeable, of watching the happiness of guests, of providing suitable social mixtures– the art, in fact, of pleasing. In later life Virginia thought that something of it had leaked into her ink–not when she was writing her novels, but in her reviewing. Here she was, she felt, too polite, too much the young lady, altogether too deferential.

The task was not an easy one. Leslie was a social problem. He could be amusing and sometimes he enjoyed being reminiscent; but he was easily bored and when he was bored he would groan to himself. Leslie's groans were, indeed, one of the more disheartening phenomena of Hyde Park Gate. He would groan in despair at his bereavement; he would groan over his bank balance; it was also said that he was heard one night slowly ascending the stairs, groaning at each step and loudly exclaiming: "Why won't my whiskers grow? Why won't my whiskers grow?"

But Leslie's teatime groans were, only too often, the prelude to something far worse. Leslie was deaf enough not to hear, or to pretend not to hear, his own conversations with himself.

"Why won't that young man go?" he would suddenly demand in a dreadfully audible voice. Or again, when his old friend Frederick Waymouth Gibbs had, for a space of twenty minutes or so, imparted a great mass of information concerning the Dominion of Canada, Leslie would produce an enormous groan and remark, in a deafening whisper: "Oh Gibbs, what a bore you are." Then some young woman–Kitty Maxse very likely, for she had every social accomplishment at her finger tips, would have to coax and flatter the indignant (but undeniably boring) Mr Gibbs back into a good humour again.

The day was always full of social arrangements; arrangements to spare Leslie unwelcome visitors, to see that someone would be in when someone else called, to cope with various horrors, such as Aunt Mary, Cousin Mia and so on. And when the social difficulties of tea had been negotiated the far more perilous business of the evening had to be managed. Before dinner the family retired to dress, no matter how quiet the evening that lay before them. The Duckworth brothers were, of course, impeccably got up; but, despite the presents that they received, the young ladies were hard put to it to make an acceptable toilette. Acceptable that is to George, who would examine his half-sisters with the keen and pitiless eye of a sergeant major inspecting a recruit. If he detected the least contravention of decorum as he understood it, as for instance when Virginia had the bright idea of making her evening dress out of cheap green furnishing material, he would express his displeasure with curt and brutal acerbity. And then, later in the evening, when Leslie, who had spent the interval between tea and dinner in his study, returned thither to read Hobbes or Bentham, to smoke innumerable clay pipes—each a virgin used but once,* so that his fender was littered with their shattered debris the next morning— George would carry his sisters out into the great world.

George was bitterly disappointed in Vanessa; she seemed determined to spoil her own chances in life. She fell in love with the wrong person and when he, George, poured gifts into her lap she was so unreasonable as to protest. How could any girl in her senses (particularly one with an allowance of fifty pounds a year) complain at being given fans, necklaces, dresses, flowers, an Arab mare for the Row and invitations to half the great houses in London? But Vanessa did complain, although at first her protests were probably silent. Indeed, to begin with she did enjoy being taken to dances, even though she was still wearing mourning—very beautifully confected mourning—for Stella; but soon her feelings changed and although she loved pretty clothes a time came when she began to look upon her evening dresses as a penitent looks upon her sheet. She was shy, she was awkward, she was naturally silent; she danced

* Tobacco was a male prerogative. Vanessa and Virginia were forbidden to smoke in their father's presence. Once, when a lady guest lit a cigarette, she was roughly told by Leslie that his drawing-room was not a bar parlour. (MH/A 5). See also: VW, 'Leslie Stephen': *Collected Essays*, Vol. IV, p. 79.

badly; but even if she had talked and danced with ease she would have found George's friends excruciatingly boring. George moved in stuffy, upper class society; but it was not only that Vanessa could find nothing to say to these people; it was worse than that: she found George himself a bore. He could spoil a party by his mere presence: when Vanessa dined with old friends whom she liked he could and did damage the evening by turning up uninvited after the meal and making polite conversation until it was time to escort his sister home. For him, indeed, parties were not designed for pleasure; his sisters were taken out, not to enjoy themselves but to practise their profession, the great profession of getting husbands; he was there as an arbiter of elegance, a censor and a chaperone; every entertainment was to be considered an examination, and their performance would be judged with ruthless severity. The people whom they met might not please them, that did not matter; these were the 'right' people and to meet them was a duty.

Presently Vanessa began to resist. Each new invitation brought a struggle. George would implore and entreat, sometimes he would actually burst into tears, if still thwarted he would sulk; he would mobilise the family – Aunt Mary Fisher was always a sure ally – and the family would, loudly, angrily and repeatedly, fail to understand how Vanessa could be so foolish, so obstinate, so unwomanly, so downright ungrateful, as to reject George's generosity. And even when Vanessa thought that she had escaped she would find that George had secretly accepted an invitation in her name and that she was condemned to another evening or another week-end of misery and exasperation.

A time came, about the year 1900, when Vanessa's opposition became so troublesome that George decided he had better see whether he might not have better luck with Virginia. He gave her a brooch and told her that Vanessa's unkindness was such that it would drive him from home and – this was emotionally implied rather than said – he would find consolation in the arms of whores. It was for Virginia to rescue him from this awful fate by being a good sister and venturing into high society. Virginia, who had been to the Trinity Ball and had found it sufficiently amusing (it was made more so by the presence of Thoby's friend Bell), thought that perhaps Vanessa's complaints were exaggerated and agreed without too much difficulty.

She soon discovered her mistake: Vanessa had been bored; *she* was terrified. After all it was not so very long since she had been unable to endure the company of any stranger; now, faced by all the apparatus of a very dull section of 'good society' she found that, despite Stella's lessons, she was unable to dance at all gracefully, nor could she converse with the slightest ease in a ballroom. She went through agonies of embarrassment, miserable humiliating evenings when she couldn't find a partner, ghastly meaningless conversations which got bogged down and left her blushing and wordless.*

... the truth of it is, as we frequently tell each other, we are failures. Really, we cant shine in Society. I don't know how it's done. We aint popular—we sit in corners & look like mutes who are longing for a funeral. However, there are more important things in this life—from all I hear I shant be asked to dance in the next....

Things were made a little worse by the fact that George, for all his social ambitions was, in practice, rather ham-handed. When he made Vanessa go with him to stay for the weekend at the Chamberlains they arrived at the wrong time and at the servants' entrance. Virginia remembered one evening when an even more ghastly mistake occurred.

On this occasion George took Virginia by herself to dine with the Dowager Countess of Carnarvon and her sister Mrs Popham of Littlecote, the dinner to be followed by a visit to the theatre. The evening began well enough; the two ladies seemed kind and Virginia felt encouraged to talk. In fact she began to speak with confidence and abandon. It was necessary, she said, that one should understand the need for expressing one's emotions. Had Lady Carnarvon read Plato? If so she would remember ...

Here Virginia said something awful, something appalling. We shall never know what it was, and perhaps she was simply talking too much; but she always had a terrifying way of forgetting her audience and, in the first years of the twentieth century, Plato could easily lead to topics which might appal Lady Carnarvon or Mrs Popham, topics entirely unsuitable for a young woman. Indeed, as George explained later, in the course of his reprimand: "they're not used to young women saying *anything*." Whatever it was that she said Virginia only became aware of her mistake when she observed that George was crimson with embarrassment. At once a new topic was started and Virginia knew that she had failed again.

* A quarter of a century later she wrote: "The heat has come, bringing with it the inexplicably disagreeable memories of parties, and George Duckworth; a fear haunts me even now, as I drive past Park Lane on top of a bus and think of Lady Arthur Russell and so on. I become out of love with everything ..." AWD (Berg), 25 May 1926.

But that was not the end of this disastrous evening. They had tickets for the French Actors. They put on their cloaks and left, Virginia still burning with shame but able to notice, despite the agitated efforts of Mrs Popham, that George gave his hostess a passionate kiss behind one of the pillars of the hall. And then there was the play. At first Virginia's misery was such that she hardly noticed what was going on upon the stage; moreover the French dialogue was too rapid for her ears; but presently the action became so dramatic that it compelled her attention. A gentleman was chasing a lady around the room, he gained upon her, she fell upon a sofa, he leapt upon her, at the same time unfastening his buttons and–the curtain fell.

Lady Carnarvon, Mrs Popham and George rose in consternation; together they beat a hurried retreat, shepherding Virginia before them out into the street, where the ladies departed in a brougham.

George, vexed with Virginia, and no doubt by his own social folly in taking his sister to such an entertainment, insisted nevertheless that the social duties of the evening were not over. They drove off in a hansom cab to Melbury Road to an evening party at the Holman Hunts where they found the Master with a large company explaining the sublimities of *The Light of the World*, which had recently returned to his studio after touring the principal cities of the Empire. There at least Virginia might feel safe from impropriety; but not for long. That night, in her bedroom she had once more to withstand the ardent embraces of George.

The incident may help to qualify the picture which Virginia drew of her relations with George at this time. She saw herself as the defenceless victim of George's social ambitions; she was snubbed, bullied, and compelled to jump like a lame dog through whatever circus hoops he might place before her. The picture, I fancy, is true enough as far as it goes; but this was not the whole picture. Virginia respected George's sex, she quailed before his authority, she was aware of her own poverty and of his affluence; but she was never guilty of weak submission.

As a child of I know not what age, she wrote a History of the Duckworths. It has been lost but the opening passage was something like this:

> One day when William Rufus was hunting in the New Forest he shot a duck. It fell into the middle of a pond and could not be recovered; but an active little page boy waded out into the water and recovered the bird. The king drew his sword and dubbed the lad saying: "Arise Sir Duckworth, for surely thou art worth many ducks."

George and Gerald were not amused and one may surmise that this little *jeu d'esprit* was meant to pain them. It expresses lightly, but not without malice, Virginia's estimate of the Duckworths. She was from an early age convinced that although the pattern of inheritance might give them beauty it did not give them intelligence. For that, the sharp wits of the Stephens were more to the purpose. George and Gerald could easily be mocked and Virginia was not the person to neglect such an opportunity; her social gaffes were painful to her, but she probably drew some satisfaction from her realisation that they were even more painful to George. On one occasion, when she was at a party, her drawers fell down while she was in the very act of saying goodbye to her hostess; she gathered everything up in a bundle and shuffled away as best she could; but on returning to Hyde Park Gate and finding George at home she came into the drawing-room and flourished the errant garments in his face. George was speechless with indignation.

And yet, her miseries were real enough. She could make a joke of them and tease George with them; but the fact remained that she and Vanessa were, as she said, "failures." In an essay written at this time she discussed her lack of success and then goes on to consider the merits of the man or woman who shines at dances. She is at some pains to be fair. She rejects the common view that the artificiality, the downright insincerity of the socially successful person is reprehensible. It represents the desire to please and to be pleased and that after all is not a bad thing: rather there is a certain gallantry, a certain philanthropy in this cultivation of the graces. The grapes, she seems to be saying, are not sour. And again, writing to an intimate friend:

> I went to *Two Dances* last week, but I think Providence inscrutably decreed some other destiny for me. Adrian and I waltzed (to a Polka!) and Adrian says he can't conceive how anyone can be idiotic enough to find amusement in dancing – and I see how they do it but feel all the really young Ladies far removed into another sphere – which is so pathetic – and I would give all my profound Greek to dance really well – and so would Adrian give anything he had.

But she did not always fail socially; the desire to succeed, though not quite in the way that George envisaged, was there. Few girls, conscious that they had more than their fair share of wits and beauty, could altogether renounce the *beau monde* at whose doors Virginia found herself. She could see clearly enough that most of its inhabitants were stupid; she could see that success, as George understood success, was a pretty dismal thing. There was much in Good

Society that she found hateful and frightening; but there was always something in it that she loved. To be at the centre of things, to know people who disposed of enormous power, who could take certain graces and prerogatives for granted, to mingle with the decorative and decorated world, to hear the butler announce a name that was old when Shakespeare was alive, these were things to which she could never be wholly indifferent. She was in fact a romantic snob. It was something which she never allowed to distort other values but it did play a part–quite an important part–in her life. In her youth she was ready to look at the world of rank and fashion, if only it could be sympathetically presented to her, and so was Vanessa. What they needed was a guide, not a tyrant but a friend, not a man but a woman–a woman with the tact, the imagination, the kindliness that could rob Mayfair of its terrors and make Kensington delightful. Living in and for society such a person would no doubt be at some points limited but the limitations would be so nearly transcended that, to a shy, intelligent girl, they would hardly be apparent; such a person might act as an evangelist of good society and be able, almost, to make one believe that it is possible to be at once worldly and unworldly. Virginia attempted to draw such a woman when she wrote *The Voyage Out*; she made a deeper, a more extensive examination in *Mrs Dalloway*. In real life she and Vanessa found her in Kitty Maxse.

Kitty Maxse had been a Miss Lushington; the Lushingtons were connected at a great many points with the Stephens, with Julia's family, with India, Clapham, the Bar and the Pre-Raphaelites. Mrs Vernon Lushington had been Julia's greatest friend, and had known the Stephen children for many years. Julia it was who had made the match between Kitty and Leopold Maxse which, it may be remembered, was settled under the jackmanii at Talland House. Leo Maxse was an invalid, enough of an invalid to be unable to take the active part in politics that he would have enjoyed; he was, nevertheless, the editor of the *National Review*. He was a difficult husband; there were no children. She was smart, with a tight, neat pretty smartness; her blue eyes looked at the world through half-closed lashes; she had a lovely mocking voice; she stood very upright.*

In some measure she inherited the Stephen girls. She was grateful

* Mrs Maxse was certainly the original of Mrs Dalloway, but I do not think that novel provides, or was meant to provide, an exact portrait. Lord David Cecil, who knew Mrs Maxse, does not see any close resemblance. Virginia comes closest to exact portraiture when she loves her model. She did not love Kitty Maxse.

to and had been deeply attached to Julia; she adopted a quasi-maternal attitude towards her daughters. Vanessa, as the eldest, most needed her help in dealing with the great world and she was quite sharp enough, quite sensible enough to perceive, even if Vanessa did not tell her, that George was not the perfect Cicerone for a tour of London Society. Guided as she was by excellent feelings and good principles, she proved really sympathetic and really helpful when Stella died; thereafter she became one of Vanessa's two most intimate friends. (The other, Margery Snowden, was a dowdy, desperately serious art student.)

Thus, with Kitty's assistance and in her own manner, Vanessa went into society.

Virginia was rather left behind on this excursion. She found Kitty far less sympathetic than did Vanessa; perhaps she was a little jealous; but also she detected a certain worldly brilliance, a kind of enamelled glitter that she did not like. She was continually telling herself that Kitty *was* a very good woman and yet, when she met her, recoiling. But she certainly had the entrée to a feminine aristocratic circle which was easier, less pretentious and quite as glamorous as that which George frequented. Lady Bath and her daughters Beatrice and Katherine Thynne (who married Lord Cromer), and their friend Lady Robert Cecil, these seemed to Virginia to have, not only rank, beauty and easy, pleasant good manners but a kind of lazy pagan majesty, a natural grace which fascinated her; she saw a good deal of them and enjoyed their society enormously; her guide thither was not Kitty but a friend of her own.

Before coming to this important friendship let us note that the years 1900, 1901 and 1902 progressed, so far as the Stephen family were concerned, sadly but without any very remarkable events. 1900 had been a year of crisis in the relationship between Vanessa and Jack Hills; thereafter it would seem that Jack gradually disengaged himself; at all events the affair died down, not, one may imagine, without pain to the principals and to Virginia. George must have been pleased but his own affairs were not progressing very well. He fell in love with Lady Flora Russell and, having learnt *Love in the Valley* by heart in order to impress her, went off to propose. This mnemonic feat succeeded in its object and he was able to write home announcing his engagement. The news, as may be imagined, was greeted with enthusiasm. Virginia telegraphed her congratulations, "She is," she wrote, "an Angel," and signed with her usual nickname. The telegram reached Islay thus: SHE IS AN AGED GOAT. It did not help matters but was not, it seems, the reason why the match was almost immediately broken off. George returned crestfallen and miserable and retired to bed, suffering, it was said, from shock.

That year 1902 saw the Coronation and a large distribution of honours. Leslie was offered a KCB. He seems to have felt some reluctance to accept such an honour but was apparently pressed to do so by his children and, notably, by Thoby. Earlier in the same year he had an illness and consulted Sir Frederick Treves, who recommended an operation; just what he said we cannot tell, but Leslie wrote: "I consider this to be equivalent to a warning that my journey is coming to an end." In fact he probably knew that he had cancer. At the end of the year he wrote to his eldest son: "They have, I suppose, explained my state to you. I do not think that they have quite taken in the fact–it *is* a fact–that the trouble is now steadily increasing."

That summer the family was at Fritham again. It was their third stay there. The young people enjoyed riding in the New Forest and Sir Leslie, although his illness kept him pretty close to the house, liked the place. Amongst their visitors were Clive Bell and, more important from Virginia's point of view, Violet Dickinson.

Violet Dickinson was a friend of the Duckworths, and had been intimate with Stella; she became a Quaker but one with aristocratic connections: she was related to the Edens. Leslie noted that "her only fault is that she is 6 feet high." She had he observed "taken a great fancy to the girls, who went about with her all day & discoursed upon literary & other matters continuously–Miss D. told me many pleasant things about the two and admires Ginia's intelligence greatly." The admiration was mutual, though why Virginia was so bowled over by Violet it is not altogether easy to say. At the time of this visit to Fritham, when the friendship was still fairly new, Virginia attempted to describe Violet in words:

We . . . showed her to her room & left her to dust her long travel-stained limbs. She came down to dinner in flowing & picturesque garments–for all her height, & a certain comicality of face, she treats her body with dignity. She always wore suitable & harmonious clothes –though she made no secret of the fact that they had lived through more seasons than one. Indeed she was singularly unreserved in many ways; always talking & laughing & entering into whatever was going on with a most youthful zeal. It was only after a time that one came to a true estimate of her character–that one saw that all was not cheerfulness & high spirits by any means–She had her times of depression, & her sudden reserves; but it is true that she was always quick to follow a cheerful voice. In that lies much of her charm– . . .* To a casual observer she would appear, I think, a very high spirited, rather crazy, harum scarum sort of person–whose part in life was [to] be slightly ridiculous, warmhearted & calculated to make the success of any kind of party. She has a very wide circle of acquaintances mostly of the landed & titled variety in whose country houses she is for ever staying– & with whom she seems to be invariably popular. She is 37– & without any pretence to good looks,–which she knows quite well herself, & lets you know too–even going out of her way to allude laughingly to her gray hairs, & screw her face into the most comical grimaces. But an observer who would stop here, putting her down as one of those cleverish adaptable ladies of middle age who are welcome everywhere, & not indispensable anywhere–such an observer would be superficial indeed.

At which point the MS comes to an end, or rather, the page on which it is written is cut away.

Virginia's numerous letters to Violet have been preserved and from this it is clear to the modern reader, though it was not at all clear to Virginia, that she was in love and that her love was returned. For they are passionate letters, enchanting, amusing, embarrassing letters full of private jokes and endearments, letters in which Virginia invents nicknames for herself, imagines herself as some shy half-wild animal, a pet to be fondled and cherished; and from which one tries to conjure up a picture of the recipient.

She was certainly a very good woman, a woman gifted with humour, intelligence and patience. "You remind me," said Virginia, "of Mrs Carlyle" and then warned her not to risk that lady's fate and go rushing with too warm a heart after her pets. She attracted Virginia, I surmise, because she was so very unlike her; she had a breezy masculine assurance, a cheerful imperturbable balance, she was a lofty and reassuring tower of strength. But she must have had something more than strength, a certain real greatness of mind and character. She could take mockery, give sympathy, understanding and love with immense generosity. The other Stephen children, none of whom was stupid, all of whom were inclined to be critical, liked her. I would guess that they found her reactions to their taste. She would always have been on the side of decency and kindliness and good sense.

Like Madge Vaughan, Violet Dickinson fulfilled a need. She provided sympathy and stability at a time when it was badly needed. I do not think that she made any very great contribution to Virginia's

* Passage excised in the original

intellectual development. Virginia did indeed send her manuscripts for criticism (she also wrote a kind of joke biography of her friend) but I doubt whether Violet's criticism as distinct from her encouragement was very important to her. Her gifts were chiefly moral and, when other and more remarkable people came into Virginia's life, passion slowly faded into kindness. One must think of this friendship as an affair of the heart, where I think that in fact it remained; while the affair was at its height, that is to say from about 1902 to 1907, it was intense.

Violet Dickinson's sympathies were to be put to the test. When she came to stay at Fritham in 1902 Sir Leslie was anticipating an operation. In December it could be no further postponed; it seemed doubtful whether he would survive but in fact he made a good recovery, good enough to allow his children to celebrate Christmas boisterously, and was back at home in January. But in April 1903 it became clear to Dr Seton and the nurse that the disease was spreading and that the patient must soon die. This news was communicated to Vanessa, who told her brothers and sister and thought it best that Sir Leslie should, if possible, be kept in ignorance.

The word "soon" in Seton's report was given a more precise meaning by Treves, who saw the invalid in May and gave him six months to live. There was nothing that they could do but try and make his dissolution as easy as possible. It was a melancholy and unpleasant time for everyone, but of the children none, I think, suffered so much as Virginia. They all felt some affection and some guilt. Vanessa who, more than any of them, was relieved–glad even–to be orphaned, dreamed after her father's death that she had committed a murder and although she had never heard of Freud, realised the connection and promptly stopped such dreaming. Thoby no doubt was upset; but with his sanguine character, his abundant and optimistic plans for the future, the thing was not too great a blow, while Adrian had very little affection for his father. But Virginia, although she had felt hatred, rage and indignation at Leslie's conduct to Vanessa, felt also very deep love for him. She saw that he was reluctant to die because his children had at last got to an age at which he could know them, and knowing, love them. He wanted to see what would become of them. In his present state he could no longer be a tyrant and his tyranny might be forgotten. Between him and Virginia a special bond had been established. She loved him and he, for his part, had for some time felt a special tenderness towards her. "Ginia," he wrote, "continues to be good to me and is a great comfort," and again: "She can be most fascinat-

Virginia Stephen, 1903

Right Mrs Leslie Stephen
with Virginia, 1884

Right Leslie Stephen, 1900

Left Virginia and Vanessa, St. Ives, 1894

Below Sophia Farrell with maids and dogs, 1899

Above Vanessa, Stella, Virginia, *c.* 1896

Left Jack Hills

Opposite above Stella Duckworth

Opposite below Adrian and Virginia, 1900

Opposite above Sir Leslie Stephen, K.C.B., 1902

Opposite below Vanessa Stephen

Left Violet Dickson and Virginia, 1902

Below Cub hunting at 5 a.m., Fritham 1901. James and Lytton Strachey, Thoby, Adrian and Virginia Stephen, and Gurth

Above Thoby Stephen

Below Lady Beatrice Thynne

Above   Lady Robert Cecil

Below   Violet Dickson

Opposite above   Walter Lamb

Opposite below   Adrian Stephen
at Fitzroy Square

Left   George Duckworth

Below   Madge Vaughan

Above   Clive Bell, *c.* 1906

Left   Lytton Strachey by
Duncan Grant

Opposite above   The Emperor of
Abyssinia and his suite
Standing, left to right: Guy
Ridley, Horace de Vere Cole,
Adrian Stephen, Duncan Grant
Seated: Virginia Stephen,
Anthony Buxton

Opposite below   Caroline Emelia
Stephen

Right   Roger Fry

Below right   Virginia Stephen

Opposite above   Clive, Virginia and Julian, Blean, 1910

Opposite below   Saxon Sydney-Turner, Clive Bell, Virginia Stephen, and Julian, Studland, 1910

Above   Asham House

Left   Virginia and Leonard Woolf

ing." Thus, for her, the conflict of feelings was most acute and most miserable.

That summer they went to Netherhampton House, near Salisbury. Sir Leslie was still able to walk a little and Virginia took him to Wilton and Stonehenge. In the autumn, the usual chorus of female sympathisers came wailing down Hyde Park Gate. The dying man was apt to consider them with some impatience:

> The amiable ladies who come to see me are not many & I fear are rather apt to bore me. One has been here just now, talking very fast till I had to look as tired as I could to get her to go.

Caroline Emelia came to see him and could think of nothing to say. He groaned in manifest boredom and she descended, blowing her nose hard, the tears pouring down her pendulous cheeks. Kitty Maxse turned up and asked briskly why Leslie hadn't been to call on her for so long. "Rather too fashionable" was Virginia's comment. Aunt Anny was a constant visitor; she was in excellent spirits and had no doubt at all that Leslie would be himself again in no time; to at least one observer her cheerful optimism seemed positively cruel. Caught in the perpetual stream of interviews a gentleman and a lady sat in the drawing-room silent and unintroduced. At last the gentleman said: "I am Henry James." "I am Violet Dickinson", replied the lady and that was the end of their conversation.

But many, far too many, having bid adieu to the deaf and dying man upstairs had then to unburden themselves upon his daughters. They wept and insisted that the Stephen girls should weep with them. The relations seemed more numerous and more lachrymose than ever before. "Three mornings have I spent," declared Virginia, "having my hand held–and my emotions pumped out of me–quite unsuccessfully. They are good people I know but it would be merciful if they could keep their virtues and their affections and all the rest of it to themselves." "This illness" she observed, "is a revelation of what human nature can be–in the way of sentimentality and uselessness." Nor could Virginia keep these rebellious sentiments to herself. There was a break with Aunt Adeline (the Duchess of Bedford) and a row with Aunt Mary, who considered that Virginia failed in her duty to her relations. Altogether it was a time of mounting and almost unendurable distress. "Why must he die? And if he must why can't he?" Such, roughly, were Virginia's sentiments. Death was no stranger in that house but never before had he come with so deliberate a tread.

Leslie was clearly dying, and after a time he clearly wished to die, but still death would not come. The six months allowed by Sir Frederick Treves was at an end. A sad Christmas was followed by a gloomy New Year. On Christmas Eve Sir Leslie had attempted his yearly performance, a recital of Milton's *Ode on the Nativity*. He still knew the poem by heart but was too weak to utter the words.

In January there was a crisis, but even the crisis was prolonged and it was not until 22 February that death came at last.

Chapter Five

1904-1906

EVEN before their father's death, the Stephen children had agreed on the need to get away from Hyde Park Gate. A complete and permanent removal was already contemplated; but the immediate need, when once the decencies had been observed, was to escape from that dark and all too accessible house of mourning. They went with George to Manorbier on the Pembroke coast, a wild desolate place which clearly they all liked, for they were to return. Indeed Virginia's return in later years is no small tribute to the therapeutic power of the neighbourhood, for she was not happy, or, at least, much of her was unhappy. While the others set off in pursuit of birds or landscape subjects she began to write and it was here that she first got an inkling of the kind of thing that she wanted to write about.*

But now the writing did not go well; nothing went well; how could it ? She had lost her father, and the event, which seemed terrible in anticipation, now appeared more heart-breakingly tragic. She was more than ever convinced that he had wanted to live and that the true and happy relationship between him and his children was only just beginning. She had never done enough for him; he had been lonely and she had never told him how much she valued him. At night she dreamed that he was alive again and that she could say all the things that she had meant to say. When they went for walks she kept thinking that they would find him waiting for them when they got home. His faults were forgotten, his kindness, his quickness, his intelligence were not.

All this produced a sadness which was natural enough and a feeling of guilt which is not uncommon when those we love are dead; but there was also something else–a feeling of profound irritation. She was irritated by the letters of condolence, by the obituaries–they missed the point; they gave no true idea of what her father had been

---

* "[At sixteen] . . . I was for knowing all that was to be known, and for writing a book–a book–but what book? That vision came to me more clearly at Manorbier aged 21, walking the down on the edge of the sea." AWD (Berg), 3 September 1922.

like. She was irritated also by her brothers and sister and indeed with herself. "I wonder how we go on as we do," she wrote, "as merry as grigs all day long." In her exasperation she could write only to Violet Dickinson and to Janet Case and tell them something– not much–of what she felt. Her grief, as she later realised, was something feverish, something morbid, something which made her feel isolated and afraid. In her attempts at writing she was, as she put it later, trying "to prove to myself that there was nothing wrong with me–which I was already beginning to fear there was."

Perhaps it was because of her condition that the Stephens decided on a more radical change. Manorbier was beautiful, but it lacked diversions. Gerald was going to Venice: Violet Dickinson was going to Florence; they decided that they too would go to Italy. They sailed on Good Friday; their train passed through the St Gotthard in a snowstorm; but at Como there was brilliant sunshine and at the end of two days' travelling they stepped into a gondola.

There were fatigues and annoyances; the Humphry Wards were on the train; Gerald was sometimes cross; he was not the perfect companion for such a journey.* And then, they had failed to book rooms and must hunt all through Venice at midnight looking for somewhere to sleep. But Virginia, who had hardly been further afield than Boulogne, was amazed and delighted. For a day or two she, and indeed all of them, were in a state of childlike astonishment and joy; they could hardly believe that the place was real.

This interval of delight was short lived; foreign travel distracts the mind, but it also tries the temper. Vanessa, to be sure, was having a fine time, discovering Tintoretto, finding fault with Ruskin and generally taking a professional interest in the scene which Virginia could not share, but, after ten days, even she was ready to leave Venice; they felt caged in the city, they longed to see some green country. They went to Florence; there they found some old friends– the Rasponis, whom they liked–but also Lytteltons, Humphry Wards, Carnarvons, Prinseps and even Aunt Minna. By this time Virginia, who had been delighted by her first sight of the Italians, was becoming disenchanted.† Also there were far too many Germans and "a strange race that haunts Hotels – Gnome like

* "Somehow Gerald's figure never did make part of the Venetian foreground I have in my mind." VW to Violet Dickinson, [March 1904].

† ". . . our travelling is not so delightful that we wish more than is necessary. There never was a *beastlier* nation than this in its railways, its streets, its shops, its beggars, & many of its habits. My dear Toad, where is a decent woman to look sometimes?" VW to Emma Vaughan, 25 April 1904.

women, who are like creatures that come out in the dark. An hotel is a sort of black Cave." There were of course compensations; but, comparing Vanessa's letters with those from Virginia, it seems that there was practically nothing that the elder sister did not like and very little to please the younger.

Violet Dickinson, who met them in Florence and who accompanied Virginia and Vanessa for some time, clearly had a good deal to put up with, and so did they all; Virginia had what she called "her tantrums." By the end of April they were all on their way home. They stopped a week in Paris where they found Beatrice Thynne. They sat in cafés, smoked cigarettes with a sense of great daring and talked to two young men: Thoby's friend Clive Bell and *his* friend Mr Kelly (later Sir Gerald Kelly, P.R.A.). These were admirable guides to Paris: they went to the Salon, they went to the *Chat Blanc*, they went to Rodin's studio. In fact they had a very satisfying taste of Parisian life; but once again the real treat was for Vanessa.

This I think was an element in the storm that was now brewing. Vanessa had got what she wanted–her freedom. Now she could paint as she chose, see whom she chose, live as she chose and would no doubt marry as she chose. Her happiness in being delivered from the care and the ill-temper of her father was shockingly evident. She was clearly and unequivocally delighted, and Virginia, emotionally strained, exhausted and exasperated by the long months of Sir Leslie's last illness, still guilty and still inconsolable, found this more than she could bear.

We do not know, although we may fairly guess, that there were headaches, sudden nervous leapings of the heart and a growing awareness that there was something very wrong with her mind. In May she felt desperately anxious to be at work on something, something big and solid that would keep her restless thoughts occupied and, on the day after their return to London when Emma Vaughan came to borrow some letters, Virginia hardly knew what she was saying or doing.

In the breakdown that followed she entered into a period of nightmare in which the symptoms of the preceding months attained frantic intensity. Her mistrust of Vanessa, her grief for her father became maniacal, her nurses–she had three–became fiends. She heard voices urging her to acts of folly; she believed that they came from overeating and that she must starve herself. In this emergency the main burden fell upon Vanessa; but Vanessa was enormously helped by Violet Dickinson. She took Virginia to her house at Burnham Wood and it was there that she made her first attempt to commit suicide. She threw herself from a window, which, however, was not high enough from the ground to cause her serious harm.* It was here too that she lay in bed, listening to the birds singing in Greek and imagining that King Edward VII lurked in the azaleas using the foulest possible language.

All that summer she was mad. It was not until early September that she was able to leave Burnham Wood, thin and shaken, but sane enough to be able to live at peace with Vanessa. The Stephen family stayed that summer at Teversal in Nottinghamshire. Here Virginia was able to write short letters, to play a little tennis and to walk. Nurse Traill, who had looked after Sir Leslie, cared for her and presently she was able to do some Latin with Thoby. Her sanity had returned but she felt physical pains—headaches and neuralgia.

> Oh, my Violet, if there were a God I should bless him for having delivered me safe and sound from the miseries of the last six months! You can't think what an exquisite joy every minute of my life is to me now, and my only prayer is that I may live to be 70. I do think I may emerge less selfish and cocksure than I went in and with greater understanding of the troubles of others. Sorrow, such as I feel now for father, is soothing and natural and makes life more worth having, if sadder. I can never tell you what you have been to me all this time—for one thing you wouldn't believe it—but if affection is worth anything you have, and always will have mine.

Her letters to Violet Dickinson are optimistic—over-optimistic; she was impatient to start writing again and believed herself to be more completely cured than she in fact was. Dr Savage, her specialist and an old friend of the family, insisted that she should live very quietly and, if possible, away from London. When, in October, the Stephens returned to Hyde Park Gate and began to make preparations for leaving it, it was felt that Virginia should not be involved in the turmoil of house-moving. She went therefore to stay with her aunt Caroline Emelia in Cambridge. Here she could see Adrian who was still at Trinity (Thoby had come down that summer), and the milieu was sufficiently quiet, for 'The Quaker' or 'Nun,' as Virginia called her aunt, led a life of tranquil benevolence in her small house, The Porch.

Moreover in Cambridge Virginia could find a useful and sedative

---

* It has been suggested that Virginia attempted to kill herself at the time of her first breakdown (i.e. in 1895). I can find no evidence of this; but that she was interested in the idea of self-destruction before the year 1904 seems likely enough, witness a remark made to Jack Hills at Queen Victoria's funeral: "Jack, do you think I shall ever commit suicide?" (p. i., Lady Hills).

employment for which she was well fitted. F. W. Maitland, the historian, had been one of the young men who used to stay with the Stephens at St Ives; he had married Florence Fisher, Virginia's cousin; Sir Leslie liked him and had asked, if there should be a 'Life', that Maitland should write it. He was already working on this biography when Virginia went to Cambridge; there were letters which he felt should be read by her before he could see them – chiefly love letters between her parents – and she was to select and copy them. In addition he asked her for a few pages describing Leslie's relationship with his children: it was the first thing of hers that ever found its way into print. She was also almost certainly the source of some passages which followed this, passages in which Maitland touches, tenderly and discreetly, on Leslie's faults in matters of education and housekeeping and which conclude with a statement – it certainly expresses Virginia's belief – that at the end he felt and expressed nothing save affection for his children.

Jack Hills offered his advice on this occasion; he was afraid that Virginia might be injudicious in her choice of material; he wrote with all the prudent authority of a brother-in-law and a solicitor. Virginia's reply was fierce. She "cared 10,000 times more for delicacy and reserve where her parents were concerned than he could"; he had never really known or understood Leslie and if he wanted to offer criticism and advice he should offer it to Maitland; he was – but this she kept for Violet Dickinson – "a poor little red-tape-tied parchment Solicitor" and "had no more thought of what a book ought to be than the fat cow in the field opposite." Vanessa really agreed with her, but of course Vanessa was weak where Jack was concerned and therefore took his part. This was not her only quarrel with Vanessa, for Virginia after a fortnight was becoming restive at Cambridge; why could she not return to her own room in her own house? The doctors might forbid it but doctors, in her experience, were always wrong; they could guess at your disease but they could not cure you. Here, in Cambridge, she was sleeping badly; the Quaker got on her nerves and her nerves were things that her family understood and could allow for, whereas a Quaker aunt could not. But Vanessa took the exasperating view that doctor's orders were doctor's orders and must be obeyed; unfortunately she added, or Virginia persuaded herself that she added, something to the effect that it didn't much matter to anyone whether Virginia was in Cambridge or London. And this, of course, did not mend matters.

In the end a compromise was made: Virginia returned for ten

days to the new house in Gordon Square and then went to Giggles-wick School in Yorkshire where her cousin Will Vaughan was now Headmaster. Vanessa wrote to Madge Vaughan:

> She is really quite well now–except that she does not sleep very well–& is inclined to do too much in some ways. . . . She ought not to walk very far or for a very long time alone. . . . Now she goes out before beginning to write in the morning for ½ an hour alone . . . then she walks alone again before luncheon for ½ an hour–but in the after-noon she is rather dependent on someone else for a walk. Of course if she could go out with the children sometimes it would do perfectly. She goes to bed very early as I think you do & she is in all other ways absolutely normal in her doings.

Virginia surveyed the Vaughan household with some curiosity. Her first impression was that Will was by no means worthy of Madge. He was domineering and thoroughly conventional. He was always afraid that Virginia would entertain Madge with "morbid" subjects; also she told the children stories which, if not precisely "morbid", were held to be unsuitable to the Sabbath, a day devoted to 'Sunday Books' of exemplary dullness. Madge had to perform all the chores, not only of a mother but of a headmaster's wife; it was taken for granted that her own work as an author would take second place. Virginia revised this opinion for a time–this was always to be her way–and discovered unsuspected moral and conjugal qualities in Will; but her first impression became her final opinion: Madge was yet another of the women whose lives and talents were to be sacrificed to their husbands.

Madge, who liked Virginia and "believed in her genius," was nevertheless sensible of Virginia's scrutiny and rather alarmed by it. After the visit we find Vanessa writing to reassure her:

> Don't be afraid that I shall quote what you say as "comic"–I know you think us all very critical–but really I dont think we criticise un-fairly– & we certainly dont laugh at people behind their backs & treat them affectionately to their faces. So dont ever be afraid that we shall talk of your "fads"! Ginia has talked to me of you & Will only in the most appreciative way– & I do think that the safeguard with her is that she always does see the real good in people. She is too clever not to find a great many people bores–& I think she often enjoys giving vigorous expression to feelings which though true are quite temporary –but when one knows her ways one can always tell how much is per-manent & how much will change–& I think I can honestly say that I have never heard her say a really unkind thing about anyone. So I dont think the criticism matters. Everyone who has brains must be critical

when they are young. She is sure to get more tolerant, & even now it does come partly from having a high standard in most things.

It is possible that Madge did not find this letter entirely reassuring. The visit to Giggleswick was memorable, not only because Virginia was able to learn something more about a person whom she had once adored and still liked, but because it provided her with a subject for her first published article.* While she was in Yorkshire she visited Haworth Parsonage and wrote an account of it which she sent to *The Guardian*, a London weekly newspaper catering for a clerical public; Mrs Lyttelton, the editor of the Women's Supplement, was a friend of Violet Dickinson. Virginia felt that she ought to earn some money, if only to recoup some of the expenses of her illness, and she was pretty sure that she could do as well as most of *The Guardian*'s reviewers, although she allowed that there was a certain knack of writing for the newspapers which she had still to learn.

Thanks to Violet Dickinson's initial introduction and continued encouragement, Virginia found in *The Guardian* a fairly regular outlet for her early attempts at journalism. She had been training herself to be a writer for a long time. That is to say she had been reading voraciously and writing assiduously. Her journals during these years consist, almost always, of careful essays written as though for publication: attempts to describe a day in the country, a visit to Earl's Court, a night spent listening to the music of a neighbour's dance, attempts to do very much the kind of thing that she achieves in the Haworth article. About this time she was also writing comic lives of Caroline Stephen, Aunt Mary Fisher and George Duckworth, all of which have alas perished; it is difficult not to suppose that they would have been more amusing than the essays in her journals. For these essays are not of biographic interest except in so far as they attest to the high seriousness and immense thoroughness with which Virginia prepared herself for the profession of letters. Her constant, almost compulsive reading and writing were intended to compensate for the fact that she had not had what she called "a real education," by which she meant a University education. Her practice in writing gave her a certain fluency, an ease of address unusual in a very young journalist; her indefatigable reading makes her appear, to modern

---

* Her review of *The Son of Royal Langbrith* by W. D. Howells was published by *The Guardian* on 14 December 1904; the Haworth article appeared a week later; but in fact the review was written after the article. See VW/VD, 26 November 1904.

eyes, by no means an ignoramus but a quite affectedly literate person. We live in a society which has less time for books and which is less dependent on the written word; we no longer take it for granted that all educated people are perfectly at home in English and French literature and will at once recognise a quotation from Johnson or La Rochefoucauld; it was a natural enough assumption for the daughter of Sir Leslie Stephen.

From now on, Virginia was regularly employed as a writer of short articles and reviews. She would turn her hand to almost anything.

From Giggleswick she returned to London and again to Cambridge and then went with the other Stephens to Aunt Minna's cottage in the New Forest (Aunt Minna was away). This Christmas holiday was to some extent marred for Virginia by *The Cornhill*, which had curtly rejected an article on Boswell's letters, and by Mr Haldane, the Liberal statesman, who wrote unenthusiastically to Violet Dickinson about Virginia's Haworth article.* It was Virginia's first taste of literary adversity and she did not like it. Nevertheless there was fun; Thoby and Adrian went out hunting; in the evening there was much eating, drinking and jollity. They sought out the silliest novels that they could find in Aunt Minna's bookcase and read them aloud roaring with laughter; they were young, irreverent and unrestrained. One curious occupation of Virginia's leisure during that holiday—her working time was mainly given to the writing of her contribution to Maitland's *Life of Leslie Stephen*—was drawing, and a few weak but not insensitive copies of Blake and Rossetti were the result.

Early in the new year, Virginia had an interview with Dr Savage; to her delight, he told her that she was completely cured and could now lead a normal life. This meant that she could return to London and join the household that had been established in her absence at No 46 Gordon Square, Bloomsbury.

When the Stephen children planned this move their friends and relations had been astonished and a little shocked. Kensington was a good address; Bloomsbury was not. "Kitty," wrote Virginia,

---

* "Also Haldane isn't exactly warm in his praise, and altogether I feel, as you read in the Bible, despised and rejected by men." (VW/VD, January 1905). What Haldane actually said was:

"Dear Miss Dickinson,

Thank you for showing me Miss S[tephen]'s article on Haworth—a place, as you know, of deep interest to me. What merits—but I think the writer can get still more inside her subject. This is a beginning however, and it shows talent . . ." R. B. Haldane to Violet Dickinson, 27 December 1904.

"already screams against Bloomsbury" (this was in March 1904), and probably she was the first to do so. But it was precisely the virtue of the place that it lay so far from that dark house of many tragedies in which they had grown up. It was far from the favoured haunts of Aunt Minna, Cousin Mia, Aunt Mary and the rest. Also, it was cheap. Sir Leslie's children had not inherited much capital and they were rather vague about their income—a topic which shall be discussed upon a later page—but certainly they had every inducement to go to a district where rents were far lower than in Kensington. Vanessa had the additional motive of wishing to be close to the Slade School which, for a time, she attended.

No 46 Gordon Square was more spacious and much better lit than No 22 Hyde Park Gate, and Vanessa, when she took it over in the autumn of 1904, emphasised its qualities. Her ideas of interior decoration had been very much influenced by Charles and Katherine Furse,* in whose house she had admired big bare surfaces of white distemper on which pictures could stand in bold, emphatic isolation. It was part of a larger redirection in her ideas about art, and she told Clive Bell that she had succeeded in persuading Virginia that "there was nothing to be said" for that family idol, G. F. Watts. Watts belonged to the dark Victorian past; the new generation wanted air, simplicity and light. The move to Bloomsbury was to be an escape from the past and all its horrors.

There was, however, one fatal, one appalling drawback. Gerald was glad to part company with the Stephen children and to set up a bachelor establishment of his own; but George, always affectionate and kind, could not bear the idea of leaving his sisters with nobody but Thoby and Adrian, who from a social point of view were worse than useless, to look after them. He must be included in the party; he regretted no doubt that they should insist on going so far from the fashionable part of town, but, after all, it is not impossible to reach the West End from Gordon Square and go with them he ought and must. This resolution was received with dismay by the rest; but they hardly knew how to oppose so much well-intentioned fraternal feeling. They were in fact weak to the point of pusillanimity: for the long story of George's attentions had at length been made so far public that he could surely have been called to account. When Virginia went mad in the summer of 1904 Vanessa told Savage of

* Charles Furse, a member of the New English Art Club very much influenced by Whistler, had married Katharine, the youngest daughter of J. A. Symonds, and was therefore the brother-in-law of Madge Vaughan. He died just at this time (16 October 1904).

what had been happening and Savage, it seems, taxed George with his conduct.* Even George might then have felt that his presence under the same roof as his half-sisters was no longer desirable. But he was invulnerably dense and incapable of pursuing a course that ran counter to his feelings and so, faced by his amiable insistence, they weakly acquiesced. Gone then were all their hopes of flying from the past: the past was coming to live with them.

And then, like a Goddess from a Machine, came Lady Margaret Herbert. George proposed; she accepted him and they were married "with immense pomp" while Virginia was still convalescing at Teversal in the autumn of 1904. Vanessa was a bridesmaid, and Adrian distinguished himself by losing all her luggage. The Bloomsbury ménage was saved from disaster.

The household to which Virginia returned in January of 1905 consisted therefore of the Stephen children and no one else.

> I often wonder [wrote Vanessa to Madge Vaughan] how our doings now would strike someone who had known & lived with us years ago . . . it is really very ideal to have to arrange for a household all of much the same age. It makes most things very easy & all the difficulties of trying to meet opposite claims & of different generations are done away with. . . I only wish we could always go on like this–but after all we may for a long time yet. I dread every day to hear that Thoby is in love!

In a young establishment, unsupervised, unchaperoned, tired of the conventions that made Hyde Park Gate so tedious and so painful, all kinds of possibilities began to present themselves. Why dress for dinner? Why tolerate bores? Why bother about 'Society'? Why not make friends with people who would talk about art and literature, religion and love without humbug? Everything seemed possible. Or so it appeared; but in fact the liberties that the Miss Stephens now sought were, even by the standards of their own age, modest. Their immediate aims were of a negative kind; they wanted to be released from the continual and galling interference of their relations; they claimed liberty; but they certainly did not shout for licence. They scarcely in fact detached themselves from the conventions of a society which was still restrained by very strict

* "George would fling himself on my bed, cuddling and kissing and otherwise embracing me in order, as he told Dr Savage later, to comfort me for the fatal illness of my Father–who was dying three or four storeys lower down of cancer." (MH/A 16). I infer that the only people who could have told Savage of this were Vanessa or Virginia; the occasion must have been Virginia's madness in 1904. The only witness on whose evidence Savage would have spoken to George would have been Vanessa.

rules. Virginia's innocence at this time was of a kind that would hardly be credible today; for all her reading she could not suppose that people of her acquaintance could be unchaste, and although she had met Corydon in the pages of Virgil she would have been horrified to learn that he was a friend of Thoby's and a visitor in Gordon Square. Leonard Woolf recalled that the first time he ever saw Virginia and Vanessa they were chaperoned by their cousin the Vice-Principal of Newnham, although they had only come to Trinity to call upon their brother. Leslie, who was old enough at the time of Virginia's birth to be her grandfather, belonged to the generation which came to maturity in the 'sixties; he was in fact 'early Victorian' and his agnosticism made him not less, but more, anxious to observe the proprieties. In this he was supported by the female relatives and of course by George. Thoby also was on the whole a guardian of established usages and his sisters were shy— Virginia desperately so. One can see how hard it must have been to break with the conventions and in fact Virginia lacked not only the courage but the desire to do so at that time.

That break may be dated from 16 February 1905, when Thoby, who was now reading for the Bar but wanted to see his Cambridge friends and had for this purpose announced that he would be At Home on Thursday evenings, entertained Saxon Sydney-Turner at 46 Gordon Square. On this first occasion he and his host and the dog Gurth formed the entire company. It must have been a quiet evening, for Saxon Sydney-Turner was not a lively companion. Indeed most of Thoby's friends seemed extremely silent and when the Miss Stephens began to put in an appearance on Thursday evenings Virginia, at all events, found their silence disconcerting. Two of them, Sydney-Turner and possibly R. G. Hawtrey, came to stay in Cornwall with the Stephen children that summer and Virginia observed them with amazement. They were, she declared:

> . . . a great trial; they sit silent, absolutely silent, all the time. Occasionally they creep to a corner and chuckle over a Latin joke. Perhaps they are falling in love with Nessa; who knows? It would be a silent and very learned process. However I don't think they are robust enough to feel very much. Oh women are my line and not these inanimate creatures. The worst of it is that they have not the energy to go . . .

What had they done with this vast privilege of University education that had been denied to her, Virginia? It seemed to have struck them dumb and made them dismal. They had a tremendous opinion of themselves and were more than a little affected, and their superior airs hardly seemed justified when from the mountain of their pretensions they extracted a somewhat ridiculous mouse–it was called *Euphrosyne*. This was a volume of poems, published privately in 1905, to which Clive Bell, Lytton Strachey, Walter Lamb, Saxon Sydney-Turner, Leonard Woolf and some others contributed and to which they seldom alluded in later life, so that the book would have been forgotten if Virginia had not been careful to keep its memory green. It was certainly an anti-climax; none of the contributors were true poets. Virginia laughed at it and began a scathing essay upon it and its contributors. (See Appendix C).

So these were Thoby's remarkable friends. Here was Clive Bell who was supposed to be a mixture of Shelley and a country squire, and Sydney-Turner who was credited with–of all things–brilliance.

"If you mean wit," replied Thoby, "then no, he is not witty; but he is truthful, and if he is silent it is because he is careful to speak the truth," and, after a time, Virginia began to admit that there was something in what Thoby said. The reserve of these odd young men was not like that of the young men at the parties to which George had taken her; theirs were not the silences of men who are seeking for an appropriate banality. And when they did speak Virginia found that she was listening to a kind of conversation that had never come her way before. A chance remark, a discussable statement, something, let us say, about beauty in pictures, would suddenly breed loquacity. The question would be discussed at a higher and higher level and by fewer and fewer people.

> It filled me with wonder to watch those who were finally left in the argument, piling stone upon stone, cautiously, accurately, long after it had completely soared above my sight . . . One had glimpses of something miraculous happening high up in the air. Often we would still be sitting in a circle at two or three in the morning. Still Saxon would be taking his pipe from his mouth as if to speak, and putting it back again without having spoken. At last, rumpling his hair back he wd. pronounce very shortly some absolutely final summing up. The marvellous edifice was complete, one could stumble off to bed feeling that something very important had happened. It had been proved that beauty was–or beauty was not–for I have never been quite sure which– part of a picture.

Now this was rather different from those parties at which an exquisitely dressed young man might content himself with the simple phrase 'sort of' repeated with slight changes of emphasis throughout the evening. At these gatherings in Gordon Square no one was exquisitely dressed; certainly not the Miss Stephens. Here they were being asked to do something that had not been required of them before–to use their brains. The rest of them didn't much matter. For whereas the tacit purpose of a party in Belgravia was the pursuit of matrimony, the purpose of a party in Bloomsbury was to exchange ideas. It was this, the purely cerebral attitude of Thoby's Cambridge friends, or at least of most of them, which made them interesting to Virginia, and she was glad to be free of the marriage market.

In June 1906, rather less than a year after Virginia had written to Violet Dickinson describing Sydney-Turner and his friend as "inanimate creatures," Virginia wrote a short story in which she describes the life of two young women, Phyllis and Rosamund. They are the daughters of a high official, and live an entirely social life: "They seem indigenous to the drawing room." It is their place of business, the market-place in which they are to sell themselves for as much as they will fetch. Virginia considers them with sympathy, they have their decencies and their loyalties, they are neither insensitive nor stupid; nevertheless, drilled by their mother, they are destined to pass through a joyless courtship to a loveless marriage. Virginia sends them to a Thursday Evening at Gordon Square–it is as though the Miss Stephens of 1903 were to call upon the Miss Stephens of 1905. Phyllis and Rosamund are disconcerted by the indifference of these people to the mundanities of life, by the frank brutality of the conversation. Love is discussed, but for these people love was not the delicate game of adornment and enticement that Phyllis and Rosamund understood so well, it was "a robust, ingenuous thing which stood out in the daylight, naked and solid, to be tapped or scrutinised as you thought best." The visitors were unable to cope with this kind of frankness, they return home half attracted but on the whole displeased by what they have seen; such is not, they decide, the life for them.

And certainly, as it developed, Bloomsbury became more and more disconcerting. George, sweeping in proudly with his aristocratic bride upon his arm, with a bow and a flourish presented Sydney-Turner to her. Sydney-Turner was, as usual, lighting a pipe, nor would he stop doing so; he made a slight and slovenly pretence of rising from his chair, half nodded and kept his match alight. Their clothes were no better than their behaviour. "Oh darling, how awful they do look!" wailed Kitty Maxse. "Deplorable, deplorable! How could Vanessa and Virginia have picked up such friends?" groaned Henry James.

And so, almost at once, the Stephen children were in trouble. Thoby's friends were 'unsuitable' and that they should remain talking, unchaperoned, with Thoby's sisters until three in the morning was even more 'unsuitable.' Inevitably a choice would in the end have to be made between the old friends and the new, but in 1905 Virginia could hardly imagine that such a choice was possible.

> I have been splashing about in racing society since I saw you, that is dined with George at Lady Carnarvon's—*young* Lady C. this time, thank God. It was the night of the Kemptown races, and we talked about horses all night, which are probably more interesting than books. Then I have seen Margaret [Lady Margaret Duckworth] who is a nice woman, and our acquaintance begins to grow promising. We shall have to know each other all our lives, so we can take time about it.

'All our lives,' that was the term imposed by so close a relationship. Vanessa, I surmise, was already half-minded—if this were to imply dinner parties wholly devoted to the turf—that the sentence might be commuted, or indeed set aside. But even she, in her most wildly optimistic moments, could not then have supposed that when, many years later, an urbane gentleman enquired after "that delightful person your sister-in-law," she, Vanessa, would be at some pains to frame an answer that would not reveal the fact that she did not know whether the lady was alive or dead. For this was how the matter ended; Bloomsbury grew not only by the making, but by the breaking, of friendships.

Between the 'good society' and the 'bad company' that they entertained there could be no real choice, although it was many years before this became apparent. George and his smart friends presented no problem. Kitty Maxse and Violet Dickinson had superior claims to friendship and in 1905 a break with *them* must have seemed unthinkable; but already it was becoming clear that these "deplorable" young men represented the kind of values that Vanessa and Virginia most respected and, as they began to speak, they revealed characters which were not unattractive.

Virginia exaggerated (and perhaps I also have exaggerated) their silence; they can perhaps be divided into a central core, the mute circle of seekers after truth who sat puffing their pipes around the discreet shrine of G. E. Moore—Saxon Sydney-Turner, Leonard Woolf and Lytton Strachey—and an outer circle, more worldly and more garrulous, which, on the Thursday Evenings of 1905 and 1906, would include Thoby himself, Clive Bell, and Desmond MacCarthy who, though a thorough Mooreist, was never taciturn. Here it should be noted that these particular young men who were later to become Virginia's most intimate friends were not, at that time, separable as a group from the others–such as Ralph Hawtrey, Hilton Young, Jack Pollock, Walter Lamb or Robin Mayor–who had also been Thoby's friends at Cambridge and were welcomed by him on Thursday Evenings. It would be wrong I think to imagine an inner coterie distinguished from the rest.

One of the first of Thoby's friends to be invited to Gordon Square was Leonard Woolf, though he came only to say farewell on the eve of his departure for Ceylon. He dined with the Stephens on 17 November 1904; Virginia, in London for a week between her visits to Cambridge and Giggleswick, was present. He remembered her as being perfectly silent throughout dinner and noticed how ill she looked. But she observed him and collected stories about him. Lytton Strachey said that he was like Swift and would murder his wife. He despised the whole human race. He trembled all over, he was so violent, so savage; he had pulled his thumb out of joint in a dream; he was, in short, a serious and powerful figure; but he had gone off to live in a jungle and no one knew whether he would ever return.

Leonard Woolf was a mysterious figure in the distance; Saxon Sydney-Turner was an enigma in the foreground. He, undoubtedly, had a gift for silence and sometimes when he spoke he would endlessly and most eruditely discuss subjects of no conceivable interest, or he might be entirely cryptic. And yet he could also be illuminating; he was, obviously, extremely intelligent and extremely gifted; he wrote poems, he painted pictures; he was intensely musical, a fanatical concert and opera-goer who regularly made the pilgrimage to Bayreuth and could tell you who sang what part in which opera ever since Bayreuth began. He was also a composer and in a rare moment of expansion disclosed to Clive Bell:

... my last Sonata [is] unique among my works for the appreciation it has found and containing passages that rank among the most beautiful ever written: my wish is to have it printed when I have polished certain parts of it but I don't know how to set about doing this.

This was in March 1906. Was it already apparent to Sydney-Turner's friends that he would never find out how to finish his Sonata, that it would remain unperformed and perish along with all his other compositions? I don't know. After the publication of *Euphrosyne* Virginia can hardly have supposed that he was to be a great poet, but he might be a musician; certainly it appeared that so astonishing a mind must one day achieve some spectacular feat.

"His friends," wrote Virginia when she attempted to write about him,

> continued to believe in him. He was going to be one of the great men of his time. Probably he was working at a poem, after office hours, when he came back to that dreary London lodging in a back street. "When is it coming out?" they pressed him. "Anyhow, show us what you've written." Or was it a history? Or was it a philosophy? . . . He was studying counterpoint. Also he was teaching himself to paint. He was studying Chinese . . . Nothing was actually published. But "wait a little" his friends said. They waited. . . .

That Lytton Strachey would also make a name for himself one day seemed equally clear. In so far as these young men had a leader it was he. Like Saxon Sydney-Turner he was a very silent man; but his silences were of an even more alarming kind; for whereas Sydney-Turner, when he surfaced, might bring with him a pearl of wisdom, Strachey showed sometimes a rakish fin and sometimes a row of wicked teeth. With one pungent, economical sentence he could reduce a party to helpless laughter or a fool to spluttering rage—and you might be the fool. Strachey was, perhaps, one of the reasons why Virginia was herself very silent at these Thursday evening meetings. She found him, I suspect, very frightening (almost any man was in some degree frightening); it was not until later that she was to discover how kind and sympathetic he could be. The Stracheys were always on the margin of her life and Lytton's sisters were what one might call her natural friends, for they belonged to very much the same world as the Stephens—the educated upper middle class of London. They were all of them formidable and they had a way of speaking that could strike terror. They could apply a verbal stress which gave their irony, their incredulity, their sudden shocked amazement at ignorance, dishonesty or inhumanity, a memorable quality. Their family jokes were numerous and arcane; they were far more of a clan than the Stephens, tied as they were to the older generation by a happier relationship and happier circumstances. It was only by degrees that Lytton became, for Virginia, the most important member of his family.

Desmond MacCarthy seemed even more certain of success than Lytton Strachey. He was of a slightly older generation at Cambridge— he came down as Thoby arrived there—and he was the most worldly of the younger Apostles. He went into London Society where he had seen the Miss Stephens looking, as he put it, "like slaves." He had the world at his feet; he was handsome, brilliant and talented. He had not much money but he had, I surmise, an easy chair, a cheerful fire, a desk, a ream of smooth writing paper, virgin save perhaps for three magnificent arresting words–the title of a novel. For when those virgin sheets were violated he was to be the great English novelist of the twentieth century. His shoulders were ready to accommodate the mantle of Henry James and, hearing him talk–for *he* certainly was not silent–you could not but conclude that he had so charmed and domesticated that intractable creature the English Language that it would do anything for him, give him a force, a range of subtlety that would take him anywhere–into the empyrean if he so wished, and with that, so much native genius and so much good nature. Even in those bright years of his early manhood Desmond MacCarthy was, no doubt, a trifle dilatory, a shade unreliable in the performance of tasks or the keeping of appointments, just a little exasperating. But did anyone, then or at any other time, dislike him? It is impossible to believe. He had, I suspect, a good deal to do with the genial social climate of Bloomsbury, with the reconciliation of difficult and angular characters and with the general spirit of tolerance and compromise which triumphed over the disputes and acerbities which were also a part of that environment.

Clive Bell also undoubtedly helped to temper the austerities of that society. He was, in a way, the strangest of the group. George noted with approval that he was different from the others in that he was better dressed, had a good seat on a horse and was an excellent wing shot; for while all the rest were pretty obviously intellectual, he came from a society which hunted birds, animals, and, in his case, girls. His family had made its way by means of coal to a sham gothic country house and a decent position in the County of Wiltshire. Clive, the younger son, went from Marlborough to Cambridge, where fate placed him on the same staircase at Trinity as Saxon Sydney-Turner, and where Thoby Stephen became his closest friend. At Cambridge he was, I think, underrated by his friends; they did not look in the one direction in which he was, intellectually, more alert than they. In his rooms hung a reproduction of a painting by Degas, someone of whom most of them had probably never heard, for Cambridge at the turn of the century was aesthetically blind. After he left Cambridge in 1902 he went to Paris and there made friends with Roderick O'Conor, Gerald Kelly and James Morrice. This eye for painting was a bond between him and

Vanessa, strengthened by the fact that he was able to show Thoby and his sisters something of Paris on their way back from Italy in May 1904. He had stayed for a few days with the Stephens at Teversal in September when Virginia was convalescing, and was thereafter, I think, a constant visitor to their house. In the summer of 1905 he proposed to Vanessa and was rejected; but not in such a manner as to leave him with no hope. Virginia soon became aware of this attachment and, I suspect, disapproved of it.

In 1905 Virginia began a connection with *The Times Literary Supplement* which was to last almost to the end of her life. Bruce Richmond, the editor, had invited Sir Leslie to contribute when the paper first started in 1902, but he had been able to do little. Now, a year after his death, Richmond approached his daughter, and on 10 March appeared her first article for him, a book review entitled *Literary Geography*. Bruce Richmond thought it "admirable" and sent her "another great fat book–which I don't much want as I know *nothing* of the subject."

In April Virginia and Adrian made a short trip to the Peninsula. They visited Oporto, Lisbon, Granada, Seville, saw the usual sights and had the usual experience of dirty inns, goat's milk, natural beauty and dilatory railways; the week-long journey out by sea in fine weather, the ship with its odd temporary life, its laziness, its bores, its places of refuge, made, I think, a more permanent impression upon the authoress of *The Voyage Out*. But it was clearly a satisfactory trip; they were glad to return but glad also to have made the journey. Back in London, Virginia found that Bruce Richmond had rejected her review of the "great fat book"–Edith Sichel's *Catherine de' Medici & The French Reformation*–on the grounds that it was not serious criticism from an historical point of view; but to make up for it he sent her three books about Spain. "You will be surprised to hear that I am an authority upon Spain," she wrote to Violet Dickinson, "but so it is."

There was another and more important excursion in that year; for now that it seemed that the good years had come back the four Stephen children decided, perhaps with a kind of symbolic intention, to return to St Ives. For Virginia, certainly, it was a deliberate exercise in nostalgia; the train that took them from Paddington was to carry them back into the past. They arrived at night, strolled up to Talland House as though they were still children returning from a day's outing, boldly opened the gate, mounted the familiar steps and reached the escalonia hedge through which they could see the stone urns, the bank of tall flowers, the lighted windows. The house seemed to have been waiting for them. Without breaking the spell the revenants returned in ghostly silence.

Broad daylight offered less equivocal delights. There had been changes in the town—new houses and new roads; but not enough to spoil their pleasure; here there were many remembered details to be verified with delight and many people who still remembered their parents with affection. The country, the sea, the inhabitants were all charming. They stayed until October and had the pleasure of seeing pilchards taken in the bay.

In October, Vanessa, on returning to town, realised a long meditated project—the Friday Club. This was a society which was to meet every week and to be concerned with the fine arts.* Virginia, who was not deeply interested but did attend some of the proceedings of this club, was amused by its factional disputes: "One half of the Committee," she wrote, "shriek Whistler and French impressionists, and the other are stalwart British." It was the first sign that Bloomsbury was going to be interested in the visual arts.

But Virginia herself was more involved in an activity of a rather different nature. Soon after her return to full health she had been approached by Miss Sheepshanks, a daughter of the Bishop of Norwich, who as effective Principal was anxious to recruit helpers at Morley College. This was an evening institute for working men and women which had been set up as an adjunct to the Old Vic in the Waterloo Road. Miss Sheepshanks' suggestion was that Virginia might "combine amusement and instruction—a little gossip and sympathy—and then 'talks' about books and pictures." "I'm sure I don't mind how much I talk, and I really don't see any limit to the things I might talk about," wrote Virginia to Violet Dickinson. "However as she is sure—the good Sheepshanks—that I shall be of the greatest use—I don't mind trying." Miss Sheepshanks's energy was such that she was able at one time or another to rope in the other Stephens too—Vanessa to teach Drawing, Thoby (and Clive Bell) Latin, and Adrian Greek; but, unlike Virginia, they soon lost interest.

Miss Stephen's students must sometimes have been puzzled, sometimes exhilarated, by her "talks," over the preparation of which she seems to have taken considerable thought.

* Clive Bell was on the original committee and so of course was Vanessa; Henry Lamb, Neville Lytton, E. M. O'R. Dickie, Pernel Strachey and Saxon Sydney-Turner were among the members. There were exhibitions and discussions; the discussions were not confined to questions of art. This club seems to have lasted until about 1912 or 1913.

Tomorrow also is my working women, for whom I have been making out a vivid account of the battle of Hastings. I hope to make their flesh creep!

Virginia believed that it was her task to fire the imagination of her students so that they might see "the flesh and blood in the shadows." But was she perhaps a little too imaginative? Was her version of English History rather too close to that which was later to fill the pages of *Orlando*? It appears from a later passage in the letter quoted above that the Ancient Britons were to perform at Hastings and one can understand the point of view of the authorities who persuaded her to turn to English Literature.

Then on Wednesdays I have my English Composition; 10 people: 4 men, 6 women. It is, I suppose, the most useless class in the College; and so Sheepshanks thinks. She sat through the whole lesson last night; and almost stamped with impatience. But what can I do? I have an old Socialist of 50, who thinks he must bring the Parasite (the Aristocrat)... into an Essay upon Autumn; and a Dutchman who thinks—at the end of the class too—that I have been teaching him Arithmetic; and anaemic shop girls who say they would write more but they only get an hour for their dinner, and there doesn't seem much time for writing. . . .

Or again:

I gave a lecture to four working men yesterday—one stutters on his m's and another is an Italian and reads English as though it were mediaeval Latin, and another is my degenerate poet, who rants and blushes and almost seizes my hand when we happen to like the same lines. . . . I can tell you the first sentence of my lecture: "The poet Keats died when he was 25; and he wrote all his work before that." Indeed—how very interesting, Miss Stephen.

Virginia taught at Morley until the end of 1907 and what her students got from her we cannot tell; we may however guess a little at what she got from them. Never before had she attempted to hold an intellectual discussion with her social inferiors. She felt that she must make it her business to get to know them; she got them to write essays about themselves, and there was one, a Miss Williams, who confided in her. These confidences gave her a first view of Grub Street; she found—and the discovery, though it cannot have been surprising, must have been impressive—a place almost without standards and entirely without integrity. Hacks laboured here to manufacture literary shoddy by the yard; Virginia could not but admire the intelligent industry of the particular hack who described these things to her and the frankness with which they were described; she must also have felt a kind of revolted curiosity, the feelings of a lady for a pavement drab. These revelations helped her to form a picture of what she was later to call 'The Underworld,' the demi-monde of letters, a region that was to loom large in her imagination.

But her main impression – for most of her students were consumers not producers of literature – was of hungry sheep that are not fed. She found them more intelligent than she had expected, but suffering terribly from being half-educated. Morley College could do something really useful for them; it failed and "those in authority" set her and her students to useless tasks – this at least was her view of the matter. Nevertheless she felt the need and the opportunity strongly enough to continue working at the College for three years.*

Virginia's commitment to Morley College obliged her to be in London during term time, and from the fact that she was able to fulfil it we may assume that her health remained stable. She did leave London from time to time – visiting her aunt at Cambridge, the Fishers at Oxford, the Cecils in Sussex, and Violet at Welwyn – and in 1906 she returned to Giggleswick for the Easter holiday, this time staying not with Madge Vaughan but in lodgings near her, and going for long walks on the moors alone with her dog Gurth. In August Vanessa and Virginia rented a decaying and beautiful moated house, Blo' Norton Hall, in a remote part of Norfolk, where they enjoyed what Virginia called "a sort of honeymoon – interrupted it is true with horrible guests."

But a really grand and important excursion had been planned for this year. The Stephens had decided they must see Greece. This undertaking involved the most tremendous preparations: Thoby and Adrian made their wills; boxes and stores, green veils, blue spectacles, white boots, grey felt hats, green-lined umbrellas, paintboxes and easels, medicaments and the help of Messrs Cook had all to be obtained; going to Greece was not so much a holiday as an expedition. Thoby and Adrian – after seeing their sisters settled in Norfolk – set off. They had a month's start, and rode on horseback from Trieste by way of Montenegro and Albania. Then the ladies – Vanessa, Virginia and Violet Dickinson – travelled by train to Brindisi and thence by boat to Patras. At Olympia on 13 September the two parties were reunited.

They had seen Marathon and Salamis and Athens would have been theirs too had not a cloud caressed it; at any rate they felt themselves

* See Appendix B.

charged on each side by tremendous presences. And to prove themselves duly inspired, they not only shared their wine flask with the escort of dirty Greek peasant boys but condescended so far as to address them in their own tongue as Plato would have spoken it had Plato learnt Greek at Harrow.

They were descending Mount Pentelicus and Virginia, as usual, was writing landscape:

But the descent of Pentelicus is stayed by a flat green ledge where nature seems to stand upright for a moment before she plunges down the hill again. There are great plane trees spreading benevolent hands, and there are comfortable little bushes ranged in close domestic order, and there is a stream which may be thought to sing their praises and the delights of wine and song. You might have heard the voice of Theocritus in the plaint that it made on the stones, and certain of the English did so hear it, albeit the text was dusty on their shelves at home. Here at any rate nature and the chant of the classic spirit prompted the six friends to dismount and rest themselves.

Then they conversed and of course their main topic was Greece and the Greeks; they were eloquent and argumentative and perhaps a little too conscious of their surroundings and then, suddenly, the little bushes creaked and bent, and a great brown form surged out of them. It was only a monk carrying a load of wood; he was dirty and probably illiterate; but there was such a force in the eye with which he fixed them that Virginia was moved to emotions which, in their intensity if not in their nature, might have been inspired by Pan himself.

At the beginning of this century an English traveller with a classical education might find much to delight and much to distress him in modern Greece. He came in pursuit of an idea and found instead a reality which was at times disconcerting. Thoby, it would seem, was such a traveller and Virginia observed his enthusiasms and his perplexities with amusement and sympathy. But in fact her feelings agreed with his. Her reaction to Greece was very much what might have been expected of any cultivated young Englishwoman in the year 1906. She was wholly unaware of Byzantine art and uncritical of that of the fifth century; for the modern Greeks she did not care; she preferred the uncivilised Wallachians on the Noels' estate at Achmetaga. She was, as always, fascinated by her fellow guests in hotels and made up stories about them.

Vanessa's views might have been different—the thing that most impressed her was the way in which the Greeks situated their buildings – but Vanessa had not much opportunity to observe Greek art. When they landed at Patras she was feeling unwell; the train journey from Olympia to Corinth upset her further, but after a day or two she was able to go on to Athens. They then set off by boat for the Peloponnese to see Epidaurus, Tiryns and Mycenae; the return railway journey made Vanessa ill again and the party had to stop at Corinth for her to rest. Leaving her there with Violet and, as it seemed, recovering, Virginia, Thoby and Adrian made their pre-arranged excursion to Euboea to visit the Noels; on their return to Athens a few days later they found Vanessa once again in bed, and this time alarmingly ill.

It was an odd, anxious, unhappy view of Greece. Virginia spent much of her time in an Athens hotel bedroom reading Merimée and heating saucepans of goat's milk, which of course boiled over when the *Lettres à une Inconnue* proved too interesting. Downstairs, Thoby and Adrian fell into a violent dispute concerning the Portsmouth Road: was it macadamised beyond Hindhead or was it not? This occupied them for some days,* though Thoby was sufficiently sanguine – or social – to return once more to the Noels.

After about a fortnight Vanessa improved and they were able to revert to their original plan; Thoby returned to London, the rest of the party went on by sea to Constantinople. Vanessa was still very unwell; she had to be carried and nearly fainted when she was put on board at the Piraeus, and again when she reached Constantinople; but here the doctor said that she was well enough to return to England by train. They left Constantinople, of which Virginia saw but little, on 29 October and reached Dover on 1 November. Here George was waiting with a nurse for Vanessa. He told them that Thoby was in bed at 46 Gordon Square with a high temperature. Vanessa was made to go to bed at once but she couldn't sleep; she was worried about Thoby. On the following day he seemed better, his temperature had gone down. The doctor clearly didn't know what was wrong with him; it had been a sharp attack of "something or other" but there was no reason to think that it was anything serious or that it would not get better; for the time being both he and Vanessa were to stay in bed.

Thus Virginia and Adrian found themselves in control of a house containing two invalids while Violet, who would have been Virginia's great standby, was herself lying ill at her own house in Manchester Street. Virginia described herself as living in the midst of nurses, bedpans, carbolic and doctors and, she might have added,

* See *The Voyage Out*, p. 417.

in an atmosphere of deepening gloom; for although Vanessa was said to be getting better and Savage, called in to consider various nervous symptoms, pooh-poohed them—or at least said that they were not at all serious—Thoby was not responding to treatment. This was hardly surprising since the doctors had decided that he was suffering from malaria and it was only discovered after ten days, through the discreet but desperate intervention of the nurse, to be typhoid fever. It was found that Violet Dickinson also had typhoid.

Whether this mistake by the doctors was the cause of what followed I do not know. Certainly the Stephen family seems to have been unfortunate in its physicians; as in 1895 and 1897 there seems to have been a helpless, muddled drifting towards death. Thoby passed from crisis to crisis; he became listless, weary and weak; all he had left at the end was the courage to die bravely.

For Virginia the disaster which prostrated them all and which seemed to take the meaning out of their lives was made a little more horrible by the fact that Violet, herself lying desperately ill was, according to her doctors, in a condition to be profoundly affected by Thoby's death. Virginia was told that it must, at all costs, be kept from her. And so Virginia, who wrote to her daily, had to keep up the pretence that her brother was still alive. "We are going on well through the stages," she writes on 20 November, the day of Thoby's death. "Thoby is going on splendidly. He is very cross with his nurses, because they won't give him mutton chops and beer, and he asks why he can't go for a ride with Bell and look for wild geese." Thus she wrote three days after the funeral. This grim exercise in fiction continued day after day for almost a month, until the truth came out by accident and Virginia had to write to explain.

There was now another piece of news to be discussed. Two days after Thoby's death Vanessa in her despair had turned to Clive Bell for comfort and had agreed to marry him.

In a way this was a consolation; "There will be all Nessa's life to look forward to," she wrote to Violet. But might there not be some treachery in becoming as happy as Vanessa now was, even though her happiness, like that of Bernard in *The Waves*, was so strangely divided? And Clive—Virginia's feelings about him were mixed but they were often extremely critical. Was he worthy to marry a Stephen? And was she, Virginia, who had lost her favourite brother, who might yet lose her Violet, now also to lose her sister? She would have to leave Gordon Square where she had been so happy. The good years had been very brief and the Stephens were devoted to catastrophe. All this she may have thought, some of it she did think; but she seems on the whole to have behaved extraordinarily well, to have risen to an occasion which might have broken a stouter constitution than hers and to have kept her head and her temper when she might fairly have been expected to lose them.

Chapter Six

1906-1908

THOBY'S death was a disaster from which Virginia could not easily recover. Two years later she still felt her loss acutely; it was odd to be living in a world that did not contain him, and even after twenty years it still seemed to her that her own continuing life was no more than an excursion without him, and that death would be no more than a return to his company.

Her immediate desire was to know more of him. There was so much that she did not know, for Thoby did not repay his sisters' love with open affection or confidences—they were all too reserved for that and there were, of course, things that a fellow does not discuss with his sisters. There was therefore much of his private and intellectual life which remained mysterious and could now never be discovered unless, perhaps, one of his Cambridge friends would write something. She addressed herself to Lytton Strachey who, after a year, had to confess that he found the task too difficult. Clive refused it also and she talked to Saxon Sydney-Turner, who applied to Leonard Woolf in Ceylon, but he too was unable to help.

That unknown part of Thoby was important to her partly because she loved him and she sought, as we all seek, for that which our dead have taken from us for ever, partly for a more complex reason—an amused yet resentful curiosity about the privileged masculine society of Cambridge. Twice she returns to a kind of bittersweet speculation concerning the vanished being whom we reconstruct in our mind's eye—*ex pede Herculem*—deducing Jacob from his room, Percival from the sensations of his circumambient friends.

In a manuscript written at the end of her life she wonders what he might have become. "Mr Justice Stephen . . . with several books to his credit . . ." She begins to draw the picture of a successful Stephen, typical of his country and class and then, almost correcting herself, she decides that he was not that: there was something melancholy and original about him, the ordinary ambitions of life would not have mattered much to him.

One is inclined to wonder what role this masterful and persuasive young man, together with his wife—for he would surely have married – would have played in the life of his sisters; how would he have regarded Vanessa's increasing libertinism and Virginia's growing tendency to flirtation? Would he have had what is called 'a steadying influence'? How would he have reacted to the Post-Impressionists, to the war and to his sister's novels? I suspect that, if he had lived, he would have tended to strengthen rather than to weaken those barriers of speech and thought and custom which were soon to be overthrown amongst his friends. It was his death which began to work their destruction: Mr Sydney-Turner and Mr Strachey became Saxon and Lytton, they were at Gordon Square continually and in her distress Virginia wanted to see no one save them and Clive – Thoby's Cambridge friends. It was then that Virginia discovered that these young men had not only brains but hearts, and that their sympathy was something different from the dreadful condolences of relations. As a result of Thoby's death Bloomsbury was refounded upon the solid base of deep mutual understanding; his death was also the proximate cause of Vanessa's marriage.

On New Year's Eve 1906 Virginia and Adrian joined Vanessa and Clive at Cleeve House, the home of the Bells, near Devizes. Virginia sat and wrote at a table which was furnished with an inkpot fashioned out of the hoof of a favourite hunter. The animal's name and the date of its death were inscribed upon a silver cartouche. She often adverted to that inkpot in later life: never, in her experience, had there been an inkpot like it; it seemed a note of the entire house. The place was populated by stuffed animals and to a large extent by living ones; animals dominated the conversation, yielding only occasionally to lawn tennis, hockey and the weather. The human inhabitants had something of the bucolic health of brutes, something of their ferocity, something of their niceness and a good deal of their intellectual limitations. It was all new to Virginia, quite different from Kensington or the world of Kitty Maxse or the Duckworths; this in fact was Philistia and for Vanessa, as a multitude of despondent letters bear witness, it was Tomi, a desolate place inhabited by Scythians to which she was periodically banished by the exigencies of marriage.

The two Miss Bells came down to dinner in pale blue satin with satin bows in their hair. Mr Bell presided, bluff, gruff and cordial at one end of the table, Mrs Bell, an attenuated rabbit-faced woman with strong religious principles, sat opposite him. What they made of Virginia, who seems to have been in one of her more fantastic moods and who on the following day exploded at lunch, lost her temper, strode out of the house and returned in the evening with the settled wish to be as charming as possible–heaven knows. They only saw her once again and the only member of the family, save her brother-in-law, to whom she was to become at all attached was Clive's brother Cory and he, it would seem, was not then present. In the 1920s, when she had become celebrated, they would refer to her with a diffidence, a kind of bewildered curiosity, as though she had two heads but was, nevertheless, a duchess–not the kind of thing to which they were accustomed.

Virginia's volatile behaviour probably had more to do with Vanessa than with Vanessa's new relations. Certainly, having seen the Bell family, she regarded the alliance with dismay; but her objections to the match had a deeper origin.

Vanessa was lost to her, ravished away and ecstatically, monstrously happy. It was intolerable, unbearable. And Clive was simply not good enough. He was pompous, polished and slight; how her sister–Thoby's sister and Sir Leslie's daughter–could match herself to such an absurd little creature was more than she could understand. And then, seeing them together, she allowed that Clive had after all very considerable good qualities; he was kind and clever and sensitive; he did understand Vanessa very well and made her beautifully happy. To be sure he was no genius, but then neither was Vanessa and Vanessa, it was apparent, was made for marriage. It would be intolerably, odiously egotistical to find fault with an arrangement that seemed so perfectly designed to bring felicity to two–at least two–amiable human beings. And yet . . .

So it went on; she was at war with herself: divided between an agonised perception of her sister's happiness and her own jealousy, a state of delight and of rage which endured for months and years and was to be qualified only by another sentiment which heightened, rather than relaxed, the tensions within her.

The immediate problem was the actual ceremony. It was fixed for 7 February. Henry James came to see Vanessa not long before; his views of the bridegroom were even more unfavourable than those of Virginia in her most hostile moods.

However, I suppose she knows what she is about, and seemed very happy and eager and almost boisterously in love (in that house of all the Deaths, ah me!) and I took her an old silver box ("for hairpins"), and she spoke of having got "a beautiful Florentine teaset" from you. She was evidently happy in the latter, but I winced and ground my teeth when I heard of it. She and Clive are to keep the Bloomsbury house, and Virginia and Adrian to forage for some flat somewhere–

Virginia having, by the way, grown quite elegantly and charmingly and almost "smartly" handsome. I liked being with them, but it was all strange and terrible (with the hungry *futurity* of youth;) and all I could mainly see was the *ghosts*, even Thoby and Stella, let alone dear old Leslie and beautiful, pale, tragic Julia—on all of whom these young backs were, and quite naturally, so gaily turned.

The night before the wedding they all went to *Fidelio*. "I hate her going away," wrote Virginia, "but I really have been quite good tempered." The marriage took place at St Pancras Registry Office. George lent his smart car for the occasion; the chauffeur, having never before been in such a plebeian quarter of the town, lost his way, causing Vanessa and Virginia to be late for the ceremony and the young couple, who had been persuaded by Virginia to go to Manorbier for a honeymoon, to miss their train at Paddington; the delay gave Vanessa time to write an affectionate note to her sister from the station. On the following day Virginia described herself as being "numb and dumb."

Virginia and Adrian planned to move into a new home before Clive and Vanessa returned from Manorbier, taking Sophia Farrell, the family cook, with them.* Virginia found a pleasant house (which had been Bernard Shaw's) at 29 Fitzroy Square; Adrian and Sophy both approved of it but there were others who did not. "Beatrice [Thynne] comes round, inarticulate with meaning, & begs me not to take the house because of the neighbourhood," she wrote to Violet, and Violet herself was wary. Virginia was not yet brave enough to defy her relations: "If I hint at any question of respectability to George, Gerald and Jack," she complained, "they will refuse to let me take it." She sought the advice of the Police and they, it seems, were reassuring; for late in March 1907, she and Adrian moved in.

To them the situation was entirely eligible: it was an agreeable house and not so close to Gordon Square that the Stephens became a mere annexe of the Bells, nor yet so far that the two households could not meet whenever they chose. It was ideally placed for the purposes of those friends who got into the habit of visiting one of the houses and then strolling over to the other. Bloomsbury now had two centres separated by a very convenient distance.

It had been Virginia's purpose in taking this new house to make

---

* Sophy, who was very stout, declared: "I ought to be able to cut myself up among the lot of you," adding more gravely: "but it must be Miss [Virginia]; she's such a harum scarum thing she wouldn't know if they sold her. She don't know what she has on her plate." MH/A 13e.

VIRGINIA WOOLF

a home for Adrian. Adrian has not played a very large part in this
story but now he was to be Virginia's chief companion. She had
described him in 1903 as being "fifteen years younger than all the
rest of us" although he was then nearly twenty and her junior by
only eighteen months. Like so many of Virginia's hyperboles it contained a good deal of truth. In a family of slow developers he was
the slowest. As the youngest he tried very hard to keep his end up:
while the others were enthusiastic butterfly hunters he held aloof
ostentatiously; when Thoby and Virginia started the *Hyde Park
Gate News* he began a rival journal. He made two attempts, but
the competition was too cruel; the editors of the *News* were con-
descending and advised him to become one of their contributors.
Leslie gave the same advice, but it was not taken; the *Pelican News* and
its successor, *The Corkscrew Gazette*, soon petered out. His mother
had been his great ally and advocate; he had been her favourite and
he looked to her for love and protection. His father's heavy-handed
attempts to teach him were frightening and bewildering; his record
at Evelyn's and Westminster was undistinguished and he was compared, unfairly but inevitably, with Thoby.*

He had inherited something of his father's moral and physical
characteristics; he was sensitive and rather nervous, a thin, bony,
almost stunted little boy known in the family as The Dwarf and very
unlike his robust elder brother. This, oddly enough, was a reproach
he was able to rebut. At the age of sixteen he began to sprout, at
the age of eighteen he was six feet two inches high and he attained
six feet five inches. The dwarf had become a giant; but this
beanstalk effort seemed almost a repetition of *The Corkscrew Gazette*:
he had made himself taller than any of them, but to no purpose, and
indeed he seemed physically exhausted by the effort. At Cambridge
he appeared no more than the evening shadow of his brother, less
brilliant, less charming. Embarking, as usual, on an independent line,
he refused to follow current intellectual fashions; he did not believe
in G. E. Moore who was, he declared, a fraud. Moore's followers,
and Lytton Strachey in particular, resented his attitude and were
snubbing.

Cambridge gave him a third and he went down in 1905 with no
very clear idea of what he wanted to do. Gifted with an acute mind

* When Adrian was being analysed, in 1923, his analyst is reported to have said
that he was "a tragedy"; "and this tragedy consists in the fact that he cant enjoy
life with zest. I [Virginia] am probably responsible. I should have paired with him,
instead of hanging on to the elders. So he wilted, pale, under a stone of vivacious
brothers and sisters." AWD (Berg) 13 May 1923.

and a strongly argumentative disposition he looked, as might have been expected, to the law for a profession, but it was not to be a lasting vocation.

Virginia found him by turns a depressing or an exasperating companion. He could be maddeningly lethargic, lamentably silent, unable to find interest in anything except the constant rehearsal of old family reminiscences which were, indeed, always his favourite topic. And yet there was another side to his character and he could, on occasion, be gay, enterprising and high-spirited; but such occasions were few and, with his sister, his intelligence and his humour were diverted into a habit of mocking surveillance and quiet irony, a devastating appreciation of other people's faults, and, above all, a merciless vein of pleasantry. Her flightiness brought out his sardonic Stephen matter-of-factness, her enthusiasm his scepticism, her arguments his ridicule. He was a tease and found in Virginia an eminently teasable subject. They were in fact, both of them, highly gifted in the arts of reproach and carried their sallies to great lengths. At Fitzroy Square Sophy used to prepare the butter in little round pats, spheres which Adrian and Virginia used as missiles when other arguments failed, so that the walls were starred with flattened projectiles; there is at least one witness who has seen an argument end in an exchange of butter.

They were genuinely fond of each other–indeed in all that family fraternal sentiments were profound, more profound perhaps than any other, and after Thoby's death brother and sisters were in a new way united. Certain reserves were broken down; they began to talk more freely, above all about the dead, who had hitherto been taboo–so much so that, for years after Stella's death, her name had not been mentioned–but I doubt whether Virginia and Adrian ever hinted at their love for each other. That deep feeling remained unexpressed, in public at all events; it was the arguments in the drawing-room and the butter on the walls that the visitor noticed.

It was all very well for Virginia to go off and live in a perhaps rather disreputable neighbourhood with her younger brother but, said her old friends, that younger brother was by no means so youthful that he could not very well look after himself, and the person who manifestly needed looking after was Virginia. Vanessa's spell of duty was over; Adrian, that irresponsible luggage-loser, was not the man for the job; what Virginia clearly and emphatically needed was a husband. "Virginia," they declared, "must marry."

She was irritated by the suggestion and wrote to Violet, "I wish everyone didn't tell me to marry. Is it crude human nature breaking

VIRGINIA WOOLF

out? I call it disgusting." Nevertheless she was not so utterly opposed
to the very notion as she seems hitherto to have been. Whether it
was the spectacle of her sister's felicity, or a new sense of her own
loneliness or the disappearance of him who had been, after all, the
man she loved best, one cannot tell, but certainly the year 1907
marks a distinct change in her emotional disposition.

Hitherto men, as lovers, seem to have played no role at all in her
imagination. There is nothing in her letters or diaries to suggest
that any man had inspired her with the slightest erotic excitement.
All her passions, her jealousies and tenderness are kept for her own
sex and above all for Violet; but now, although very far from falling
in love with any man, she was at least ready to flirt.

It is not altogether surprising that the first man with whom she
flirted was almost old enough to be her father. Walter Headlam
was an old family friend. Born in 1866, he had been one of the
younger men whom Julia brought to Talland House. He was now a
Fellow of King's, a man with a great reputation amongst Hellenists,
a translator who had shown a fastidious delight in the use of English
and could, in his own right, be considered a poet. These were qualities to give him an immediate claim upon Virginia's attention: she
had a kind of reverence for Greek scholars, felt them to be rulers over
a territory into which she had attempted to journey and, equally,
she could not fail to be interested in one who, like herself, was devoted to the art of letters. Moreover his character was in some respects
engaging; he had a certain eccentric absurdity which was endearing
because it resulted from a complete absorption in his work. The confusion, the learned turmoil of a life spent largely in a single-minded
hunt for truth, the occasional reckless sallies into practical affairs, of
which he had but the vaguest understanding, the ingenuousness
with which he wandered into the most ludicrous misadventures
from which he emerged baffled, perplexed but always convinced
that the most important thing in his life was, after all, properly to
achieve the restoration of Herodas—all this was not unsympathetic.*

Virginia respected and liked him and according to Vanessa he had
a great belief in her genius—and this was a lovable trait. But both
Vanessa and Violet considered the friendship with some misgivings.
Walter Headlam was, in their opinion, a shocking flirt and his real
passion in life, so it was said, was for little girls.†

* Headlam may have served as a model for Mr Bankes in *To the Lighthouse*.
See George Duckworth to VW, 28 May 1927.

† Violet Dickinson's attitude towards Mr Headlam may have been coloured by
Stella Duckworth—who had been her particular friend. In September 1893 he

Not long after Thoby's death—in fact while she was still keeping up the fiction of his survival—Virginia wrote excitedly to tell Violet that she was to send all her "unpublished works" to Walter Headlam "for sober criticism"; further, that he wished to dedicate his translation of the *Agamemnon* to her, instead of to Swinburne, "in gratitude for 3 papers of the finest criticism known to him which I wrote and despatched 4 years ago!" Thereafter they corresponded (he wrote to her "as to a sister") and met frequently; he would come to tea—once with Lytton Strachey, when Virginia complained that she hated "pouring out tea & talking like a lady"; at another time they had "a serious interview"; he declared himself miserable because Virginia didn't marry but sat moping alone, thinking she must be "a d——d failure." They discussed the matter for two hours, greatly to the advantage of their feelings no doubt. She saw him at Cambridge when she went, as she periodically did, to visit her aunt; he took her to the Opera at Covent Garden.

Presently he accused her of being fickle; he was pathetic, dignified, injured and then, so it would seem, the affair petered out with no great harm done to anyone. When he died very suddenly and unexpectedly in June 1908, Virginia's grief was not immoderate.*

---

stayed with the Stephens at St Ives; Stella wrote in her diary (21 September): "Mother & Mr Headlam came home late for dinner, looking tired & unhappy. *Drat* Mr Headlam. What *has* happened?" and (22 September): "Mr Headlam went at 10.30. I cannot think of him without a shudder & yet he is much to be pitied—it is awful."

* Virginia preserved one of Headlam's letters. Erudite and flirtatious, it may serve, probably, as an example of his manner to her.

King's College,
Cambridge.
Saturday.

Dear Virginia

I had thought of writing to say please don't write to thank me for the book, which you had already said thank you for – you talk of me as always giving things away, but this is the only thing I can remember ever asking you to take from me – and now before the letter comes I find this book from you. I thought at first it must be something I had left behind me, though what I knew I had left behind me was not this. I was going in any case to take the Life abroad with me and your MSS. It must seem strange that I have never read them yet, but I want to enjoy them in the holidays.

You musn't say Christian to me: that must be left for me to say to you; it's what you have been in coming to that dismallest of chambers every week and never failing, and it's well there has been Christianity, or I should never be able to say bless you.

Χαῖρε φίλη [Hail Mistress]
Walter Headlam

VIRGINIA WOOLF

Virginia had believed, or had affected to believe, that when once Vanessa was married she would be entirely changed and that she and her sister would never meet again on the old footing. Clive would destroy their intimacy. When she returned from her honeymoon Vanessa set herself to reassure Virginia on this point: Virginia must spend a great deal of her time at Gordon Square and she, Vanessa, insisted on coming frequently to see Virginia. They all went off to Paris together, and talked of finding a country house to share for the summer; there were far too many servants at No 46 and if two thirds of them were dismissed it would be easy to finance such a scheme. Discussions such as these, the patent fact that Vanessa was not essentially changed, that they met almost every day, and that they continued to have long tête-à-têtes together—all this had its effect in relieving Virginia from the too gloomy fancies in which she had indulged at the time of Vanessa's marriage.

When they were apart the sisters corresponded daily; together, they discussed Virginia's suitors, Vanessa always fancying that every man whom Virginia met would at once propose to her. Meanwhile, at Fitzroy Square, Virginia was forced to stand on her own feet in her own drawing-room and to talk a little. In the autumn she and Adrian began shyly to entertain and to revive Thoby's Thursday Evenings.

From the first Virginia's ideas of acceptable company were very different from those of Vanessa. She invited Bloomsbury—the word can now be used with a little more confidence—and also other young men who had been at Cambridge and at 46 Gordon Square in Thoby's time—Charles Tennyson, Hilton Young, Theodore Llewelyn Davies—and one rather older Cambridge figure. A scholar, a linguist, a critic, a lawyer, Charlie Sanger was also, according to his friends, a saint; he had been elected to the Apostles at the same time as Bertrand Russell and did, I fancy, exert a considerable influence over his younger friends, with whom he was on terms of perfectly easy familiarity. These, the intellectuals, might find themselves at Fitzroy Square in the company of 'Ozzie' Dickinson (Violet's brother), Lady Beatrice Thynne, Lady Gwendolen Godolphin Osborne, Margaret Vaughan, Janet Case,* Miss Sheep-

---

Thus by an allusion to the pious inscriptions of the Catacombs, where $\phi\iota\lambda\eta$ has a chaste meaning, Headlam is able boldly to address her as 'mistress.' (I am much indebted to my colleague Dr Shiel for pointing out to me the extent of Headlam's ambiguous dexterity.)

* "I remember having tea with you one day after the Greek lesson time was over and done with, and V. established in the new odd Bloomsbury life and I didnt

shanks, or any of the Hyde-Park-Gaters–though the latter were more likely I think to be invited to dine than to drop in after dinner on Thursdays.

Virginia was always curious about people and we find her adventuring into decent society there to listen to the current talk of the Establishment: "Country going to the dogs . . . we have no fleet . . . the Germans menace us from without, the Trades' Unions from within . . ." For the Duckworths still represented authority and there were occasions when she felt like a child in their presence, a child who might be scolded because George was 'hurt.' He never saw his family now, he complained; really Clive and Vanessa had treated him very ill; they were drifting apart. And this was true, for things were very different at Gordon Square. Clive was much more easily bored and much more selective in his invitations, while Vanessa enthusiastically slammed the door against old friends and relations. It was almost certainly Vanessa–although the story is told of both sisters–who tried to hide from Mrs Humphry Ward by standing behind a lamp post in the Piazza della Signoria, and it was certainly Vanessa who pushed her neglect so far that Richmond Ritchie–Aunt Anny's husband–cut her dead at the Opera. The Bells really did attempt to be exclusive and it was with a touch of malice that Virginia observed in November 1907 that

> Nessa & Clive live, as I think, much like great ladies in a French salon; they have all the wits & the poets; & Nessa sits among them like a Goddess.

They regarded their drawing-room as a work of art and did not welcome intruders.

Virginia's drawing-room was not a work of art; for one thing it was inhabited by the dog Hans, which delighted in extinguishing visitors' matches with its paw, which interrupted several parties by being sick, and on one occasion, when Virginia was giving Lady Strachey tea, eased itself upon the hearthrug–a performance which both guest and hostess thought it best to disregard.

Despite her training at Hyde Park Gate Virginia was not, I think, in any sense a leader of the society within which she moved. She was often silent, respectfully–or sometimes abstractedly–silent; she affected to feel, and really did feel, awe in the presence of Saxon or of Lytton; even the admirable but unattractive Miss Sheepshanks could

---

think she'd have any further use for me, and felt shy of going [presumably to Fitzroy Square] and *you* told me to stick to her. She'd like it–so thank you for that." Janet Case to Violet Dickinson, 19 April 1937.

put her down with the devastating enquiry: "Miss Stephen, do you *ever* think?" Nevertheless, with her own social life to conduct, Virginia was probably happier than she had expected to be, and, for comfort, she could still turn to her sister.

It was agreed that the two households should spend the summer holidays of 1907 within reach of one another. Virginia and Adrian rented a cottage at Playden, a little to the north of Rye; the Bells, who came a little later after visiting the Bell family residence in Wiltshire, stayed in Rye itself. Guests were to some extent shared and, of course, there were constant meetings. While she was there, in addition to some journalism, Virginia started to write an account of her father and mother, of life in the nursery, of Stella and Jack and her half-brothers; it was in the form of a Life of Vanessa written for her children (Vanessa was by now pregnant). She was also writing descriptions of light and mist, night scenes and rural life, and now also she was attempting, with a novelist's intention, to look at states of mind; she tried to enter the mind of a Sussex farm labourer, she considered the pathetic fallacy in novels, the habit of reading the novelist's sentiments into those of very different kinds of people—or for that matter of animals. Also she was reading Henry James, but without great enthusiasm.*

Amongst the monuments of Rye was the Master himself and a visit was called for. Vanessa had written to Virginia from Wiltshire, hoping that "old Henry James won't be too monumental and difficult." He was monumental enough, as may be seen from the following letter to Violet Dickinson.

. . . we went and had tea with Henry James to-day, and Mr and Mrs Prothero at the golf club and Henry James fixed me with his staring blank eye, it is like a child's marble, and said "My dear Virginia they tell me, they tell me, they tell me, that you—as indeed being your father's daughter, nay your grandfather's grandchild, the descendant I may say of a century, of a century, of quill pen and ink, ink, inkpots, yes, yes, yes, they tell me, a h m m m, that you, that you, that you *write* in short." This went on in the public street, while we all waited, as farmers wait for the hen to lay an egg,—do they? nervous, polite, and now on this foot, now on that. I felt like a condemned person, who sees the knife drop and stick and drop again. Never did any woman hate 'writing' as much as I do. But when I am old and famous I shall dis-

* " I am reading Henry James on America; & feel myself as one embalmed in a block of smooth amber; it is not unpleasant, very tranquil, as a twilight stroll—but such is not the stuff of Genius: no, it should be a swift stream." VW to Clive Bell, [18 August 1907].

course like Henry James. We had to stop periodically to let him shake himself free of the thing; he made phrases over the bread and butter, "rude and rapid" it was, and told us all the scandal of Rye. "Mr Jones has eloped I regret to say to Tasmania leaving twelve little Jones's and a possible thirteenth to Mrs Jones, most regrettable, most unfortunate, and yet not wholly an action to which one has no private key of one's own so to speak." Well, this ceases to interest you ...

The Bells arrived, also Saxon and Lytton. As we have seen, Henry James did not care for Clive; Saxon he seems to have liked even less. Neither the Bells nor the Stephens returned to Rye, nor did Virginia see very much of Henry James in later years. One may suppose that he was attracted to her on principle–she was Leslie Stephen's daughter–but she hardly conformed then, and was to conform less and less, to his notions of delicacy, decorum and reverence. He could not possibly approve of her scrubby, gritty friends. Virginia, for her part, regarded him with a kind of amused awe, respected his work but respected it with reservations and, as we may perceive from the letter that I have quoted, enjoyed his company only in retrospect.*

On 27 December 1907 there was a meeting at Gordon Square at which Saxon, Vanessa, Clive, Adrian, Lytton and Virginia read Vanbrugh's *The Relapse*. Lytton excelled as Lord Foppington, Virginia was both Berinthia and Miss Hoyden. This was the first of many such meetings. They took place on Friday evenings during the year 1908, usually at Gordon Square, always with the same readers, who may be regarded as the core of Bloomsbury at this period. Walter Lamb, a friend of Clive's, who had been at Trinity and of whom we shall hear more, once took part. He was then a schoolmaster at Clifton and could never have been a regular participant. Saxon kept the minutes for a time, giving the cast and a comment on each reading; Clive, who became Secretary in April 1908, did likewise; the minute book is interesting in that it provides a notion of the taste of the group. It was catholic: the Restoration and the Elizabethans, Milton, Shakespeare, Swinburne, Ibsen. Virginia failed, according to the Secretary, to convey the feeling of concentrated nervous force required in the part of Rebecca West in *Rosmersholm* but she excelled as Althaea in *Atalanta in Calydon*.

---

* "[Henry James] asked much after Virginia and Vanessa. Can't cultivate Gordon Square because of the unpleasant presence of 'that little image' Clive. 'Tell Virginia–tell her–how sorry I am that the inevitabilities of life should have made it possible even for a moment that I would allow any child of her father's to swim out of my ken.'" Sydney Waterlow, *Diary (Berg)*, 10 March 1912.

The Relapse was hardly the kind of play that Sir Leslie would have cared to have heard his daughters reading aloud in the company of young men. Nor, while he was alive, would Virginia, who in her letters ventured no stronger expression than 'd—n,' have imagined herself capable of such an audacity. In the four years that had elapsed since her father's death, there had been a change in the moral climate.

Virginia, after her first relief at finding that the young men from Cambridge did not pursue her, began to find their lack of interest dull; her flirtation with Walter Headlam had inclined her to take a more adventurous attitude. And then Lytton, whose heart had been opened by their common grief and who was now so close a friend, found it intolerable that the pruderies and reserves of the past should be allowed to continue.

It was a spring evening. Vanessa and I were sitting in the drawing room. The drawing room had greatly changed its character since 1904. The Sargent-Furse age was over. The age of Augustus John was dawning. His Pyramus filled one entire wall. The Watts portrait of my father and my mother were hung downstairs if they were hung at all. Clive had hidden all the match boxes because their blue and yellow swore with the prevailing colour scheme. At any moment Clive might come in and he and I should begin to argue–amicably, impersonally at first; soon we should be hurling abuse at each other and pacing up and down the room. Vanessa sat silent and did something mysterious with her needle or her scissors. I talked egotistically, excitedly, about my own affairs no doubt. Suddenly the door opened and the long and sinister figure of Mr Lytton Strachey stood on the threshold. He pointed his finger at a stain on Vanessa's white dress.

"Semen?" he said.

Can one really say it? I thought & we burst out laughing. With that one word all barriers of reticence and reserve went down. A flood of the sacred fluid seemed to overwhelm us. Sex permeated our conversation. The word bugger was never far from our lips. We discussed copulation with the same excitement and openness that we had discussed the nature of good. It is strange to think how reticent, how reserved we had been and for how long.*

* MH/A 16. Virginia gives the impression that this occurred in about 1909, but a letter from Vanessa to Virginia which can confidently be dated 11 August 1908 makes it clear that by then Lytton's private life was well known to both sisters, while a letter from Maynard Keynes to Duncan Grant, dated 2 August 1908, contains the following passage:

"Lytton seems to carry on a good deal with his females. He has let Vanessa see his most indecent poems–she is filled with delight, has them by heart, and has made many typewritten copies for Virginia and others."

We may therefore place this *éclaircissement* not later than the summer of 1908;

This was an important moment in the history of the *mores* of Bloomsbury and perhaps in that of the British middle classes; but although Virginia's entire social climate was altered from now on–and this had all sorts of consequences–the libertine speech of herself and of her friends had no radical effect upon her conduct or, I think, upon her imagination. She remained in a profound way virginal and for her the great event of the years 1907–1908 was not the beginning of Bloomsbury bawdy talk, but the birth of *Melymbrosia*.

Melymbrosia may, indeed, have had its beginnings in Virginia's imagination at some earlier date; perhaps even at Manorbier in 1904. But it is now that we hear it mentioned by name in her letters, now that she asks for advice and gives some indication of her struggle in writing it.

Melymbrosia was to occupy her for the next five years and to become, eventually, *The Voyage Out*. We do not know much about her earlier attempts at what she called "a work of the imagination." She had conceived a play, to be written oddly enough in collaboration with Jack Hills:

> I'm going to have a man and a woman–show them growing up–never meeting–not knowing each other–but all the time you'll feel them come nearer and nearer. This will be the real exciting part (as you see)–but when they almost meet–only a door between–you see how they just miss–and go off at a tangent, and never come anywhere near again. There'll be oceans of talk and emotions without end.

This interesting but remarkably intractable scenario was devised about 1903; so far as I know it never materialised.

A few fragments remain: the beginning of a novel and a short story, to which reference has already been made. There were also, it seems, some works of an unusual kind. We only know of these because Virginia and Madge Vaughan sent each other manuscripts and criticisms. It is clear that Virginia's early attempts at fiction (if that is what they were) disconcerted Madge a good deal and Virginia found it necessary to explain something of her purpose by way of justification.

> My only defence is that I write of things as I see them; & I am quite conscious all the time that it is a very narrow, & rather bloodless point

---

unless Virginia invented it. That it was not wholly imaginary is made probable by the fact that it was read to the Memoir Club (in about 1922). That audience would not have been troubled by inaccuracies but it would not have accepted a complete invention.

of view. I think–if I were Mr Gosse writing to Mrs Green!–I could explain a little why this is so from external reasons; such as education, way of life &c. And so perhaps I may get something better as I grow older. George Eliot was near 40 I think, when she wrote her first novel– the Scenes [*of Clerical Life*].

But my present feeling is that this vague & dream like world, without love, or heart, or passion, or sex, is the world I really care about, & find interesting. For, though they are dreams to you, & I cant express them at all adequately, these things are perfectly real to me.

But please dont think for a moment that I am satisfied, or think that my view takes in any whole. Only it seems to me better to write of the things I do feel, than to dabble in things I frankly dont understand in the least. That is the kind of blunder–in literature–which seems to me ghastly & unpardonable: people, I mean, who wallow in emotions without understanding them. But, of course, any great writer treats them so that they are beautiful, & turns statues into men & women. I wonder if you understand my priggish & immature mind at all? The things I sent you were mere experiments; & I shall never try to put them forward as my finished work. They shall sit in a desk till they are burnt!

No doubt they were burnt; so, it would appear, were seven different versions of *The Voyage Out*.

She continued to do a good deal of reviewing. A series of *Cornhill* articles published during 1908 gave her the chance to be a little more ambitious than she had been in her contributions to *The Guardian*, *The Times Literary Supplement* and other journals, for here she had more room for manœuvre; but she published no fiction until she was thirty-three.

Her literary taciturnity was partly the result of shyness; she was still terrified of the world, terrified of exposing herself. But with this was united another and nobler emotion–a high regard for the seriousness of her profession. To produce something that would meet her own criteria it was necessary to read voraciously, to write and rewrite continually and no doubt, when she was not actually writing, to revolve the ideas that she was expressing in her mind.

Having discovered, more or less, the direction in which she wanted to proceed, she would have lived very close to her work. No one who has any experience of creating a work of art will need to be told how completely such a process, when once started, dominates the mind. It becomes the stuff of one's waking life, more real than anything else, a delight and a torment. Thus, in considering the events of this period in her life, a period in which Virginia embarked with some recklessness and, it must be said, with very little scruple, upon emotional adventures of a sufficiently desperate kind, it is to be remembered that, for the greater part of the time, she lived in a world of her own making and, as will be seen, some of her least creditable actions were related to the necessities of that world.

Chapter Seven

1908-1909

A S we have seen, Virginia was always being told that she should marry; but, when one considers the men who formed her immediate circle in the year 1908 it must be allowed that her chances of doing so were not encouraging. The field of search had been narrowed, or at least the pitch had been queered, by her discovery that most of the young men who most interested her were buggers.*

Saxon she would hardly have thought of as a husband; although he did not inspire love in her, she perhaps did in him. In a letter to Lytton, Leonard Woolf speculated on the possibility that she might end by marrying Saxon; but his qualifications as a lover were questionable. He had his peculiarities in love, as in so much else, and it was, perhaps, in order to make his position clear that he discussed them with Virginia.†

On paper, so to speak, Duncan Grant was also a possible husband. Virginia had met him when she was with the Bells in Paris in 1907; he was then an art student in that city. He had liked the Bells and thought that Virginia was extremely witty and "amazingly beautiful." Clive and Vanessa had found him charming and hoped to see a great deal of him when he returned to London.

They did; Duncan Grant was to become a familiar figure in Gordon Square and an even more familiar figure in Fitzroy Square, where he had a studio. He would wander into No 29 at any hour, hitching up his trousers, which always seem to have been in a precarious condition and which, at that time, were frequently borrowed from someone less slim than he; then he would borrow twopence for a tram fare and presently wander out again. He was never unwelcome, although Maud, the housemaid, was slightly scandalised by his informality: "that Mr Grant", she complained,

* Buggers, a coarse and perhaps an inaccurate word. Nevertheless I use it, for Virginia and her friends used it (*q.v.s.* p. 124) and would have thought most of the alternatives over-refined and–in that they do not remind us of persecuted heresy–impoverished.

† "What a very odd talk you seem to have had with Saxon. I cant believe that that mild little man is really a Sadist or whatever its called." VB/VW, [16 March 1909].

"gets in everywhere." I doubt whether Maud remained insensible to his charm; certainly Virginia did not; she would have been pleased to know that Duncan praised her beauty and that he once told his cousin, Lytton Strachey, that he might like to be married to her.*
She would not, however, have taken this remark very seriously; she was well aware that if, at this time, his affections were given–or lent–to any member of the family they were for Adrian.

Probably the person whom Virginia's Bloomsbury friends most frequently thought of her marrying was Lytton Strachey. And yet, considered as a husband, Lytton would appear to have been a non-starter and this for two reasons: he was an impossible character and he was the arch-bugger of Bloomsbury. Nevertheless, Virginia certainly considered the idea of marrying him and he half wanted to marry her. Where both the principals are inclined to make a match it is clear that the spectator cannot dismiss the thing out of hand and it is worth enquiring into the disabilities which, at first sight, made the marriage so unlikely and seeing whether, as stated here, they are not somewhat exaggerated.

That Lytton was a pretty thorough-going homosexual cannot be denied. Once, in considering Virginia's suitors, her sister remarked:

> I should like Lytton as a brother in law better than anyone I know but the only way I can perceive of bringing that to pass would be if he were to fall in love with Adrian– & even then Adrian would probably reject him.

Nevertheless, in matters of sex we are few of us entirely consistent; indeed Clive at one moment suggested that Lytton had become a womaniser. Lytton's attentions to Virginia were of a kind to suggest that such a transformation might occur and his later history shows that he could, to some extent, respond to a woman's affection. Conceivably Virginia might have saved him for her sex; but it was not only his sexual inclinations that needed saving.

The picture that we have of him at this period when he was thought of as a possible husband for Virginia, is a dark one. I think that it is fair to say that it is the picture of a creature torturing and self-tortured, slipping from one agony to another, a wretched,

---

* The remark should be read in its context:

"I think I could almost marry Vanessa, and I could altogether? Clive." Lytton Strachey to Duncan Grant, 6 November 1907.

"I think I might manage to like being married to Virginia–but not to Clive. I suppose you think this odd?" Duncan Grant to Lytton Strachey, [8 November 1907].

sighing, hand-wringing misfit, a quite impossible person. And yet a great many people found him not only possible, but easy and, when he was naughty, as he certainly very often was, they forgave him. Why? The reason is not altogether flattering to Lytton; he was forgiven because neither his sorrows nor his crimes were taken very seriously. Despite his real and sincere emotion at the time of Thoby's death, Virginia felt misgivings about Lytton, not because he was lachrymose but rather because he had so few tears to shed. Socially this made him much easier than the weepy monster of popular imagination. In fact, socially he was easy enough. He might be cruel or spiteful but this ill-humour was as superficial, as histrionic, as his affected groans and his mock lamentations. Virginia thought that he lacked what she called magnanimity, and by this I think that she meant the kind of greatness of feeling which enables one to disregard criticism, the quality, perhaps, that makes a true poet. When Clive sent her some of Lytton's verses to read, she wrote:

> Yes, they are exquisite, & a little anthology I have here of minor Victorian verse shows none better. But (you will expect that but, & relish it,) there is something of ingenuity that prevents me from approving as warmly as I should; do you know what I mean when I talk of his verbal felicities, which somehow evade, when a true poet, I think, would have committed himself? "Enormous month", "unimaginable repose", "mysterious ease", "incomparably dim"; when I come upon these, I hesitate; I roll them upon my tongue; I do not feel that I am breasting fresh streams. But then I am a contemporary, a jealous contemporary, & I see perhaps the marks of the tool where Julian [i.e. the next generation] will see the entire shape. I sometimes think that Lytton's mind is too pliant & supple ever to make anything lasting; his resources are infinite. Jealousy—no doubt!

And no doubt she was jealous; certainly she was critical and her criticism shows some acumen, a just appraisal of Lytton's limitations, if not of his virtues. It was at once the advantage and the difficulty of their relationship that both still had their way to make in the republic of letters and that each divined that the other could become a formidable rival. Virginia must have felt that their union would have been one of competitive powers. But for this very reason it could appear an attractive proposition. As a fellow writer Lytton was a rival but he was also congenial and, from a literary point of view if from no other, he was respectable, more respectable than her other friends; for Saxon, she must by now have suspected, would produce very little, and both she and Lytton were inclined to dismiss Clive as a man of letters. But, for all her strictures, she and her friends had a firm belief in Lytton's potential. She liked him very much; in a way she feared him and perhaps she might—in a way—come to love him.

But, judged by the common standards of marriage, the only one of Virginia's friends who could be regarded as a desirable *parti* was Edward Hilton Young. He was born in 1879, the same year as Vanessa; his father, Sir George Young, had been a friend of Sir Leslie, and Hilton and his brothers had bowled their hoops in Kensington Gardens with the little Stephens. Sir George climbed mountains, sat on Royal Commissions, wrote a study of Homer and the Greek accents and was, in fact, another of those solid Victorian characters who seem to have been so abundant in the older generation.

Hilton seemed to be cast from the same smooth and well-proportioned mould as his father—even, like him, becoming President of the Union at Cambridge; nobody was surprised when in later life he made a name for himself in war and in politics, ending with a peerage, a string of decorations and some estimable volumes of prose and verse. On coming down from the University he read for the Bar and later on, when the Stephen family had moved to Bloomsbury and began to entertain on Thursday evenings, he renewed his acquaintance with them, and became a fairly regular visitor at both Gordon and Fitzroy Squares. He found himself at first rather intimidated by the company with its intellectual brilliance and uncompromising scrutiny of accepted opinions and conventions. He certainly *was* conventional by their standards; but they were tolerant as well as charming and accomplished; he was genial and well-endowed: he grew to value their opinions and they learnt to value him.

He was attracted to Virginia but never—I should suppose—was deeply in love with her; she accepted his attentions with pleasure and yet, when it came to the point, thought him a little unsubtle. As Vanessa characteristically put it, he was "like an elephant in a china shop."* Somehow his perfections bored Virginia; he had all the good qualities and yet failed to be more than interesting. But he *was* interesting and for some years she saw a good deal of him and felt that it might be nice to be married to him or at all events to be proposed to by him. We shall meet him again later but first we must

---

* VB to VW [11 August 1908]. Vanessa's use and misuse of proverbs was an unfailing source of delight to Virginia. "It's an ill worm that has no turning," "to take the bull by the udders," "a stitch in nine saves time" etc. It is uncertain which were invented by Virginia herself.

VIRGINIA WOOLF

discuss an admirer of a different kind, a much more agitating and distressing lover than Hilton, Saxon or even Lytton.

In February 1908 Vanessa bore a son, Julian. In April, after the very long convalescence then thought necessary, Clive, Vanessa, and Adrian joined Virginia, who was at St Ives for Easter. With them of course went the baby and his nurse. Virginia had no experience of very young children. The little creature screamed, as it seemed to her, like an ill-omened cat; it seemed a completely inhuman thing, something alien and appalling which created endless bother.

Vanessa felt all that a young mother might be expected to feel; but her maternal sentiments were very highly developed, so much so that they bred a kind of obtuseness, for to her it seemed that the baby was as important, as interesting, as conversable as any adult; all its activities, even its screams, were of delightful interest and she found it almost impossibly hard to believe that there were those who could not share her feelings and would not admit that, the baby being the centre of life, other topics could, for a distraction so entirely charming, be postponed. To Virginia this was incomprehensible; all the comforts of sisterly intercourse were destroyed. She turned to Clive and found that his sentiments were nearly the same as hers. They were both, in a way, jealous of the child.

Clive was in many ways an excellent father, kindly, generous, and if occasionally exasperated beyond endurance by his children, never resentful. But before he could set himself to charm and amuse the young he had to have some common ground on which to meet them. In the case of a small baby he was at a loss. He hated mess – the pissing, puking and slobbering of little children distressed him very much; so did their noise. Naturally anxious and easily alarmed for everyone's health, he was disturbed by the fragility of babies. If a baby howled he would certainly conclude that it was desperately ill and if it continued to howl he would himself be made ill by its noise. So now, at St Ives, tortured alike by compassion and exasperation, he fled the house, taking refuge in long walks through the countryside. With a sense of desertion and of treachery, but to some extent consoled by a sense of her own uselessness, Virginia accompanied him.

Out of earshot of that dreadful caterwauling they could be comfortable again; they could talk about books and friends and they did so with a sense of comradeship, of confederacy, against the fearful tyrannies of family life. In such converse it was easier for Virginia to discover her brother-in-law's good qualities: the real good humour which lay beneath his urbanity, the tenderness for other people's feelings which could make him appear fussy, his almost invariable good temper, his quick sense of the absurd, his charm. He, for his part, had never doubted that she was a remarkable, an exhilarating, an enchanting companion; but perhaps it was now that he noticed, in certain lights and in certain phases of animation, that she was even more beautiful than Vanessa. Clive could never carry on more than five minutes' conversation with a personable woman and refrain from some slight display of gallantry; now perhaps he was a little warmer than mere homage required and–this was the crucial thing–she, who would ordinarily have repulsed all advances with the utmost severity, was now not entirely unkind. An ardent and sanguine temperament such as his was excited by resistance and fortified by the least hint of success. In a word, Clive, after fourteen months of marriage, entered into a violent and prolonged flirtation with his sister-in-law.*

I use the word flirtation, for if I called this attachment an 'affair' it would suggest that Clive succeeded in his object, which was indeed no less, and I think not much more, than a delightful little infidelity ending up in bed. Many years later Virginia accused him of being a cuckoo that lays its eggs in other birds' nests. "My dear Virginia," was his cheerful reply, "you never would let me lay an egg in your nest." In fact I doubt whether the business would have lasted for so long or, for a time, have become so important to them both, if Virginia had given him what he wanted. But this she never did and, in a very crude sense, her conduct may be described as virtuous.

What then did she want? She was not in the least in love with Clive. In so far as she was in love with anyone she was in love with Vanessa. She wrote and received letters daily when they were separated and her letters are much like love letters. If nothing came for her from Vanessa she at once imagined that her sister was ill or dead, or at least in the midst of some fearful calamity. She longed for the comfort of Vanessa's presence. But it was because she loved Vanessa so much that she had to injure her, to enter and in entering to break that charmed circle within which Vanessa and Clive were so happy and by which she was so cruelly excluded, and to have Vanessa for herself again by detaching the husband who, after all, was not worthy of her.

In October 1907 Virginia had written of the Bells "it will be some

* Guesswork: the flirtation may have started earlier; but the date that I suggest is probable.

time before I can separate him from her.' This was a lapsus—her ostensible meaning was: before I can distinguish him from her"— but the slip may have betrayed a velleity of which Virginia herself was unaware at this time. The manifest success of the marriage would have reinforced such feelings. She perceived the happiness of her sister's life as one standing on a cold pavement looks enviously through a window at pleasant firelit intimacies. Her own life with Adrian was a cheerless substitute, nor could she have imagined Lytton, Saxon, or even Hilton Young, making with her the same cheerful domestic blaze that she envied at 46 Gordon Square. Fate had thrust before her a quite exceptionally fair example of normal connubial sensuality; and it left her feeling lonely and frightened by her own loneliness. It was now within her power to make an end of that particular torment and she did not know how to resist the temptation of doing so.

What she must soon have realised, or rather, what she must have known perfectly well from the beginning, was that Vanessa was deeply in love with her husband and that an attempt of this nature, whatever its cause, could not but arouse the deepest resentment in her whom she wished above all things to attach.

Vanessa's situation, as Virginia must have understood, was in the highest degree painful and called for a remarkable exercise in prudence and in fortitude. An outright quarrel with high words and accusations never took place; it is probable that both sisters shrank from the notion of 'a scene.' In letters to Clive and to Virginia, Vanessa takes things lightly, easily, with a show of humour; inwardly she was both hurt and angry; she could, she said, have forgiven Virginia if Virginia had felt any passion, had been genuinely or indeed at all in love with Clive. But this clearly she was not; her conduct was therefore inspired by nothing save a delight in mischief. It made Clive irritable; it made her—Vanessa—very unhappy. What satisfaction did Virginia herself gain from it? None, it may be thought, save that which comes to him who teases an aching tooth with his tongue.*

And yet there was a sense in which Clive's attachment was of real service to Virginia. She was not, I think, of that unamiable temperament which loves to arouse male lust only in order to disappoint it. Her conduct in other affairs of the heart, and indeed all that we know of her temperament, points in a different direction—she was in fact

---

* "My affair with Clive and Nessa . . . For some reason that turned more of a knife in me than anything else has ever done." VW to Gwen Raverat, 22 March 1925.

very shy of arousing any sexual feeling in anyone. But she did enjoy being admired—admired for her looks, her brains, her personality—and by being flattered by a man who well understood the art of making himself agreeable to women. It was something quite new in her life, something that she had certainly not had from Madge or Violet, or indeed from Walter Headlam. Clive had the special charm of normality. This meant, not only that he valued Virginia for her sex (whereas Lytton valued her despite her sex), but that he did not belong to that little *cénacle* of Apostolic buggers from which Virginia was necessarily excluded and which she regarded with apprehension, irritation and distaste. I suspect that he succeeded, far more than Walter Headlam, in making her aware of her own normal proclivities, in making her feel the need, which she had not hitherto felt, for a man.

To this was added something of greater moment: Clive believed, as Madge and Violet believed, in Virginia's genius (it was the word that they used), but unlike Madge or Violet, Clive was able to offer acceptable criticism. In this respect he was indeed much more serviceable than Lytton. Lytton was admirable for a discussion of literature in general, but not when it came to the writings of Virginia Stephen. Then he was too serious a rival. With him she was perpetually on her guard, for him she adopted her best literary behaviour, with the result that the letters she sent him were about the dullest and most pretentious that she ever wrote. Clive, though a valuable critic, was more sympathetic and less formidable; with him she could let herself go and he was, therefore, able to offer some useful advice and to make a real contribution to the writing of *Melymbrosia*. (See Appendix D).

Returning to London from St Ives Virginia forgot her copy of John Delane's *Life* which she was reviewing at some length for *The Cornhill*. She had wanted to read it on the train, but remembered when it was almost too late that she had left it in her lodging house. Clive ran back for it and, rushing after the moving train, tried to thrust it through the window of her compartment, slipped, fell, and hurt himself. The incident furnished a pretext for epistolary gallantries: he would not write, he declared, "about the honourable wounds gained in your service. . . ." Half mockingly she commiserates: "You brought a tear to my eye & a blush to my cheek, by speaking of bandaged hands & crippled knees." "Do you remember," he writes, "our talk about intimacy and the really exciting moments in life? Did we ever achieve the heights?" And "On the top of Rosewall, I wished for nothing in the world but to kiss you?" "Why?," she responds, "do you torment me with half uttered and ambiguous sentences?" ". . . though we did not kiss— (I was willing, & offered once . . .)—I think we 'achieved the heights' as you put it."

Meanwhile, Vanessa was writing to Virginia:

> I wonder what *you* have said about us—"Of course Nessa was quite taken up with the baby. Yes, I'm afraid she's losing all her individuality & becoming the usual domestic mother & Clive—of course I like him very much but his mind is of a peculiarly prosaic & literal type—And they're always making moral judgements about me. However they seem perfectly happy & I expect its a good thing I didnt stay longer. I was evidently beginning to bore them." Now Billy*—on your honour havent you uttered one of these sentiments?

Presently the Bells followed Virginia back to London and no doubt the flirtation continued with manœuvres and counter-manœuvres on both sides; but it is only when the players were separated that we can get any notion of the state of play.

The 'game' such as it was (for all the participants were losers) was complicated by irritations and social distresses. There were moments when general conversation, particularly his style of robust male conversation, failed to reach Virginia at all and Clive would find her disconcertingly inattentive; there were times when she would allow Miss Sheepshanks to spoil a tête-à-tête. Then there was Lytton; as the summer progressed his interest in Virginia did like-wise—or so it appeared. And then, to aggravate Clive's jealous exasperations, there was Hilton Young. He was certainly regarded as a serious admirer, and Virginia herself believed that he would propose to her that summer. When he did not, she was distinctly disappointed, having hoped at least to have an offer of marriage to her credit.

For the first part of the summer holidays Virginia was on her own; Adrian had gone with Saxon to Bayreuth, the Bells as usual were at Cleeve House. To be within reach of them yet independent, she settled on Wells, where she went with two dogs on the first of August, determined to work at her novel. She had finished—or at least she had written—a hundred pages; Helen Ambrose was coming to life, so was Rachel Vinrace; but at this moment she was called Cynthia. At Wells, Virginia decided that this would not do.†

---

* i.e. Billy-Goat. Virginia, in writing to Vanessa, contracts this to a 'B'.

† *The Voyage Out* was the only one of Virginia's novels in which she worked more or less in public, asking for advice, showing portions of her manuscript to

She wrote asking Vanessa to find her another name. Vanessa was willing enough to act as god-mother; she suggested Penelope, Perdita, Chloe, Euphrosyne. "Couldn't you," she added recklessly, "call her Apricot?" Clive, for his part, thought Belinda very suitable. Belinda was too dainty, answered Virginia; besides, the girl's father was a sea captain who would give his child a foreign name – Cintra, perhaps, or Andalusia. "Or Barcelona," exclaimed Clive, rather nettled by the rejection of Belinda, "though Polly or Catherine would be adequate to my taste." Virginia then observed, rather inconsistently, that the changing of names was the most trivial of occupations.

At first it seemed that Mrs Wall's lodging house in Vicar's Close, a place where the fat slumbers of the church seemed gently audible, would provide the tranquillity that Virginia needed; but then she was disturbed by Mrs Wall's attempts to provide her with company in the form of a timid theological student, so she moved to a verger's house in Cathedral Green, abandoned her study of Mrs Wall, for whom she had by now constructed an entire life, and studied the children in the street below. But it was difficult to write in a room without a table or a desk and with Prince Albert staring down at her between his whiskers, and so she removed to Manorbier. Its poor rough austerity compared favourably with Wells and it seems to have been a better place for writing. On 30 August she confided to Violet Dickinson that she had begun to believe that she would "write rather well one of these days," and to Clive:

> I think a great deal of my future, & settle what books I am to write – how I shall re-form the novel & capture multitudes of things at present fugitive, enclose the whole, & shape infinite strange shapes . . . but tomorrow, I know, I shall be sitting down to the inanimate old phrases.

There is a letter to Emma Vaughan written during this stay at Manorbier, a kind of crazy joke of a letter which suggests a sudden lapse into something very near to insanity. But in other respects, and judging by all her other letters of this period, she seems to have been in good health.

Clive and Vanessa had done their duty by Clive's parents by staying with them first in Wiltshire and then in Scotland. In September they were free to take a real holiday. Virginia went

others and discussing her progress with her friends. In the later stages of writing the book she was, I think, less communicative. No one was allowed to see anything of her later novels until they were finished.

with them to Milan, Pavia, Siena, Perugia and Assisi. She kept a notebook in which, as usual, she describes the landscape. She also considers with some interest the ceremonies of the Church which, in Siena, seemed very different from those which she had observed in Wells. She describes the characters in hotels: the greedy old spinster who has become a permanent wanderer from *table d'hôte* to *table d'hôte* in foreign lands (Virginia began to make up stories about her and her education in the 'sixties and her family in England), and the thin clean lady with two simple friendly daughters quietly looking for husbands.

Of pictures and architecture she does not usually say much; but she was struck by the frescoes in the Collegio del Cambio in Perugia, and was moved to make certain rapid and disjointed notes which, however, are not uninteresting.

I look at a fresco by Perugino. I conceive that he saw things grouped, contained in certain and invariable forms; expressed in faces, actions— [?which] did not exist; all beauty was contained in the momentary appearance of human beings. He saw it sealed as it were; all its worth in it; not a hint of fear or future. His fresco seems to me infinitely silent; as though beauty had swum up to the top and stayed there, above everything else, speech, paths leading on, relation of brain to brain, don't exist.

Each part has a dependence upon the others; they compose one idea in his mind. That idea has nothing to do with anything that can be put into words. A group stands without relation to the figure of God. They have come together then because their lines and colours are related, and express some view of beauty in his brain.

As for writing—I want to express beauty too—but beauty (symmetry?) of life and the world, in action. Conflict?—is that it? If there is action in painting it is only to exhibit lines; but with the end of beauty in view. Isn't there a different kind of beauty? No conflict.

I attain a different kind of beauty, achieve a symmetry by means of infinite discords, showing all the traces of the mind's passage through the world; achieve in the end, some kind of whole made of shivering fragments; to me this seems the natural process; the flight of the mind. Do they really reach the same thing?

There was equal interest, if less speculation, to be derived from the little collection of India paper novels that she brought with her. She read *Two on a Tower* by Thomas Hardy and considered him too clumsy a writer to be accounted a classic, but there was a kind of bleak force about him, a sort of "rude honesty" which was very much to her taste. She also read *Harry Richmond*. Meredith was, I think, an early enthusiasm; but now "Meredith fails to satisfy me"; she finds in his conceit, his verbal brilliance, the shadow but not the likeness of something magnificent, a world of his own, but a world of flats and flies. Such then were Virginia's intellectual diversions that September.

How her emotional diversions progressed it is harder to say. There was some kind of violent quarrel in Perugia; she and Clive walked through the narrow and precipitous streets of that city screaming at each other, and again in Siena.* But, on the whole, things seem to have gone very well. Clive wrote to Saxon: "Vanessa and Virginia are both well & incredibly charming," to which Saxon replied in characteristic manner: "Does it savour of paradox if I say that I can quite well believe that Vanessa and Virginia are incredibly charming?"

Virginia at the end of the holiday told Violet that Clive was "an admirable man"; from which we may deduce that matters went smoothly enough.

This autumn and indeed during all these years Virginia was busy, not only with her novel and a good deal of journalism, but with her education. Although Janet Case had ceased to be her teacher she remained a friend and Virginia may have profited by her advice. At all events she continued to read the Greek and Roman authors.† In August, when she was at Manorbier, she had attacked that work which her Cambridge friends regarded practically as the gospel of their time: G. E. Moore's *Principia Ethica*. She read it with some difficulty and great admiration. It is a little suprising that she should for so long have postponed what was, one imagines, almost compulsory reading in Bloomsbury (not that Vanessa or Duncan Grant ever attempted it) and I fancy that it was Clive, who rather liked to use Moore in his arguments, who persuaded her to read it.

Clive at this time was her authority, and guided her reading in modern French literature. Also, and this was much more important, he became her literary confidant. Letters have been preserved which show that in 1908 and 1909 he was offering and she was accepting very long and detailed criticisms of the early drafts of *The Voyage Out*. There was a good deal that he did not like, passages which seemed to him crude, immature or derivative. But on the whole he was very enthusiastic; he considered that her words had a force

* On a picture postcard showing a view of the Viale della Fortezza in Siena, posted 17 June 1935, to Clive, Virginia wrote: "It was on the spot now marked by a cross that Clive Bell quarrelled with his sister in law in Sept. 1908. I dropped memory's tear there under the orange blossom. V.W."

† In 1907 Virginia was reading Juvenal, in 1908 the *Odyssey* and Plato; in 1909 the *Ion*, the *Ajax* and *The Frogs*; she made a fairly extensive commentary on these works in a notebook. MH/A 21.

"that one expects only in the best poetry" and came "as near the truth underlying them as it is possible for words to come." It is clear that she was fortified by his praise and very glad to have some assurance that her writing was not "all vapour"; also she was able to accept and, it would appear, to use, some of his strictures.*

These exchanges formed the most cheerful and the most constructive part of what was, in other ways, an increasingly unhappy entanglement.

* See Appendix D.

Chapter Eight

1909

ON 17 February 1909 Lytton came to 29 Fitzroy Square, proposed to Virginia and was accepted.

In the very act of proposing, Lytton realised that the idea, an idea which he had been meditating for some time and saw as a solution to the problems of his very complicated private life, was in fact no solution at all. He discovered that he was alarmed by her sex and by her virginity; he was terrified by the notion that she might kiss him. He perceived that his imagined "paradise of married peace" was an impossibility; it would not do at all. He was horrified by the situation in which he had placed himself, all the more so because he believed that she loved him.

She perceived something of this, and with sympathetic tact helped him to escape. After a second meeting, at which he finally declared that he could not marry her, while she assured him that she did not love him, they contrived a gentle disengagement.

For Lytton this was probably the end of the affair; he must have become fully aware of the nature of his feelings and it is hard to suppose that he could again have contemplated such a marriage.

But for Virginia it was different. Although she must have realised that the chances were remote, she still considered the possibility of marrying him. She had told Lytton that she was not in love with him. Nor was she, I think. She might accept his personality but not, when it came to the push, his person. She had always been, as she was later to admit, a sexual coward and her only experience of male carnality had been terrifying and disgusting. But she did want to be married; she was twenty-seven years old, tired of spinsterhood, very tired of living with Adrian and very fond of Lytton. She needed a husband whose mind she could respect; she valued intellectual eminence above everything and in this respect no rival had yet appeared. Lytton's homosexuality might even have been a source of reassurance; as a husband he would not be sexually exigent and a union with him, almost fraternal in character, might perhaps grow by degrees into something real, solid, and deeply affectionate.

But if she continued, as I think she did and as Vanessa certainly did, to hope for such a marriage, her expectations must indeed have been faint when once Lytton's offer had been withdrawn. It was, certainly, a deeply disappointing and saddening experience.*

Lytton retired to Brighton to soothe his agitated nerves; Virginia continued to lead a very busy but, I should guess, a very unhappy life. It was at this time that a stranger, watching her at the Queen's Hall and noticing how lonely and how melancholy she looked, sent her anonymously a ticket for Galsworthy's *Strife* which was then playing at the Haymarket, sat next to her, spoke to her and later wrote asking for her friendship. This she felt that she could not give; but she preserved his letter.

During these early months of 1909 Virginia had embarked upon another and perhaps even more dangerous adventure. Someone among her friends invented a letter-writing game in which the players – Virginia, Lytton, Walter Lamb, Clive, Vanessa, Saxon, and probably Adrian, each took the part of an imaginary character and was provided with a false name – the idea was to produce a novel in letters.† But although the names were imaginary it soon became clear that the characters and the events that they described in their letters were not; it was in fact a kind of epistolary *bal masqué* in which the disguises served only to embolden the participants. From behind his mask Clive felt able to renew his gallantries with unusual openness and ardour; Lytton discusses them frankly with Virginia and adverts to the pain that Vanessa must feel. Virginia replies with agonised evasions; Vanessa chides her for her deplorable weakness with regard to Hilton Young. It is not astonishing that the game ended about the time of Lytton's proposal. "Life," wrote Virginia, "is certainly very exciting. . . . Oh how I wish I could write a novel!"

The Bells suggested that she should go with them to Florence for a month towards the end of April. She had planned to take

* At the very moment when Virginia seemed in danger of drawing the wrong card the right one emerged momentarily from beneath the pack. Lytton, in a letter to Ceylon, suggested that it was really Leonard Woolf who should marry her. He replied: "Do you think Virginia would have me? Wire to me if she accepts. I'll take the next boat home." [1 February 1909.]

† Virginia was Elinor Hadyng, Clive and Vanessa were James and Clarissa Philips, Lytton was Vane Hatherley, Walter Lamb was Humphry Maitland, Saxon, Mr Ilchester. (Lady Ottoline Morrell, referred to as Caroline Lady Eastnor, Philip Morrell as Sir Julius, and Hilton Young apparently as Roger, were not, I think, participants in the game.) See *Virginia Woolf and Lytton Strachey Letters*, 1956, p. 28.

ship with Adrian to St Malo, landing "as the first cock rises to crow on Easter Day." But on 7 April Aunt Caroline Emelia, who had been ill for some time, finally died. Between writing an obituary* for *The Guardian* and attending the cremation she sent a postcard to Vanessa saying that she would after all come with them. Clive was of course delighted and wrote ecstatically; she replied with a very flirtatious letter.

But Florence was unsatisfactory. She did not like "that unnatural Florentine Society," in which she met the formidable Mrs Ross, who patronised her–she did not enjoy being patronised–and Mrs Meynell the poetess, lean and bony "like a transfixed hare"–not an encouraging specimen of the literary lady. Virginia was happier scrutinising the less distinguished members of the English colony and, in particular, one Mrs Campbell, an elderly body who had turned the *Life of Father Damien* into verse. It was one of those odd things that stuck in Virginia's mind and found their way into her novels.†

Her diary also contains some preliminary notes for a life of Clive. It looks as though she intended to produce a perceptive and not unsympathetic portrait of a sensitive, honest, kindly man, a little too carefully polished and a little too conscious of his own social gifts. He was, we may surmise, very much on her mind at the time. Their relationship was an unhappy one; how could it be otherwise? Clive's attentions might be a welcome solace after Lytton's evasions; but she, in her own way, was as evasive as Lytton. She would neither take Clive nor leave him; he continued to be exasperated, delighted, thwarted and enraged by her coquetry. She lived, he declared, by the head and not by the heart, and when they were not flirting they were quarrelling. To her it seemed that he took his revenge for her coldness in a way that hurt her abominably, that is to say by the simple expedient of making love to his wife. The slightest, the most natural demonstration of affection–an endearment, a kiss–could make her feel unloved, unwanted, and excluded. "I was," she wrote later, "unhappy that summer and bitter in all my judgments." Probably she was enervated and chafed by the excitements and disappointments of the previous months. No doubt she was quarrelsome; there were scenes; she was, as Vanessa put it, "tiresome" in the Bargello, and after a fortnight she decided that she must cut short the holiday and go home.

* This obituary was published in *The Guardian* on 21 April 1909.
† See *The Voyage Out*, chapter xi, p. 165 and *Jacob's Room*, chapter xxi, p. 263.

Vanessa and Clive urged her to stay: there were strikes in France; she had little French and less Italian; she was miserably bad at catching trains. But she was resolute and she left them.

It was rather melancholy [wrote Vanessa to Margery Snowden] to see her start off on that long journey alone leaving us together here! Of course I am sometimes impressed by the pathos of her position & I have been so more here than usual. I think she would like very much to marry & certainly she would like much better to marry Lytton than anyone else. It is difficult living with Adrian who does not appreciate her & to live with him till the end of their days is a melancholy prospect. I hope some new person may appear in the course of the next year or two for I have come to think that in spite of all drawbacks she had better marry. Still I dont know what she would do with children!

The expedition had been a failure; she returned to England and failure of another kind. In May she visited Cambridge and it was here, in a punt on the Cam, that Hilton Young proposed. There was much to recommend him, she had not discouraged him, his person and his character were admirable; moreover he might have seemed to provide a solution to all her difficulties, for by now her hopes of marrying Lytton must indeed have been faint, while her philandering with Clive had brought more pain than pleasure. But when it came to the point, she knew she did not love him and that she could not marry him. It was perhaps as a kind of excuse that she told him she could marry no one but Lytton.

It was at about this time that her social life received an important addition.

"We have just got to know a wonderful Lady Ottoline Morrell, who has the head of a Medusa; but she is very simple & innocent in spite of it, & worships the arts."

I think that Virginia was right in describing her as innocent and that she was indeed extremely simple and not very clever. But it is hard to believe. Her appearance made one think that she was vicious, devious and complicated to a degree. For she was as decorative and as outlandish as an Austrian baroque church and from the remarkable edifice that she inhabited there issued a voice that had something of the cooing of a dove, something of the roaring of a lion; it seemed to be rolled out upon her improbable Hapsburg chin; and withal she had a certain grace, a certain majesty of address which was at once intimidating and seductive. She arrived at one of Virginia's Thursday Evenings with Dorelia and Augustus John, figures as beautiful and almost as improbable as she (together they must have made a rare spectacle, for Ottoline could by herself draw a sizeable crowd in the street); Philip Morrell, Ottoline's husband, came with them.

Presently Ottoline wrote to ask Virginia for the names and addresses of all her "wonderful friends"; they were all to come and see her at home in Bedford Square. "Then," wrote Virginia—and the word "then" means in the course of the next two or three years—

> we were all swept into that extraordinary whirlpool where such odd sticks and straws were brought momentarily together. There was Augustus John very sinister [?] in a black stock and a velvet coat; Winston Churchill very rubicund all gold lace and medals on his way to Buckingham Palace; Raymond Asquith crackling with epigrams; Francis Dodd* telling me most graphically how he and Aunt Susie had killed bugs: she held the lamp; he a basin of paraffin; bugs crossed the ceiling in an incessant stream. There was Lord Henry Bentinck at one end of the sofa & perhaps Nina Lamb at the other. There was Philip [Morrell] fresh from the House of Commons humming and hawing on the hearth rug. There was Gilbert Cannan who was said to be in love with Ottoline. There was Bertie Russell, whom she was said to be in love with. Above all there was Ottoline herself.

Who, we may add, for the spirit of rumour was reckless in Bedford Square, was said to be in love with Virginia. I don't think that anyone ever suggested that Virginia returned her love; but in sober truth she liked Ottoline, found her comic, fascinating, improbable, like Royalty or the Church, a portent rather than a woman, a character from the fiction of another age; but also quite simply likeable. Certainly she contributed something new to the life of Bloomsbury—a mundane glamour and a very strong heterosexual element which Virginia welcomed. She brought petticoats, frivolity and champagne to the buns, the buggery and the high thinking of Fitzroy Square.

From 6 June to 16 July Adrian kept a diary in which he describes one of his and Virginia's Thursday Evenings and the description seems worth quoting because it gives a notion of what a Bloomsbury party was like at this time, and illustrates Adrian's view of Virginia.

* Francis Dodd (1874–1949; R.A. 1935). At his request, Virginia gave him several sittings for her portrait between October 1907 and July 1908. He etched four plates of her from drawings, one of which is in the National Portrait Gallery, London, and another in the collection of Mr Benjamin Sonnenberg, New York. 'Aunt Susie' was Miss Isabel Dacre (1844–1933), a member of the Manchester Academy of Fine Arts, and a close associate of Dodd's.

Thursday July 1st.

On my way home I went to Gordon Square where I found the Goat and walked home with her. We dined alone together and after dinner waited a long time before anybody appeared. Saxon as usual came in first but was quickly followed by Norton and he by James and Lytton Strachey. We were very silent at first, Virginia and Lytton and I doing all the talking, Saxon being in his usual state of torpor and Norton and James occasionally exchanging a whisper. Later on Vanessa and Clive came in bringing with them Duncan Grant. After this the conversation became more lively. Vanessa sat with Lytton on the sofa and from half heard snatches I gathered they were talking about his and James's obscene loves. Whatever it was they were discussing they were brought to an abrupt stop by a sudden silence, this pleased them very much, especially Vanessa, and I kindly added to their joy by asking why they stopped. Soon afterwards Henry Lamb came in having returned from doing some portraits at Oxford. The conversation kept up a good flow, though it was not very interesting, until about half past eleven Miss Cole arrived.

She went and sat in the long wicker chair with Virginia and Clive on the floor beside her. Virginia began in her usual tone of frank admiration to compliment her on her appearance. "Of course, you Miss Cole are always dressed so exquisitely. You look so original, so like a sea shell. There is something so refined about you coming in among our muddy boots and pipe smoke, dressed in your exquisite creations." Clive chimed in with more heavy compliments and then began asking her why she disliked him so much, saying how any other young lady would have been much pleased with all the nice things he had been saying but that she treated him so sharply. At this Virginia interrupted with "I think Miss Cole has a very strong character" and so on and and so on. Altogether Miss Cole was as unhappy and uncomfortable as she could be; it was impossible not to help laughing at the extravagance of Virginia and Clive and all conversation was stopped by their noisy choruses, so the poor woman was the centre of all our gaze, and did not know what to do with herself. At last, a merciful diversion was made and Virginia took my seat and I hers and with, I may say, some skill I managed to keep Clive under control.

James and Lytton Strachey left and we played an absurd game which Vanessa and Clive had learnt at the Freshfields. The principle of the game was as follows: that person won who in half a minute could say the most words beginning with any given letter. Clive held the watch and gave us each a turn. Norton being given G. started off with Jerusalem and Jesus, which I am afraid must have added another pain to poor Miss Cole's already lengthy list. We all had our turns, Vanessa trying to sail as near to the wind as she could, she is always trying to bring out some bawdy remark and is as pleased when she has done it as a spoilt child. Miss Cole went at one and Duncan Grant at about the same time, when a great discussion was started, I know not by whom, about vice. Very soon Virginia with exquisite art made herself the centre of the argument making the vaguest statements with the intensest feeling and ready to snap up anybody who laughed. Her method is ingenious and at first is rather disconcerting for when someone has carefully examined her argument and certainly refuted it she at once agrees with him enthusiastically saying that he has put her point exactly.

The argument such as it was degenerated into mere phrase making and so regarded was quite amusing; this gave way in its turn to the game of bantering Saxon. He was chaffed and laughed at for all his little peculiarities and all the time he kept his silence, only giving an occasional smile. He could not be provoked into saying anything even by Virginia's most daring sallies which never fail of their guffaw when Clive is present. At last everybody went except Saxon. Saxon went on to discuss different ways to Germany having obtained further information from Cooks. Virginia and I were however so sleepy that we managed by sheer indifference to oust him. We got to bed as the dawn was coming up about 5.

Poor Miss Cole was unlucky. It was never easy to know what to do with the image of oneself that Virginia could fabricate and then gaily, publicly, even generously (for she loved her inventions too well not to believe in them) toss back at one's shuffling feet. But it must have been harder still when Clive, whose gallantries were not always well judged, joined forces with her and boisterously amplified the most extravagant of her compliments. The cruelty which sometimes accompanied Virginia's conversational extravagances lay, not in their animus–indeed I do not think that she was (usually) malicious–but rather in their sincerity. The image that she created was fanciful, but the victim–the slender basis upon which she built–could have dismissed such fancies easily enough had they not been advanced with such overwhelming force; and that force arose, not from a desire to misrepresent, but from conviction. Miss Cole may or may not have looked like a sea shell:* there was no doubt some elegance about her nacreous enough to stir Virginia's imagination (it was easily stirred), but almost at once Virginia would have come to believe in the reality of the glittering edifice that she had so easily raised. In truth it was she who was being absurd and, in later years at all events, it was she and not her victim who was laughed at when she allowed her fancy to take liberties with people.

Another less guilty anecdote belongs to this period and may be recorded because it shows, in a rather pure form, how Virginia's mythogenic capacity could create distress and confusion.

It was in Cornwall; Virginia, Vanessa and Clive and, I think,

* In 1910 Miss Cole became Mrs Neville Chamberlain.

Adrian were having lunch in a lodging house. The maid – a dimmish, timid, mousy maid – came to clear away the remains of mutton and two vegetables.

"What's the pudding?" asked Virginia.

"Mount St Michael's Pudding, Miss."

Virginia's imagination took fire; she saw how it would be and seeing could not but describe her vision. Her exact words are lost; but there was something about a soaring convexity of chocolate surmounted by a castle of dazzling sugar, battlemented, crenellated, machicolated, crowned with banners of crystallized angelica and at its feet a turbulent ocean of lucent jelly, flecked with creamy foam and graced by heaven knows what sweetmeats fashioned to resemble vessels, mermaids, dolphins, nereids. . . . For Virginia's relations the chief interest in listening to this inventory lay in the face of the serving girl, who stood amazed by Virginia's eloquence and appalled by the knowledge that she would, in a few minutes, produce a steamed pudding, not unlike a sand castle in shape and texture, parsimoniously adorned with a dab of strawberry jam.

This was one of the difficulties of living with Virginia; her imagination was furnished with an accelerator and no brakes; it flew rapidly ahead, parting company with reality, and, when reality happened to be a human being, the result could be appalling for the person who found himself expected to live up to the character that Virginia had invented. But even when reality happened to be an umbrella it could cause havoc.

Later in the summer of 1909, when she was at Bayreuth, she went out shopping with Adrian and bought a penholder. This was always an affair of the utmost difficulty, for the actual manual exercise of writing delighted her. She loved the feel of a good stiff nib cutting letters over the paper, and was miserable with inferior implements; from the age of fifteen certainly, probably from an even earlier age, she was continually trying new pens and penholders and was of course madly difficult to please. Thus from Adrian's point of view the expedition started badly. It was made worse by a visit to a bookshop where Virginia created havoc in her search for a Tauchnitz edition of *The Autocrat of the Breakfast Table* which she was writing about and should have brought from England. Here at least she knew what she wanted. Unfortunately the shop had not got it and had to send to Leipzig for a copy. More unfortunate still, she found it in her bag when she got home. With feminine insouciance she proposed that Adrian should accompany her on a second visit to the shop to countermand the order. Adrian refused; he couldn't face the people again. This however was after the purchase of the parasol, which was an even longer and even more harrowing business. She said that she needed a white parasol and every white parasol in the shop was brought out; but they were not what she had imagined; a white parasol, she explained, was no good without a green lining. There were none of this kind, so then she asked for a coffee-coloured one and eventually bought the cheapest brown holland thing in the shop.

All through her life Virginia was a vague, undecided and exasperating shopper; she must have reduced many poor shop assistants to the verge of blasphemy or of tears, and not only they but her companions suffered intensely when she found herself brought to a standstill by the difference between that which she had imagined and that which in fact was offered for sale.

This digression has taken me to Bayreuth and I must explain why Virginia was there in the month of August 1909. In later years it was the last place in which one would have expected to find her. She was not, in any strict sense, musical. She played no instrument; I do not think that she could follow a score with any deep comprehension. Music, it is true, delighted her; she enjoyed the family pianola (when Adrian did not play it for too long), as she was later to enjoy the gramophone; it formed a background to her musings, a theme for her pen; during the period at which Adrian kept a diary she was frequently at concerts and very frequently at the opera,* which she enjoyed as a spectacle and a social event. But her taste for opera was, as Adrian's had been, probably stimulated by Saxon; certainly he must have been responsible for the marked homage which she now paid to Wagner, for Saxon was, and always remained, a fervent Wagnerian, sitting through cycle after cycle of *The Ring*, relishing every bar of *Tristan* and of *Parsifal* (already, in 1910, he was able to celebrate his 300th operatic performance), and I think it must have been his strong, silent pressure that made Virginia who, even then, would have preferred to listen to Mozart, travel to the shrine of Wagnerism, encountering Germans who seemed to her distressingly ugly, old family friends from England whom she would rather not have met, lodgings and meals that aroused no enthusiasm.

* Adrian records that she went, in a space of six weeks, twice to *Don Giovanni* and twice to *Louise*, to the first performance of *The Wreckers*, to *Aida*, *Madame Butterfly*, *Faust*, and *Orpheus and Eurydice*; she attended several concerts and heard works by Cimarosa and Delius (*The Mass of Life*), went to two plays, and also went with the Morrells to see the Russian dancers at the Coliseum.

VIRGINIA WOOLF

They remained a fortnight in Bayreuth. Each morning Adrian and Saxon went for a walk while Virginia wrote at a shaky desk made by balancing her box on a commode. They met at lunch, and in the afternoon went to the opera.

> We must be a curious sight [wrote Adrian to Vanessa] as we leave the Opera House between the acts; there is the Goat carrying a parasol, a large leathern bag, a packet of cigarettes, a box of chocolates, and the libretto of the opera, in one hand and at the same time vainly striving to hold up a long white cloak & skirt which insist upon trailing in the dust however high she pulls them; then there is Saxon humming to himself with an impassioned voice and gesticulating so wildly that one thinks that every bone in his body must be out of joint; then I come holding my head very high & pretending that nothing particular is happening & at the same time trying to lead the others away from the main body of the crowd.

("... There is a great crowd & we get stared at, not for our beauty," wrote Virginia. Remembering Adrian's odd gaunt figure, his awkward manner and the fact that, even without holding his head up high, he would have towered above any crowd, one may wonder whether he did not appear the strangest of the three.)

> It is of no use trying to relieve the Goat of any of her burdens because as soon as one makes the attempt half of them are scattered upon the ground. Eventually I conduct them into a large deserted field where Virginia & I sit down and Saxon also when his rheumatics permit of it; here Saxon always becomes doubly mortish* and sour & Virginia begins to expand into the most extravagant images. At last I am driven into contradicting her flatly & she snaps back at me & then we all subside and eat our chocolate in silence & comparative peace.

Nevertheless Virginia and Adrian, driven by Saxon's lethargy to fraternise, were on unusually good terms with each other (although Adrian doubted whether this desirable state of affairs could last if Virginia insisted on doing any more shopping). Virginia also wrote, almost daily, to her sister describing their surroundings, their activities, and their fellow creatures:

> The grossness of the [Germans] is astonishing—but they seem very clean & kind. They suit Saxon very well. He thinks them so sensible.

Saxon indeed came under her constant scrutiny:

> Saxon is dormant all day long, & rather peevish if you interrupt him. He hops along, before or behind, swinging his ugly stick, & humming,

* Mortish, a word invented by Adrian to describe Saxon's deadlier moods.

like a stridulous grasshopper. He reminds me a little of father. He clenches his fists, & scowls in the same way; & stops at once if you look at him. Adrian & I wink at each other, & get caught sometimes. About 11 o'clock at night, when we begin to yawn, he brightens up, & comes out with some very acute & rather acid question. We argued till 1.30 this morning. It was about something Adrian had said two or possibly three Thursdays ago, which Saxon had not understood. He hoards things, like a dormouse. His mind is marvellously accurate; but I am rather surprised by his intellect. . . . We are rather austere, like monks and nuns, speak little, & —— oh I long for you!

And a week later:

Saxon is . . . almost sprightly. His conversation is still odd. "What did you mean, Virginia, when you said, about three years ago, that your view of life was that of a Henry James novel, & mine of a George Meredith?" I had to invent a meaning, & he actually told me that he thought me a very clever young woman – which is the highest praise I have ever had from him.

Saxon himself makes his own characteristic contribution:

. . . it begins to dawn upon me that I have written still another letter merely about letter writing . . . since no doubt Adrian has sent one of his amusing and faithful sketches of actual occurrences, and Virginia several of her brilliant and imaginative pictures of things as they ought to be, there is no need for me to go outside this humble tack and enter into individious and disastrous competition.

Altogether it was Saxon's holiday; in a sense it was his apogee as far as Virginia was concerned. Never again would he persuade her into going to Bayreuth and he, who had been the cleverest of all Thoby's friends, who for six or seven years had exerted a considerable influence and had been regarded by Virginia almost with awe, was already something of a joke and a tedious joke at that. She liked him, and she always continued to like him; but it was becoming more and more apparent that he would never do anything but solve conundrums and cultivate a number of quiet enthusiasms. It was easy to believe that he was a genius; but it was easier still to believe that his genius would never result in anything positive. As he grew older he seemed increasingly to cultivate the art of escape. He might be compared to the cuttlefish which slips silently away beneath a cloud of obfusc sepia, but he might also be likened to the porcupine which not only conceals itself but can wound the too curious investigator. He was not only a solver but

VIRGINIA WOOLF

a setter of puzzles; he loved ingenuity and took a natural pride in
his own dexterity; his elliptical utterances, his allusions, his acrostic
letters were proofs of his own erudition but they also humbled and
bewildered the recipient, and this too he enjoyed. He liked to play
games with his friends—games so subtle that they hardly realised
that any sport was afoot. Quietly he laughed at them, but there
was, I fancy, a joke within a joke; at bottom he laughed at a sad
little pleasantry of his own which he made at his own expense
and which had as its theme his own appalling life.

At the beginning of September, after spending a further ten
days with her two companions at Dresden, Virginia returned to
Fitzroy Square. The Bells were still dutifully staying in Wiltshire
with Clive's parents. Virginia met them at Salisbury after arrangements which almost suggest the clandestine contrivances of lovers.
Then she rented a small cottage at Studland and experienced on a
minute scale, and I suppose for the first time, the pleasures and
labours of housework, cooking her own breakfast, taking in the
morning milk and so on. She hired what she called 'a bi-sexual'
bathing dress and "swam far out, until the sea gulls played over my
head, mistaking me for a drifting sea anemone." Soon she was
joined by the Bells, who moved into a boarding house nearby and
she was able to enjoy, not only their company, but that of her
nephew Julian who, at the age of eighteen months, was beginning
to manifest charms of a kind that she could appreciate.

The Bells brought other company. Vanessa invited Lytton; but
he was undergoing a cure in a Swedish sanatorium. Walter Lamb
was asked in place of him. A contemporary of Clive's at Trinity,
he was a close friend but perhaps not quite as intimate as he would
have liked to have been. He was an occasional visitor at Gordon
Square on his journeys between Clifton College, where he taught
the classics, and Cambridge or his family home in Manchester.
Earlier in the year, the Bells being away, he was so to speak boarded
out at Fitzroy Square and reported: "I was most agreeably entertained. I had my first good talk with Virginia. The result is . . . that
I agree with everything that you say about her mind: . . . I must
make a further confession of your accuracy; for I was surprised
to find how friendly she made herself appear." Thereafter he made
and sent her a translation of Euripides. Clive commended him,
Adrian cultivated him; it seemed possible that Virginia might
grow fond of him.

But Walter Lamb was not a substitute for Lytton, to whom
Virginia wrote on 6 October:

Now we are back again, living on culture chiefly . . . and the memory—
alas it fades!—of conversations with Walter Lamb. I wish (as usual) that
earth would open her womb and let some new creature out.

She was, as always, working on her novel; but also throughout
1908 and 1909 she was busy with journalism, busier than she usually
was—or than she was to be again for several years; *The Times
Literary Supplement* had become her chief employer, although she
now wrote some longer reviews for *The Cornhill*. It was for Reginald
Smith, the editor of that journal, that she devised what was, for
her at all events, an entirely new kind of article. She called it *Memoirs
of a Novelist* and it is, ostensibly, a review of Miss Linsett's *Life* of
Miss Willatt:

> a book which one may still buy with luck in the Charing Cross Road . . .
> The volumes had got themselves wedged between Sturm "On the
> Beauties of Nature" and the "Veterinary Surgeons Manual" on the
> outside shelf, where the gas cracks and the dust grimes them, and
> people may read so long as the boy lets them.

Miss Linsett, it becomes clear, is the typical Victorian hagio-
grapher and Virginia has some fun describing her manner of writing
a biography. But it is Miss Willatt, a novelist and an almost equally
obscure figure, who really interests the reviewer: hers is one of
those lives of the obscure which always fascinated Virginia; she
regards Miss Willatt with affection, with amusement and with
compassion. Marriage was denied to Miss Willatt; she turned to
philanthropy, decided that she had no vocation and thereafter
devoted her energies to the writing of fiction. It was highly
romantic fiction.

> [She] thought it indecent to describe what she had seen, so that instead
> of a portrait of her brothers (and one had led a very queer life) or a
> memory of her father (for which we should have been grateful) she
> invented Arabian lovers and set them on the banks of the Orinoco.

At which point one becomes pretty sure that Miss Willatt is
herself an invention and so is Miss Linsett.* *Memoirs of a Novelist*
is in fact an attempt to publish fiction under the cloak of criticism,
or rather, to combine both genres and, as such, it is interesting and
could have been momentous in the history of Virginia's development as a writer. It shows, I think, that the long process of writing
and rewriting *The Voyage Out* had in some measure tried her
patience, or at all events that she was eager to spread her wings

* I have searched in vain for Miss Linsett and Miss Willatt in the catalogues of
the British Museum Library and in that of the Library of Congress.

and publish a work of the imagination; moreover, this was not to stand alone but to be the first of a series.

She showed her manuscript to Clive; he thought it clever, but he clearly had some reservations; later he explained that they were not important and accused himself of being clumsy—his critical stance was affected by the fact that he believed that she had cooled in her feelings towards him and he was anxious to make amends. In November he wrote from Cambridge to say that her series was "expected to be the chef d'oeuvre of the century." Such flattery would have been pleasant enough if it had not been followed, almost at once, by a letter from Reginald Smith who wrote: "My feeling is that you have impaled not a butterfly, but a bumble-bee, upon a pin. It is cleverness itself, but . . ." In short, he rejects it, courteously, regretfully, but most decidedly. The fact that this was a new departure and that her friends had been led to hope so much from it must have added to the bitterness of the occasion. She never published or, I think, tried to publish in *The Cornhill* again.

But the year 1909, which had brought many vexations and disappointments, closed with a new anxiety; for now it appeared that Bloomsbury itself was to be extinguished. Clive and Vanessa, very much pre-occupied by the visual arts and increasingly aware that great things were happening on the other side of the Channel, had begun to feel that they were too far from the capital of the arts. They were both very francophile, they both enjoyed the amenities and liberties of life in France and they decided that they would be happier if they lived in Paris. It would mean leaving their friends behind, but they hoped that Virginia, and perhaps Lytton, might join them. Virginia cannot have welcomed the idea; she did not wish to be separated from Clive and still less from Vanessa; but she was never at home outside her own country, she was not particularly interested in contemporary painting and, when she mentioned the scheme to Lytton, he thought it catastrophic. But if Clive and Vanessa went, then, she declared, she would go too. Vanessa forecast that, when it came to the point, Virginia would stay in England; the move was not to be made for a year or so and by then she would probably have married Lytton—or at least be engaged to him. And yet she hesitated; it was indeed a painful question to decide.

On the last day of the year Vanessa was able to report that Adrian had decided to give up the law and go on the stage, while Virginia had definitely come round to the idea of Paris.

On the morning of Christmas Eve, walking alone in Regent's Park, Virginia suddenly decided to go to Cornwall. According to her, the idea struck her at half past twelve; the train left at one o'clock. Sophy nearly had hysterics, Maud packed her amethyst necklace and left out her handkerchiefs, but she caught her train. Lelant was beautiful, the weather was soft as Spring, and she tramped the countryside, staggered up Tren Crom, and enjoyed her Christmas without festivities. For conversation there was the maid and the Ferryman, for intellectual exercise Dr Meryon's accounts of Lady Hester Stanhope. The fantastic story of that arch-eccentric delighted her, and it was with her in mind that she wrote to Clive:

> Suppose I stayed here, & thought myself an early virgin, & danced on May nights, in the British Camp!—a scandalous aunt for Julian, & yet rather pleasant, when he was older, . . . & wished for eccentric relations. Cant you imagine how airily he would produce her, on Thursday nights "I have an Aunt who copulates in a tree, & thinks herself with child by a grasshopper—Charming isn't it?—She dresses in green, & my mother sends her nuts from the Stores."

The Bells did not leave Bloomsbury, and Adrian never became an actor. Nevertheless he was to give one notable and highly successful impersonation.

Virginia at 29 Fitzroy Square, 1910
By Duncan Grant

Chapter Nine

1910 – June 1912

ON the morning of 10 February 1910, Virginia, with five
companions, drove to Paddington Station and took a train
to Weymouth. She wore a turban, a fine gold chain hanging to
her waist and an embroidered caftan. Her face was black. She
sported a very handsome moustache and beard. Of the other
members of the party three–Duncan Grant, Anthony Buxton
and Guy Ridley–were disguised in much the same way. Adrian
was there, wearing a beard and an ill-fitting bowler hat so that
he looked, as he himself put it "like a seedy commercial traveller,"
while the sixth member (and leader) of the party, Horace Cole,
was convincingly attired as an official of the Foreign Office.

The object of their excursion was to hoodwink the British Navy,
to penetrate its security and to enjoy a conducted tour of the
flagship of the Home Fleet, the most formidable, the most modern
and the most secret man o' war then afloat, H.M.S. *Dreadnought*.

Virginia came into this impudent and sketchily prepared hoax
almost by accident. It had been conceived by Adrian and by
Horace Cole. Cole was in fact the person most responsible. He
was a rich and in many ways a preposterous young man, the
author of many practical jokes, who had become a friend of Adrian's
while at Cambridge. The most spectacular of his pranks had been a
ceremonious visit to Cambridge by the Sultan of Zanzibar, or
rather, by his uncle, who was impersonated by Cole, together
with three members of his suite (of whom Adrian was one) and
an interpreter. They were formally received at the Guildhall by
the Mayor, patronised a Charity Bazaar, were shown the principal
Colleges, and seen off at the Railway Station. Cole informed the
Daily Mail, which published the story; the Mayor was cross about
it and asked the Vice-Chancellor to have the culprits sent down.
But there were no serious consequences.

The 'Dreadnought Hoax'–to give it the name by which it
became famous–was, essentially, to be a repetition of the Zanzibar escapade. Mr Tudor Castle, a friend of Adrian's, was to send
a telegram purporting to come from the Foreign Office to the

Commander-in-Chief Home Fleet announcing the impending
arrival of the Emperor of Abyssinia. The Emperor would be
impersonated by Anthony Buxton and would be escorted by Cole
as a Foreign Office official. Adrian was to interpret and there would
be a suite of noble retainers. It was here that they encountered
their first difficulty. The Abyssinian Court began to melt away
until it was reduced to Guy Ridley and Duncan Grant; this seemed
altogether insufficient to support the dignity of the Lion of Judah.
One more at least was needed. Adrian asked Virginia; she was
delighted to take part; she had two days' notice.

Vanessa was dismayed at the whole idea. To her it seemed that
the joke would certainly fail, and Virginia should have nothing
to do with it. Cole himself already had the deepest misgivings and
so, perhaps, had the missing courtiers. Adrian was the only one
who seemed happy, confident and quite determined to proceed.

They set off, relying on the Fleet to accept and not to question a
telegram *en clair* from the Foreign Office. No one had the vaguest
idea of what an Abyssinian, let alone an Abyssinian Emperor,
looked like. They depended upon a few words of what may have
been Swahili, Mr Clarkson's grease-paint, and a pretty uncon-
vincing wardrobe, intended perhaps for a performance of *Il
Seraglio*, to defeat the vigilance of the Navy. And, just to stack the
odds impossibly high against them, they had chosen to visit a battle-
ship on which Adrian would almost inevitably encounter his cousin
William Fisher, who was flag commander. This indeed, to Adrian's
sanguine temper, was an inducement; to tease the Navy would be
fun, to do so at the expense of the Fisher family was an irresistible
temptation. But if they were detected, what then? They might
very well be thrown overboard–not an agreeable experience in
the month of February and one for which Virginia was equipped
neither in mind nor body.

When the train arrived at Weymouth, a flag lieutenant advanced
to their carriage door and saluted the Emperor with becoming
gravity. Cole made the proper introductions. There was a barrier to
restrain the crowd and the Imperial party proceeded with dignity
to where a little steam launch lay in readiness to carry it out to the
fleet anchored in the Bay. On H.M.S. *Dreadnought* Virginia found
herself shaking her cousin's hand; it was hard not to burst out
laughing.

They inspected the Guard of Honour. The Admiral turned to
Adrian and asked him to explain the significance of certain uniforms
to the Emperor.

"*Entaqui, mahai, kustufani*" said Adrian, and then discovered that his stock of Swahili, if it was Swahili, was exhausted. He sought inspiration. It came, and he continued:

"*Tahli bussor ahbat tahl æsque miss. Erraema, fleet use.* . . ."*

The dismembered limbs of a poet would serve the needs of the interpreter, and the Emperor, quickly rising to the emergency, responded with tags from Virgil; Duncan and Virginia may perhaps have spoken a rather different dialect. It is unlikely that Virginia used the opportunity to air her Greek; in fact she spoke very little, and then as gruffly as she could; it was difficult, she said later, to disguise her speaking voice. "A rum lingo they speak," muttered one of the junior officers, but another struck chill into their hearts by announcing that there was a seaman who could talk to the visitors in their own language. Unluckily–most unluckily–he was away on leave.

And so they went round the ship, the captain explaining guns, turrets, range finders, the sick bay and the wireless room to Adrian, and Adrian repeating the explanation in terms of Virgil or some-times of Homer to the royal party, until there was nothing left to see. Refusing a salute of twenty-one guns and refreshments which might have dislodged the noble Ethiopians' false whiskers, Adrian indicated that the State Visit was over, and the Imperial party was escorted back to Weymouth. Going home, Cole, who had spent the greater part of the visit in the *Dreadnought*'s wardroom, insisted that the waiters attending them in their compartment should wear white gloves.

"Oh Miss Genia, Miss Genia!" exclaimed Sophy as her employer, exhausted, dishevelled, blackened and bewhiskered, let herself into No 29 Fitzroy Square late that evening.

The press should be told nothing. This at all events was the view of the majority. They had been charmingly entertained, treated in fact with such kindness that they felt rather guilty, and, at any rate, the joke had gone far enough.

But not for Cole; he had always wanted fame, and here was his chance of it. Without telling his confederates, he went to the newspapers.

The newspapers, and more particularly the *Express* and the *Mirror*, gave the story headlines and full-page photographs. Re-porters appeared at 29 Fitzroy Square; they had been particularly interested when they learnt that one of the Abyssinians (according to some accounts it was the appropriately named Ras Mendax) was

* "*Talibus orabat talisque miserrima fletus.*" Æneid iv, 437.

a young lady, "very good looking, with classical features"; they wanted her story and they got it. They also wanted her photograph in evening dress, but this, so far as I can discover, they did not get. Leader writers hesitated between indignation and amusement; distressed patriots wrote letters to editors; and at last, when the press grew tired of the matter, the House of Commons took it up.*

The nine days' wonder was over and the public almost forgot about it. But private repercussions continued. Most of Virginia's friends took it as an excellent joke. Vanessa was relieved, although she feared that it would mean they would see even more of Horace Cole, whom she found bumptious and boring. But the Stephen family was outraged. Adrian received a stately rebuke from his cousin Harry, the Indian Judge, who had been much amused by the Zanzibar exploit but felt that, although it was funny to hoodwink a municipal dignitary (the Mayor of Cambridge was a shopkeeper), a naval man–'a man of honour'–must not be made to look ridiculous. Virginia received a letter from Dorothea Stephen in which she declared that it was a silly and vulgar performance; she would not scold, she would merely point out that, clearly, Virginia's life was entirely unsatisfactory and that she stood in need of religion.

Willy Fisher and his brother officers reacted in an appropriately aggressive manner. The honour of the Navy had to be saved, and it could be saved only by the corporal punishment of the hoaxers. After a series of disappointments and of rather absurd arguments on matters of punctilio and propriety, the naval party did succeed in abducting Duncan Grant and taking him to Hampstead Heath, where they were again more than half defeated by the gentle perplexity and mild courage of a pacifist in carpet slippers.

Apart from an account of the business which Virginia wrote in 1940, nearly all of which is lost, Virginia used the 'Dreadnought Hoax' only once in her writings. In a short story entitled *A Society*† she describes how a young woman called Rose "had dressed herself as an Ethiopian Prince and gone aboard one of His Majesty's ships." Discovering the hoax the captain visited her, disguised as a private gentleman, and demanded that honour should be satisfied. The wholly ludicrous manner in which first the Navy and then Rose receive their respective satisfactions occupies no more than five hundred words; but the theme, the theme of masculine honour, of masculine violence and stupidity, of gold-laced masculine

* See Appendix E.
† Published in *Monday or Tuesday*, 1921.

pomposity, remained with her for the rest of her life. She had entered the Abyssinian adventure for the fun of the thing; but she came out of it with a new sense of the brutality and silliness of men. And this perception came, in its turn, to reinforce political sentiments which had for some time been taking shape in her mind.

1910 was a year of crisis in the affairs of the nation. In January the struggle between the House of Lords and the elected majority had entered its final phase with a general election. Ever since January 1906, when Vanessa, Virginia, George and Gerald had gone to Trafalgar Square, the girls to applaud, the gentlemen to deplore, a great Liberal victory, Virginia had, in an imprecise way, known where she stood; but now there was a complicating factor. Virginia desired the defeat of the Conservatives; certainly she was not sorry to see Clive taking an active part in politics on the radical side; but *his* battle was not entirely hers, for while he had two votes she had none. It is not surprising that in the spring of 1910 we find her addressing envelopes, almost always the fate of the youthful volunteer in political causes, on behalf of the Adult Suffrage movement. She had, for a long time, been in sympathy with the feminist cause, but it was not until 1 January 1910, Janet Case having put the arguments for political action with unanswerable force, that Virginia wrote to her saying that she could neither do sums, nor argue, nor speak, but would like in some humbler way to be helpful. Janet Case applied to Margaret Llewelyn Davies, and she in turn spoke to Miss Rosalind Nash, who made some very sensible-sounding suggestions. Virginia might like to get up the history of the franchise movement in New Zealand or might make a collection of extracts on representation. Or there were things that might usefully be said in magazine articles. Virginia, it appears, preferred to address envelopes.

Not that she liked the work–she spent "hours writing names like Cowgill on envelopes." Moreover politics, like philanthropy, seemed to her to attract a bloodless, inhuman kind of person. She found work in an office filled with ardent, educated young women and brotherly clerks too much like living in a novel by H. G. Wells. Nevertheless she did do a good deal of work; she even sat on the platform at public meetings and, despite an interval caused by illness, returned to this work at the end of the year.

Whether she addressed too many envelopes, or whether the other effects of the 'Dreadnought Hoax' were to blame, or–and this is more likely–whether she had entered into one of those states of acute nervous tension which usually afflicted her when she was coming to the end of a novel (she was now, she thought, nearing the end of *Melymbrosia*) I do not know. But certainly she fell ill in March and was again on the verge of madness.

Dr Savage was consulted; he, as usual, prescribed a quiet life, early and regular hours, plenty of rest. She went off with the Bells to Studland and tried to obey his orders. At the end of three weeks Clive reported to Saxon that she was cured.

But the cure was not radical. The distractions of London undid all the good that Studland had done; soon she was again suffering from headaches–what she called numbness in the head–insomnia, nervous irritation and a strong impulse to reject food, all the old symptoms in their most severe form. Again Savage was applied to and again he ordered her to leave London and to rest.

Clive and Vanessa rented a house–the Moat House–at Blean, near Canterbury, and here they established themselves with Virginia. They invited Saxon; he could not join them but perhaps he was consoled by the letters which Virginia sent him from the Moat House, for she wrote:

. . . more to mitigate my own lot than to please you. The rain falls, & the birds never give over singing, & hot sulphur fumes rise from the valleys, & the red cow in the field roars for her calf. In these circumstances you would address yourself to Chaucer, & master his habits before tea. I have tried, but cant persist–I pick chocolates out of a box, & worry my sister. Shortly before the rain began, three days ago, we had our windows prized open by a Smith. The decay of centuries had sealed them. No human force can now shut them. Thus we sit exposed to wind & wet by day; & by night, we are invaded by flocks of white moths. They frizzle in the candles, & crawl up my skirt to die, in the hollow of my knee. There is something unspeakably repugnant in the feel of creatures who have lost their legs. However, Nessa has done her best for us. She has invented an old woman who comes before anyone asks her, to stop the chimbleys smoking, & finds eggs, by looking for them, on the common. Then Nessa said at breakfast, "What a very large family Mr LeFevre must have!" & pointed to a photograph of gospel preachers since the time of Wiclif. The poor old man who owns this house, Mr LeFevre, called here the other day; & said that his happiest hours had been spent here, but times were changed. He alluded to the death of his prolific wife, which happened in sad circumstances which I will explain one day. At this, Nessa & Clive suddenly lost their tempers & showed their intolerant brutality in such a way that the old man was led out by his daughter (herself much moved) in tears.

If you should write to me, in one of the living languages [Saxon had a disconcerting habit of writing in Latin], preferably Romance, I should have one happy breakfast. . . .

Saxon took, or affected to take, Virginia's account of the Bells' brutality to Mr LeFevre with so much gravity, seriously considering that Clive and Vanessa were indeed uncommonly hard on any kind of sentimental effusion, that Vanessa felt obliged to protest.

> Virginia since early youth has made it her business to create a character for me according to her own wishes & has now so succeeded in imposing it upon the world that these preposterous stories are supposed to be certainly true because so characteristic.

True or not (and usually there was a scintilla although not much more than a scintilla of truth in Virginia's inventions) she was on good terms with the Bells and particularly with her intolerant and brutal brother-in-law. He indeed had been touched by her unhappiness and her pain and was now particularly considerate and attentive, writing her charming and affectionate letters when he was away, flattering and flirting with her when they were together. His real concern for her health and the absence of any rival who could excite his jealousy made them more happily intimate than they had been for a long time.

Clive was no doubt a stimulating companion, but perhaps it was a sedative that she needed; after a fortnight it was clear that she was getting no better. Vanessa went back to London and told Savage that Virginia was not recovering; worse still, she had to point out that she herself would be unable to look after Virginia much longer, for in July she was expecting another baby. With great misgivings she wrote both to Clive and to Virginia on 23 June to tell them that Savage insisted upon a period of complete rest in a nursing home at Twickenham.

Virginia accepted the decision with dismay, but with resignation; she only wished that Savage had insisted on this in the first place. She wanted to start the cure as soon as possible, to get it over and to get well again. George Duckworth sent her a kindly but fatuous letter; he deplored her ill-health – no doubt she had been smoking too many cigarettes in order to repel the mosquitoes from the moat, and invited her to his country house. She meditated a reply:

> I shall say that I expect to be confined next month & let him muddle it out for himself. He will suspect Saxon, & take immediate steps to have him promoted. He will also run down to Brighton, & negotiate a settlement with Saxon père. How tactful he would be . . . bringing down a basket of plovers eggs, I expect.

But such pleasantries could hardly alleviate the desolating prospect of a month's incarceration at 'Burley,' Cambridge Park, Twickenham, a kind of polite madhouse for female lunatics. Here her letters, her reading, her visitors would all be severely rationed, she would be kept in bed in a darkened room, wholesome foods would be pressed upon her and she would be excluded from all the social enjoyments of London. Faced by the possibility of madness she accepted her fate; but she accepted it in a sullen and rebellious spirit.

Virginia was an exceedingly difficult patient. Vanessa, immobilised by the child which was expected before the end of July but did not appear until the 19th of August, had to wage a continuous war through the post. She had to scold, to exhort, to plead, in order that her sister might behave at all prudently. Sometimes bored to extinction and near to complete despair, sometimes recklessly euphoric about her health, Virginia was always adroit enough to use her charm upon her medical advisers so that she might win them over and make them her allies in whatever plot against routine and good sense she might devise. Savage could be manipulated, so too Miss Thomas, the proprietor of 'Burley,' and also Miss Bradbury, whom Vanessa supposed to be one of the lunatics but was in fact a trained nurse. Virginia declared that they were charming and good women but spoiled by religion: "They reverence my gifts, although God has left me in the dark. They are always wondering what God is up to. The religious mind is quite amazing." But they too were amazed, and Miss Thomas in particular was captivated as Clive, who was allowed to pay visits from time to time during that miserable July and August, observed. She "was transformed . . . suddenly life, which she had found drab and dreary, had become thrilling and precious . . . everything seemed exciting or amusing . . . her own life, coloured by the presence and idle talk of her patient, [had] grown poetical . . . for the first time in her life she felt of consequence to herself; she was aware of her own existence . . . and all the trivial things that made up that existence had significance too. The magician had cast her spell."

All this was in its way pleasing, and Miss Thomas was to repay Virginia with much practical devotion. But it also made it easier for her patient to take unheard-of liberties, to wander in the garden clad only in a blanket, to break rules about rest and food, to plan, if not to effect, a sudden return to London. When attempts were made to keep her in order she wrote accusing Vanessa of plotting against her with Miss Thomas: she was "a dark devil," they were all in a conspiracy behind her back; it was "damned dull being here all alone" and she could not stand much more of it. She would throw herself from a window.

Vanessa answered as one who has reached the end of her forbearance. She quite saw the horrors of Virginia's position; but did she or did she not want to be an invalid (she avoids the frightening word 'mad') for the rest of her life? Presumably she did and she would have her own way; she could get round Savage, who could not bid her do anything that she did not want to do; but if she insisted on coming back to London she would undoubtedly fall ill again. However, she must decide for herself, even though, as Miss Thomas said: "one cannot help having her welfare very near at heart."

In the end Virginia was dissuaded from committing the wilder imprudences. Vanessa, still waiting at Gordon Square for her confinement, wrote every day preaching patience, assuring her that London was hopelessly dull, and grieving over her own shortcomings. "Oh dear," she writes, "how nice it would be if you were quite well again . . . I don't make undue fuss about you . . . really I feel that I have made only too little fuss during the last 3 years."

Virginia remained at Twickenham until the middle of August and then, having had a pretty thorough rest, she tried the effect of healthy exercise. She went to Cornwall; she can hardly have been in a state to go by herself but the devoted Miss Thomas accompanied her, and here they escaped boredom by vigorous walking. Soon Virginia began to complain that she was leading a completely animal existence with no intellectual excitement whatsoever. But Cornwall was her favourite country and it did her good; she began to feel better than she had for a long time, although she still had bad nights and occasional headaches. When early in September she returned to London to see the new baby, Vanessa thought her very much improved. But her state of mind was a little puzzling. She seemed very self-confident, she was elated and excited about the future, looked forward to fame and marriage; at the same time she was irritated by trifles, exaggerated their importance and was unable to shake off her excessive concern with them.

Her cure was to be completed at Studland with the Bells, and in a sense it was; even so, although they should have known better, Clive and Virginia provoked each other to fury (the blame was his rather than hers on this occasion). The trouble was caused, as it often was, by Lytton. Clive thought that Lytton had become insufferably supercilious; he was intimate with and confided in Virginia and Vanessa while taking not the slightest notice of Clive himself. It was not to be borne and Clive announced that in future Lytton would not be welcome at Gordon Square. This squabble agitated Virginia excessively, and they both of them found it hard to avoid the subject.

Vanessa, however, was able to make and keep the peace while they were at the seaside. Here they were distracted by babies and by numerous visitors, including Saxon, Marjorie (the youngest of the Strachey girls), and Sydney Waterlow, another Cambridge intellectual and friend of Clive's, whom Virginia found amiable but not exciting. Presently Clive went to Paris and the two sisters were able to relax and settle down to a long discussion of their favourite topic, which was, of course, Virginia herself. She talked a great deal of Lytton; they would be meeting again in the autumn but now their relationship was to be regarded as entirely platonic. Her obscure and inconclusive connection with Hilton Young still exercised her mind; but her relations with Clive himself were now, she declared, in a satisfactory state. Their former condition was, I should guess, left undiscussed.

Virginia finally came back to Fitzroy Square in the middle of October to take up her London life where she had left it seven months before. She might consider herself cured; but Dr Savage and Miss Thomas, though encouraged and relieved by her good progress, were still fearful of the effect upon their patient of London, late hours, too much company and too much excitement. They uttered appropriate warnings and Miss Thomas drew up a set of rules for Virginia to observe. Vanessa also knew, even if Virginia did not, that her health was still precarious. The question naturally arose—or so I imagine—whether it would not be a good plan if Virginia were to find some quiet and accessible place near London to which she could, when necessary, escape.

Accordingly, at Christmas time, 1910, Virginia began looking for a house in the country.

She found what she wanted in the village of Firle, near Lewes; she could hardly have hit upon a quieter place. But it must be allowed that the house which she actually chose to live in did not contribute to the repose of the village street; it was a raw, red, newly-built, gabled villa. She named it Little Talland House, for even here she could not forget the superior charms of St Ives.

Nevertheless the beauties of Sussex clearly impressed her and the lease of Little Talland began a connection with the neighbourhood which was to last for the rest of her life.

She moved into this country villa early in 1911. Vanessa helped her to make it comfortable and she was frequently there, often with friends to stay, during the Spring and Summer of that year. It would seem that the place had a therapeutic effect; she enjoyed living there, she enjoyed walking on the Downs, she was well enough to go on with her novel and to work for the Adult Suffrage movement. She was staying at Little Talland, very contentedly, in April of the year 1911 when fate suddenly carried her to the shores of the Propontis.

To understand the reason for this unpremeditated excursion we must return to 1910. Early in that year Clive and Vanessa, returning to London after a visit to Cambridge, had travelled up with Roger Fry. Clive and he had not known each other before; now they discovered common interests and common enthusiasms. Clive was excited and impressed; he thought Roger Fry the most remarkable person he had met since he left Cambridge; as a natural consequence his new friend became an intimate and indeed an element in Bloomsbury.

Roger Fry was forty-four, and at an emotional and intellectual turning-point in his life. His wife was going mad, and by the end of the year was incurably insane and in an asylum. Educated as a scientist at Cambridge, he had turned to the arts and become a rather conservative painter and member of the New English Art Club as well as a considerable scholar and connoisseur, qualities he exercised in his capacity as buyer for the Metropolitan Museum in New York, a position from which he had recently resigned. He was in fact a highly respectable and well-established figure until the autumn of 1910 when, as it seemed to many of his old friends and admirers, he had taken leave of his senses and, to his enemies, that he had wilfully and wickedly entered into a conspiracy with hoaxers, crooks and criminals of the Parisian underworld. In short, he had asked the British public to look at and to admire the works of Cézanne.

During the fierce controversy which followed the opening in November 1910 of what is now called 'The First Post-Impressionist Exhibition,' an exhibition for which Roger Fry took the responsibility and the blame, Clive and Vanessa were his fervent supporters. Virginia was not deeply interested in the Post-Impressionists; but with Roger a constant visitor in Gordon Square she could not ignore the commotion that they caused. The atmosphere engendered by him and by the exhibition made her circle a little more centripetal, a little more conscious of being revolutionary and notorious. Bloomsbury had become an object of public disapproval, a centre of disaffection, of Abyssinian Emperors and of incomprehensible aesthetics. Also, the intellectual character of Bloomsbury itself began to change. The doctrines of G. E. Moore no longer seemed quite so important when Cézanne was the chief topic of conversation, and Lytton Strachey might seem less pre-eminent when compared with Roger Fry.

It was, I have very little doubt, under Roger's influence that a party was formed to visit the home of Byzantine art. Early in April 1911 Clive and Vanessa joined H. T. J. Norton (a Cambridge mathematician) and Roger himself in Brussels, from whence they set off together by train for Constantinople. Clive embarked on this expedition with some misgivings. Vanessa had been unwell and this worried him; but his feeling of possessive jealousy for Virginia gave rise to a more intense irritation of the spirit; he had "an irrational foreboding" that something might happen to her while he was away; she might fall in love or someone would fall in love with her. He begged her to assure him that his "own little niche" in her feelings was secure.

A good deal did happen while Clive was away; but not to Virginia. At Broussa Vanessa had fainting fits; she collapsed. The place was at that time remote—a day's journey from Constantinople—the inn was archaic and there was no medical man except a chemist. Virginia, reading between the lines of Clive's letters—letters which Clive tried to make as reassuring as possible—imagined a dreadful repetition of the nightmare of 1906 and, abandoning all other plans, set off across Europe in order to be with her sister.

At Broussa she found Norton in despair, Clive in a state of solicitous and ineffectual agitation, Vanessa convalescent and Roger in command. He was in his element, organising cooks and dragomen, arguing his way with a bottle of medicine in one hand and a Turkish conversation book in the other, cajoling English tourists, constructing a litter, always finding just time enough for another rapid sketch and, as Virginia believed, saving Vanessa's life by his energy, sympathy and practical good sense.

It was now that Virginia got to know Roger really well. During the few days during which all four of them were to remain in Broussa waiting until Vanessa was considered fit to travel, Virginia was able to appreciate the extraordinary richness of his nature.

His conversation, his activity, his delighted interest in ideas, and indeed in everything that he saw or heard, astonished and impressed her. Roger was a tower of strength. He was more, he was a perpetual fount of enjoyment.

Even though he himself was suffering agonies from sciatica, Roger was able to take command of his invalid and of her companions and to bring them, together with a considerable collection of paintings, pottery and textiles, successfully to England. But Vanessa's recovery was slow. Her disease was complicated by nervous symptoms and it was many months before she was perfectly well again. For Virginia this was, naturally, a source of unhappiness, all the more so because she depended very much on her sister and needed her support. But Vanessa's fortunes affected Virginia in another way; by the time of their return to England, Roger and Vanessa knew that they were in love. Vanessa did not confide in Virginia; she thought her much too indiscreet for that; but Virginia was pretty well aware of how matters stood and must soon have been conscious that Vanessa's tolerant attitude towards Clive's flirtations was no longer determined by policy but rather by sentiment. Hitherto Clive's passion for Virginia had been a source of severe, though concealed, pain. Now it became a matter of indifference. Now indeed Vanessa would have been only too glad to see Clive more completely obsessed by his sister-in-law, instead of which, such is the perversity of things, that affair seemed to be cooling off. In fact there was a moment–or so I suspect–when Vanessa feared that her much loved but agonisingly exasperating sister might set herself to charm Roger. There was no serious cause for alarm. Virginia was fascinated by Roger and he, undoubtedly, thought from the first that she was a genius; but his passions were pre-engaged and, most unhappily for him, were not to alter for many years. Virginia, for her part, had other things to occupy her mind and heart.

On the whole the break-up of the Bell marriage, that is to say its transformation into a union of friendship, which was slowly accomplished during the years 1911-1914, made for a relaxation of tension between the sisters and a slow dissolution (never quite complete) of Virginia's long troubled relationship with Clive. Perhaps also it created a situation in which she, being no longer preoccupied by her sister's marriage, could begin more easily to contemplate a marriage of her own. For Virginia, who had envied the domesticity of the Bells, need envy it no longer; it was ceasing to exist, things were changing.

In 1908 Bloomsbury had become licentious in its speech, by 1910 it was becoming licentious in its conduct, or rather, licence was no longer the privilege of its homosexual component. Virginia once said that human nature changed in or about December 1910. She is seldom accurate in her use of dates but it is true that the world (or at least her bit of it) was at this time transformed; things were happening which would very much have astonished the maidenly Miss Stephen of 1907. As usual it was Vanessa who gave the lead; she proposed, I do not know how seriously, the creation of a libertarian society with sexual freedom for all. The world at large would not have been surprised to hear it; Vanessa and Virginia had gone to the Post-Impressionist Ball as bare-shouldered bare-legged Gauguin girls, almost—as it seemed to the indignant ladies who swept out in protest—almost naked. And it was whispered that, at Gordon Square, Vanessa and Mr Maynard Keynes copulated *coram publico* in the middle of a crowded drawing-room. The story is improbable, if only because at that time Mr Keynes was pursuing other interests. In fact I believe that there was a certain element of bravado in Vanessa's high-spirited manifestations of sexual anarchy.

The painter Henri Doucet, who was present at one of Bloomsbury's wilder parties, when Vanessa danced with such enthusiasm that she shook off most of her clothes and whirled bare to the waist, remarked—perhaps a little wistfully—"*en France ça aurait fini dans les embrassades*"; for apparently it did not; the game of promiscuity remained only a game. Sex, it was agreed, need no longer be sanctioned by marriage, but it must still be sanctioned by passion. This, for Virginia, was the escape clause. In fact, what Virginia really wanted was someone for whom she could feel passion. Instead, in the month of July, she received another offer of marriage—of a kind.

Walter Lamb, who it will be remembered was one of the party at Studland in 1909 and was a persistent visitor in Bloomsbury, continued to seek Virginia's society. In July he asked her to join him in an excursion to Richmond Park. As she is our only witness we may as well quote the account of it she gave in a letter to Vanessa which can be dated 21 July 1911.

29 Fitzroy Square, W.
Friday.

Beloved,
   It is great devotion to write, as the heat is something awful.
   We had our great expedition yesterday. It was all very odd. First of

all it was rather strained; we lay under the trees & discussed the Bedford
Sq. plan.* Then we walked, & he began lamenting the lack of noble
souls. We discussed love & women in the abstract. At last he sat down
& said "Will you tell me if you've ever been in love?" I asked him
whether he knew about the Lytton affair. He said "Clive told me a
good deal" which made me angry, but cant be helped. Then I said I
would tell him about it if he really wanted to know, & not out of
curiosity. He said he wanted to find out what I felt, & would be glad
to hear anything. I gave him an abstract. Then he said, "Do you want
to have children & love in the normal way?" I said "Yes". He said
"I do care for you very much", I said "But you're quite happy?" He
said, "There are such dreadful complications." I said, "What". He
said, "You live in a hornets nest. Beside[s] marriage is so difficult—
Will you let me wait? Dont hurry me." I said "There is no reason why
we shouldn't be friends—or why we should change things & get agitated." He said "Of course its wonderful as it is."

Then we went rambling on: & I gathered that he felt he could not
let himself fall in love because he doubted what I felt; & he also was
puzzled by parts of my character. He said I made things into webs, &
might turn fiercely upon him for his faults. I owned to great egoism &
absorption & vanity & all my vices. He said Clive had told him dreadful stories to illustrate my faults. (for God's sake, dont repeat this) I
said that I liked him, & thought we could be friends. I tried to make
this clear. Then he talked a great deal about you—how noble & divine
you were—how you frightened him—how he wished to talk to you,
how he had an aesthetic love for you &c &c. We talked of general
things after that—his gout a good deal—& then had tea & went home,
& went to the Opera. There was an enormous crowd of cultivated
ones—Sangers, Forster, Rupert, Ka, James, Wolf† &c. Walter walked
home, & came in & drank here, as Adrian was out. He began again
about our relationship, & said he would like to live near me, in
the autumn, but didn't add much. It is uneasy, because he is always
trying to find out what I feel, & I can only talk about the beauty of
friendship. Of course I liked him much better than I have ever done,
as he was quite direct & really felt a good deal (unless I'm too vain to
judge). But the thing is left in an uncomfortable state. He wants to
come to Firle in September. I do like him, but the prospect of many
very long talks, rather appals me. There is something pathetic in him.
He's so desperately afraid of making a fool of himself, & yet conscious
that his caution is a little absurd. I think I've told all I can remember—
at least the gist of it. No doubt some further compliments to you
will be washed up. Oh how I'm damned by Roger! Refinement! &

* A plan to make a communal house in Bedford Square which was later realised
at Brunswick Square. q.v.i.

† i.e. Charles and Dora Sanger, E. M. Forster, Rupert Brooke, Katherine Cox,
James Strachey and Leonard Woolf, who had returned from Ceylon in June.

we in a Post Impressionist age. You dont deserve any compliments for sending me that one. By the way, the last thing W. said before we were interrupted was that he could not see that I had a single fault. "Not even as a wife?" I said "No: not even as a wife." In my opinion he is in love with me; but that you must hush up.

I'm in great difficulties with my engagements. Eily wont answer; & I think she must have written to Firle. If she puts me off, I might come down next Thursday or Friday for the night [to Guildford, where Vanessa was convalescing] (if you'll have me). Case comes on Monday, & wont say for how long. Then Savage asks me for Thursday, & I accepted for Wednesday. Jean [Thomas] is in a fury—flings the telephone from her ear—because she thinks I'm trying to avoid dining with her—Saxon has become very pathetic about Bayreuth. Altogether, its a hornets nest, as W. said. He meant that we lived in the centre of intrigues, which distressed him, & he asked about Harry & Roger & Desmond. He asked whether I should flirt if I married. I said "not if I were in love with my husband." But that was bold.

Are you better. Does this heat hurt you! At lunch I compared you with a South American forest, with panthers sleeping beneath the trees. I also gave a passionate vision of our love—yours for me, I mean.

yrs B.

Virginia was right in supposing that he loved her. He expressed his passion in long and slightly absurd letters, but his cause was hopeless. He was amiable but unimpressive and the only passion that he aroused in her was one of indignation against Clive. She burst out in a furious letter to Vanessa who, as usual, had to try and keep the peace. Then Clive, Walter Lamb and Sydney Waterlow became involved in a three-cornered wrangle about who said what to whom about Virginia (she certainly did live in a hornets' nest), and in the end Walter Lamb, having failed to secure a wife, for he must soon have realised that he was getting nowhere with Virginia, discovered also that he had lost a friend, for Clive never spoke to him again.

Vanessa had invited Virginia to stay with her in a cottage she had rented at Millmead, conveniently close to Roger's home at Durbins, near Guildford. She felt some anxiety lest the *sequelae* of Walter's proposals should result in storms between Clive and her sister. But the weather remained fine both literally and metaphorically. Week after week of sunshine made it a time for bathing and landscape painting, for picnics and Neo-Pagans.*

* The term *Neo-pagans* was, it would appear, invented in Bloomsbury, perhaps by Vanessa. The first use of it that I have found is in a letter from her to Roger Fry of August 1911.

Of these, some must have been known to Virginia long before 1911, for they were a Cambridge group connected in many ways with Lytton and Maynard Keynes and their friends. But it was now that she began to know a few of them better. One in particular was to be of great practical importance in Virginia's life. She met Katherine Cox – Ka Cox, as she was usually called – for the first time in January 1911 in "the heart of young womanhood" – that is to say in the company of Marjorie Strachey and her Newnham friends, Ray and Karin Costelloe. "Miss Cox is one of the younger Newnhamites," Virginia wrote to Clive, "& it is said that she will marry either a Keynes, or a Brook. She has a superficial resemblance to a far younger and prettier Sheepshanks. She is a bright, intelligent, nice creature; who has, she says, very few emotions. . . ." Virginia used to call her 'Bruin' and it is thus that I imagine her – not in the fiercer or gruffer aspects of bearishness, but comfortably furry, slow-moving, warm-hugging, honey-loving, a little clumsy, a little insensitive, but not so insensitive as to be unhurtable – rather, a shade imperceptive, but, unless touched by passion, helpful and dependable. She was a confidant, almost a sister, to many of the Neo-Pagans and in particular to Gwen Darwin and Jacques Raverat (who were married in 1911), to Frances Cornford and, above all, to Rupert Brooke, the luminary of that society, who set its tone rather as Lytton had that of his generation. But the tone was rather different.*

Their background was not unlike that of Bloomsbury; they were, for the most part, the children of eminent Victorian intellectuals; but there was a heartier element, a Bedalian, Rugbeian element; many of the women had received the advantage, which Virginia so much envied, of a university education; they were not so ladylike, more practical, more commonsensical than their seniors. Both the men and the women had reacted sharply and robustly against the decadents and the aesthetes; they felt, far less than Lytton's generation, the influence of G. E. Moore and although they were concerned with and practised the arts, they were also active socialists.

There was a sort of innocent athletic camaraderie about them;

* The Neo-Pagans resemble Bloomsbury in that they were intimately connected with Cambridge and were in no sense organised. It is not very easy to say who was and who was not a Neo-Pagan. To the names already mentioned we may add those of Justin Brooke, Dudley Ward, Gerald Shove, Geoffrey Keynes, David Garnett and the four daughters of Sir Sydney Olivier, the Fabian Socialist. Amongst them also were some – as for instance James Strachey and Francis Birrell – to whom the generalisations attempted in the next paragraph hardly apply.

they met, not only in drawing-rooms, but in tents, they navigated canoes, they dressed in jerseys and bandannas, they walked vigorously, they were gay and serious and, in their loves, they looked in general to the opposite sex, with marriage as their ideal.*

Thus, when Virginia went to stay with Rupert Brooke at Grantchester, where she supplied a word for one of his poems and bathed naked with him by moonlight in the Granta, he, one may surmise, considered both these acts as being in the nature of sympathetic gestures; it was decent of her to help him to a simile and decent too not to be prudish about stripping in mixed company; it was treating him like a friend. But for her, I think, this shameless bathing was altogether more eventful; it was an act worthy of Vanessa, a gesture of emancipation. If Adrian is to be trusted, she was a little vexed that it did not create more of a sensation amongst her friends. Whether Adrian was justified in calling their friendship the 'Rupert Romance' is very doubtful. I do not think that there was a serious attachment on either side, although they got on well enough for Rupert to be able to persuade Virginia to join him and some friends in a camp at Clifford Bridge on the banks of the Teign. This visit began badly and uncomfortably. The other campers had made an excursion to Crediton leaving nothing for Ka Cox and Virginia to eat on their arrival save a rotting blackberry pudding–such are the inconveniences of the simple life. There were, however, compensations; the fine weather still held and by the camp fire at night there was music, good conversation and that peculiar serenity which attends a life passed in boundless fresh air and sunlight.

Maynard Keynes was another of the campers at Clifford Bridge that September; he was intimate with, although he certainly could not be said to 'belong' to, the Neo-Pagans; in fact he must have known all Virginia's Cambridge friends and, from 1907, had been a visitor to 29 Fitzroy Square. Although his subsequent election to a Fellowship at King's caused him to live much at Cambridge, in 1909 he took rooms with Duncan Grant at 21 Fitzroy Square and thereafter got to know Virginia very well indeed. Incredibly clever, he had a sensual, affectionate, volatile and optimistic nature which could be very attractive. He was, from the point of view of practical politics, the greatest man Virginia was ever to know

* "The group of people we're part of . . . don't copulate without marriage, but we *do* meet in cafés, talk on buses, go unchaperoned walks, stay with each other, give each other books, without marriage." Rupert Brooke to Katherine Cox [? May 1911], *The Letters of Rupert Brooke*, 1968, p. 304.

intimately and in 1911 he might already be considered the most brilliant and the most obviously destined for a great career.

The lease of 29 Fitzroy Square was coming to an end; Virginia and Adrian, tired perhaps of their long and quarrelsome tête-à-tête, proposed a domestic revolution: they would share their home–it would have to be a large home–with other friends; for this purpose they considered a house in Bedford Square, but it was at 38 Brunswick Square that in October they found what they wanted. Here Virginia was to live in rooms of her own on the second floor; Adrian was to have the first, and Maynard Keynes a *pied-à-terre* on the ground floor which Duncan Grant could also use as a studio. The vacant top floor was offered to Leonard Woolf. The expenses of running the house were to be shared, but otherwise the 'inmates' were to be as independent as possible. Service and individual meals were to be supplied by Sophy and the housemaid Maud.*

To modern eyes the arrangement looks unexceptionable, but in 1911 it seemed odd. George protested that Virginia simply could not go off to live by herself with three young men. "Oh, its quite alright, George," Vanessa explained, "you see it's so near the Foundling Hospital." This would do for George: but it was not so easy to find an answer to Violet Dickinson; for Violet, broad-minded though she was, thought that her friend was going too far. "Julia would not have liked it." Such an objection, coming from such a quarter, must have brought Virginia, momentarily at all events, to a halt. She liked and respected Violet, she valued Violet's good opinion, Violet was her best friend. Or rather–as we may see in the gradual but decisive diminution of their correspondence– Violet *had* been her best friend. Virginia would always like, trust, and admire her, always be grateful to her; but somehow the vital spirit in their friendship had evaporated and now, when it was put to the test, Virginia found that she could break away and live as she chose, despite Violet's evident disapproval. There was a coolness but no quarrel; their friendship was of too long standing for that; moreover Virginia's conduct, though unconventional, was not immoral. Still Violet had been the most important person in her

* "Meals are:/Breakfast 9 A.M./Lunch 1./Tea 4.30 P.M./Dinner 8 P.M. Trays will be placed in the hall punctually at these hours. Inmates are requested to carry up their own trays; & to put the dirty plates on them & carry them down again *as soon as the meal is finished.*

Inmates are requested to put their initials upon the Kitchen Instruction Tablet hung in the hall against all meals required that day before *9.30* A.M."

Extract from the 'Scheme of the house' prepared by VW for Leonard Woolf in December 1911.

life and the incident marks the final extinction of a great passion.

It was indeed a season of terminations and new beginnings; Virginia was leaving, not only Fitzroy Square, but Little Talland. She had found Asham,* a strange and beautiful house in a lonely and romantic situation a few miles to the west of Firle, and planned to rent it from the New Year. Vanessa was enthusiastic and agreed to share the lease. The one thing that seemed endless was her novel. In April 1911 when she was revising it for perhaps the sixth time, she had written to Clive:

> Yesterday I finished the 8th Chapter of Mel[ymbrosia]; which brings them within sight of the South American shore. This is a third of the book done, I think. From sheer cowardice, I didn't bring the other chapters here [to Little Talland]. If I thought "There! thats solid & done with" I'm sure I should have the palsy. Some of it, I'm certain, will have the pallor of headache upon it.

Although the breakdowns of 1910 were not repeated in 1911 there were no doubt plenty of headaches. In June 1911 she wrote to Vanessa describing a moment of depression, when:

> I could not write, & all the devils came out–hairy black ones. To be 29 & unmarried–to be a failure–Childless–insane too, no writer.

How frequent and how important such moods may have been it is hard to say; but if the summer was at times melancholy there is some reason to think that the autumn was happier.

In November Sydney Waterlow†–who had joined them at Studland in 1910–made a declaration of love. She seems to have had no hesitation in rejecting him, kindly though decisively, and his passion soon evaporated. One may presume that the tribute was not unwelcome even though, by then, she was preoccupied by a new and much more important relationship.

When Leonard Woolf returned on leave from Ceylon in June 1911 he naturally sought out those Cambridge friends whom he had left behind him in 1904: Lytton, Saxon, Desmond MacCarthy,

---

* or Asheham.

† Sydney Waterlow was a frequent visitor in Bloomsbury and, as the following Diary entry makes clear, on fairly intimate terms with the Bells:
"Dined with the Clive Bells; what a relief and change [from electioneering]. No one else but Virginia S. We had talk that begins to be really intimate. Vanessa very amusing on pederasty among their circle. I realised for the first time the difference between her and Virginia. Vanessa icy, cynical, artistic, Virginia much more emotional, and interested in life rather than beauty. A glorious evening." Sydney Waterlow, *Diary* (Berg), 8 December 1910.

Clive, Maynard Keynes and Morgan Forster. In so doing he was bound to meet others whom he knew much less well: Roger Fry, Duncan Grant, Vanessa, Adrian and Virginia. He had left Cambridge and had returned to Bloomsbury. Bloomsbury welcomed him easily. "Woolf came to tea," wrote Vanessa, "and we had an argument as to whether colour exists." From which it might appear that things had not changed so very much since he had left Trinity. But of course things *had* changed, and so had he. There was now a difference between him and the rest, to quote again from Vanessa:

> He is of course very clever & from living in the wilds seems to me to have got a more interesting point of view than most of the "set" who seldom produce anything very new or original.

At Cambridge Leonard had been particularly close to Lytton; he was one of the few men whom Lytton liked and trusted but did not love or see as a rival in love. They were both tremendously earnest as Apostles. It was, for them, a kind of religion. Leonard has written of their private Henry-Jamesian language and, when he read *The Golden Bowl* in Ceylon, he was surprised to find how Jamesian they in fact were.* He and Lytton were, with Saxon, notable figures in the G. E. Moore *cénacle*; they were united in their devotion to the great man and, despite their genuine passion for intellectual honesty and their remarkable personal qualities, these young men left Cambridge with a terribly precious esoteric air. They had received the Gospel of *Principia Ethica* and regarded themselves as the elect.

When, therefore, Leonard set sail for Ceylon, Lytton was bereaved and he himself was isolated. Letters from Lytton were his only link with the old world, the "real" part of it. Saxon wrote sometimes, it is true, but usually only to say at considerable length that he had nothing to say, or sometimes—and here he would furnish examples—that he had nothing worth saying. There was always an idea—it was a thing to be talked of rather than actually done, that Lytton would come out to Ceylon some day. Perhaps he ought to have done so. Lytton never got that slight baptism of fire—if we may call it fire—which fate provided for Gibbon. Gibbon knew how practical men managed and mismanaged matters, because he had practical experience of war, or at least of an army. Would

* "I have just finished *The Golden Bowl* & am astounded. Did he invent us or we him? He uses *all* our words in their most technical sense & we cant have got them all from him." Leonard Woolf to Lytton Strachey, 23 July 1905.

Lytton have given a sharper edge–a slightly deeper note of comprehension–to Gordon and to Florence Nightingale if he had sat
amidst the flies and dirt of Jaffna and Hambantota? It is hard
to say, and hard to imagine Lytton visiting, let alone ruling, a
province.

But if Leonard had never left Cambridge and London to fly the
Union Jack amongst a wilderness of monkeys it might be hard to
imagine *him* as an administrator. As it was he had that experience,
the experience of being a sahib amongst natives, utterly removed
from all those friends with whom one could be entirely open, the
jokes, the high seriousness, the intellectual communion of Cambridge. He learnt to travel and to live alone, to undertake the
duties of a policeman and to exert the authority of a magistrate,
to send men to their deaths and to watch them hang, to perform
the endless and endlessly boring tasks of empire. Hardest of all,
he had to deal with and to come to terms with compatriots who,
in a moment of impatient despair, he described as a "stupid de-
graded circle of degenerates and imbeciles." These people, in whose
hands lay the administration and the exploitation of the island,
the half-educated sahibs and their terrible memsahibs, pointed the
difference between Ceylon and Cambridge with dreadful clarity.
But to make a success of his job, and he was clearly determined
from the outset to do that, it was necessary not merely to live on
terms of intimacy, of cordiality even, with people whom as an
undergraduate he would easily have avoided, but to cultivate them,
to study them, to please them. This he did, and in so doing he
became more tolerant, recognised that they were not, after all,
homogeneous, that there were many from whom he could learn
and some whom he could sincerely like. The arrogance of the
young intellectual was tempered, his sympathies were broadened.
He found that he could get on with, be tolerated and valued by,
people who had no understanding of "good states of mind," and
this without ever essentially sacrificing that first fine perception
that Cambridge had given him.

It was on this point that Lytton had some misgivings. Leonard,
he feared, might become "interested in his work" and in that
interest others would be quenched. They almost were.

Even in his early cries of despair Leonard was, consciously or not,
adapting his tone of voice to his interlocutor. As time went on and
he rose in the Service he found the administrative game fascinating.
He purged and reformed offices, he imposed order upon chaos,
he made inefficient machinery work smoothly. His superiors soon

understood that they had a very useful man in their service. They gave him a kingdom, the Hambantota District of the Southern Province, and for two and a half years he devoted himself to the task of making it peaceful and prosperous. By 1911 he had become an extremely successful colonial servant, and Lytton's fears might have seemed to be justified.

Bloomsbury broke the spell. Leonard returned to find the seeds which he and Lytton had cultivated under Cambridge glass growing tall and no doubt in some ways strange in their flowering. But it was still recognisably the same plant. The old values were still honoured although applied to a greater world than that of Cambridge; despite one melancholy loss, old friends remained, their lives enriched and complicated by new ones and, above all, by the feminine element, that is to say by Vanessa and Virginia.

In this new, but not unfamiliar society, Leonard could discard the reserves and reservations of the intellectual turned Colonial Administrator; he felt at home once more (much more so, I fancy, than at his mother's house in Putney); he was amongst people who respected the same fundamental values, people in whom he could discover congenial characters and qualities. After a seven years' term the holiday was exhilarating; released from the burden of solitude and from the grim pleasures of efficiency he embarked upon an excursive and erratic pursuit of social enjoyments and new experiences (he even took up painting for a time); and then his interests began again to become concentrated: he rediscovered a purpose and it became all-important. Six months after his arrival in England he proposed to Virginia.

On 3 July Leonard had dined in Gordon Square with Clive and Vanessa; after dinner Virginia, Walter Lamb and Duncan Grant came in. A few days later Virginia wrote to "Dear Mr Wolf" and invited him for a week-end at her "cottage in the South Downs." As he was already committed to a series of visits he could not accept and so, while Virginia undertook her 'great expedition' with Walter Lamb and her minor excursion with Rupert Brooke and the Neo-Pagans, Leonard went, firstly to a Somerset rectory, then to a meeting with Lytton and G. E. Moore in Devonshire and finally to Scandinavia. But when he returned he ventured to remind Miss Stephen of her invitation; she repeated it and suggested that it would be nice to use Christian names; she added that it was "not a cottage but a hideous suburban villa." Leonard went there for the week-end of 16 September; Marjorie Strachey was a fellow guest. It was then that Leonard discovered how pleasant it was to walk over the Downs with Virginia; it was in his company that she discovered Asham.

This week-end visit was decisive; from now on Leonard was increasingly at Fitzroy Square and Gordon Square; he continually sought Virginia's company. In November she began living at 38 Brunswick Square and Leonard was by this time so much a part of Bloomsbury that it seemed natural to ask him to join this establishment. On 4 December he moved into two rooms on the top floor at a rent of 35 shillings a week. The rooms had been painted and Virginia assured him that there would be a bookcase.

Thus, for the last three months of 1911 Leonard and Virginia saw a great deal of each other and Leonard found himself falling very deeply in love. She obviously liked him but what her liking amounted to was clear neither to herself nor to him, and his doubts as to the strength and nature of her feelings prevented him from expressing his own.

Early in the New Year Leonard again went to stay with his old friend the Vicar of Frome in Somerset; here, in the quiet of a country parsonage, he saw that he must at once ask Virginia to marry him. On 10 January he sent a reply-paid telegram to Brunswick Square: "I must see you for an hour tomorrow Thursday I shall arrive town 12.50 and leave again 5 if I can come to Brunswick Square 1.15 can I see you then Leonard."

He saw her and asked her to marry him. She cannot have been greatly astonished; but she had prepared no decisive answer; she wanted time in which to get to know him better. Their conversation was interrupted by the arrival of Walter Lamb and Leonard had to go back to Frome. When he arrived he wrote:

Great Elm Rectory
Frome
Somerset

11 Jan 1912

My dear Virginia, I must write to you before I go to bed & can, I think, probably think more calmly.

I have not got any very clear recollection of what I really said to you this afternoon but I am sure you know why I came – I dont mean merely that I was in love but that that together with uncertainty drives one to do these things. Perhaps I was wrong, for before this week I always intended not to tell you unless I felt sure that you were in love & would marry me. I thought then that you liked me but that was all. I never realised how much I loved you until we talked about my going back to Ceylon. After that I could think about nothing else but you. I got into a state of hopeless uncertainty, whether you loved me or could ever love me or even like me. God, I hope I shall never spend such a time again as I spent here until I telegraphed. I wrote to you once saying I would speak to you next Monday but then I felt I should be mad if I waited until then to see you. So I wired. I knew you would tell me exactly what you felt. You were exactly what I knew you are & if I hadnt been in love before I would now. It isnt, really it isnt, merely because you are so beautiful–though of course that is a large reason & so it should be–that I love you: it is your mind & your character–I have never known anyone like you in that–wont you believe that?

And now I will do absolutely whatever you want. I dont think you want me to go away, but if you did, I would at once. If not, I dont see why we cannot go on the same as before–I think I can–and then if you do find that you could love me you would tell me.

I hardly know whether I am saying what I mean or feel: I am extra-ordinarily tired. A dense mist covered the whole of Somerset & the train was late & I had to crawl my way from the station for 3 miles to the house.

Dont you think that the entrance of Walter almost proves the exist-ence of a deity?

Yr L.

He wrote again the next day:

. . . I can try & write about what, with you sitting there, it was so difficult to discuss calmly & dispassionately. I dont think I'm selfish enough not to be able to see it from your side as well. From mine, I'm sure now that apart from being in love . . . it would be worth the risk of everything to marry you. That of course–from your side–was the question you were continually putting yesterday & which probably you ought to. Being outside the ring of fire, you should be able to decide it far better than I inside it. God, I see the risk in marrying any-one & certainly me. I am selfish, jealous, cruel, lustful, a liar & probably worse still. I had said over & over again to myself that I would never marry anyone because of this, mostly because, I think, I felt I could never control these things with a woman who was inferior & would gradually enfuriate me by her inferiority & submission . . . It is because you aren't that that the risk is so infinitely less. You may be vain an egoist untruthful as you say, but they are nothing compared to your other qualities magnificence intelligence wit beauty directness. After all too we like one another, we like the same kinds of things & people, we are both intelligent & above all it is realities which we understand & which are important to us. . . .

Virginia, rushing to catch a train for what must have been her last visit to Little Talland House, replied:

There isn't anything really for me to say, except that I should like to go on as before; & that you should leave me free; & that I should be honest. As to faults, I expect mine are just as bad—less noble perhaps. But of course they are not really the question. I have decided to keep this completely secret, except for Vanessa; & I have made her promise not to tell Clive. I told Adrian that you had come up about a job which was promised you.

Vanessa had liked Leonard from the first and believed that he had the qualities that could make her sister happy. She wrote at once to say:

> . . . how glad I shall be if you can have what you want. You're the only person I know whom I can imagine as her husband.

Also Vanessa hoped that Leonard was coming to her housewarming party at Asham. This he did—in fact he came to two housewarmings there; the first was, according to Virginia, on the

> coldest day for 40 years; all the pipes were frozen; the birds were starving against the window panes; some had got in, & sat by the fire; the bottom fell out of the grates; suddenly Marjorie [Strachey], who was reciting Racine, stopped dead & said "I have got chicken pox."

The second and larger party took place a week later, with the Bells, Roger and Duncan, Adrian and Virginia, and again Leonard was there. But despite these gaieties Virginia was in distress. Leonard was anxious not to worry her, she should be free to go on as before; but, inevitably, he imposed a greater strain than had her previous suitors; never before had marriage presented itself as so real, so fair and yet so alarming a possibility. Her nerves gave way; at the end of January she had been in bed for a week—"a touch of my usual disease, in the head you know," and then, after the housewarmings, the symptoms became even more severe and she was obliged to go back to the hateful but convenient shelter of Twickenham and Miss Thomas. Vanessa wrote sadly to Leonard to tell him that he must not see or write to Virginia for the time being. She hoped that all would be well in the end. It was not until the end of February that Leonard was allowed to send Virginia a studiously boring letter and when at length she was released, Vanessa dismissed him with gentle but firm benevolence to Somerset; here he received a letter from Virginia in which she declared:

> I shall tell you wonderful stories of the lunatics. By the bye, they've elected me King. There can be no doubt about it. I summoned a conclave, & made a proclamation about Christianity. I had other adventures, & some disasters, the fruit of a too passionate & enquiring disposition.

I avoided both love & hatred. I now feel very clear, calm, and move slowly, like one of the great big animals at the zoo. Knitting is the saving of life; Adrian has taken to it too. The wondrous thing is that it transmutes Stephenese into Saxonese, so much that the poor old creature thinks himself echoed, & suspects malice.

Today Lytton came to tea, & was very charming & amenable to all the strictures I made upon Cambridge life & the . . . ums.* He practically agreed with me that the Hearthrug was rotten, & the whales a-stink. I said you did too, & he groaned at the spread of light.

. . . I must go out & post this. I have got 5/- which I am going to spend on chocolates & a sleeping draught, if the shops are open, & I escape molestation. I shant want the sleeping draught–in any case.

Leonard cannot have found this letter reassuring; it has a crazy ring although some of its eccentricities probably result from private jokes rather than from a disturbed mind. A tepid lover might have wondered what kind of wife he was wooing and might well have withdrawn from the undertaking; but there was nothing in the least tepid in Leonard's love.

Virginia spent much of her time at Asham living very quietly and working at her novel. It was at this time that Ka Cox, herself in the throes of an agitating and unhappy love affair,† began to devote herself to Virginia and to show her gift for being comfortably useful.

Meanwhile Leonard's situation was becoming very difficult indeed. His feelings for Virginia were complicated by his feelings for Ceylon. His interest in the island and its people was already finding expression in a novel – *The Village in the Jungle* – which he began during the autumn of 1911; at the same time he had begun to wonder whether he ought to return as an agent of the Imperial Government and in fact he had growing doubts about the Empire itself. If Virginia would accept him, this problem would be solved automatically, for it would certainly be impossible to return to Ceylon *with* her; but how, if he lost her, could he go back *without* her? At the same time Colonial Administration had become his profession; he knew that he was good at it and he dreamed sometimes of devoting himself for the rest of his life to some remote Cingalese community; but he had other dreams which made the idea of such a lonely return to a distant station five thousand miles from Bloomsbury and Virginia melancholy indeed. The prospect

* A reference to 'The Apostles.'

† With Rupert Brooke, who had himself been having a nervous breakdown and wrote to Virginia begging her not to follow his example.

however had to be faced and, if Virginia could not love him, might have to be accepted. Virginia herself remained undecided and he was determined not to try to hurry her into a decision; he was therefore obliged to gamble on his fate, for his leave expired on 20 May and before then he had to decide what he should do.

On 14 February, realising that Virginia might need a long time in which to make up her mind, he wrote to the Secretary of State for the Colonies and asked for four months' extension of his leave in order to settle his private affairs. The Under-Secretary answered him and asked politely what these affairs might be. Leonard replied that he could not discuss them. In March the matter was referred to the Governor of Ceylon, who decided that unless Leonard could be more explicit the extension could not be granted. On 25 April Leonard sent in his resignation.

Such a renunciation could hardly be accomplished without some natural regrets. Whatever misgivings he may have felt cannot but have been increased by a week-end at Asham when, clearly, Leonard realised that things were going very wrong between him and Virginia. On 29 April, four days after he had despatched his final letter to the Under-Secretary, Leonard wrote in a rather different manner (for under the influence of passion his style became most uncharacteristically diffuse and unpunctuated) to Virginia:

. . . I want to see you to talk with you & now though I suppose I shouldn't I'm going to write utterly miserable what I should want to say to you & probably couldn't.

Since yesterday something seemed to rise up in you against me. It may be imagination on my part: if it is, you must forgive me: I dont think even you realise what it would mean to me. God, the happiness I've had by being with you & talking with you as I've sometimes felt it mind to mind together & soul to soul. I know clearly enough what I feel for you. It is not only physical love though it is that of course & I count it the least part of it, it isn't only that I'm only happy with you, . . . : It's that that I want your love too. It's true that I'm cold & reserved to other people; I dont feel affection even easily: but apart from love I'm fond of you as I've never been of anyone or thing in the world. We often laugh about your lovableness but you dont know how lovable you are. Its what really keeps me awake far more than any desire. It's what worries me now, tears me two ways sometimes—for I wouldn't have you marry me, much as I love you, if I thought it would bring you any unhappiness. Really this is true though it hurt me more than the worst physical pain your mere word, that you told Vanessa that probably you would never marry anyone.

There was much more. It was a long repetitive letter in which he seemed almost to be talking to himself, wandering from hope to despair and back again; but always beset by the fear that there was some dreadful psychological barrier which he could not surmount.

And while he was writing in this vein to Virginia a Semi-Official letter was being written to him on behalf of the Secretary of State offering him the means whereby the extension of leave might yet be granted. On receipt of this he wrote at once to Asham to ask Virginia if he might speak to her before sending a reply.

... what a career you're ruining! [she answered and then]:

It seems to me that I am giving you a great deal of pain—some in the most casual way—& therefore I ought to be as plain with you as I can, because half the time I suspect, you're in a fog which I dont see at all. Of course I *cant* explain what I feel—These are some of the things that strike me. The obvious advantages of marriage stand in my way. I say to myself, Anyhow, you'll be quite happy with him; & he will give you companionship; children, & a busy life. Then I say By God, I will not look upon marriage as a profession. The only people who know of it, all think it suitable; & that makes me scrutinise my own motives all the more. Then, of course, I feel angry sometimes at the strength of your desire. Possibly, your being a Jew comes in also at this point. You seem so foreign. And then I am fearfully unstable. I pass from hot to cold in an instant, without any reason; except that I believe sheer physical effort & exhaustion influence me.

All I can say is that in spite of these feelings, which go chasing each other all day long when I am with you, there is some feeling which is permanent, & growing. You want to know of course whether it will ever make me marry you. How can I say? I think it will, because there seems no reason why it shouldn't—But I dont know what the future will bring. I'm half afraid of myself. I sometimes feel that no one ever has or ever can share—something—Its the thing that makes you call me like a hill, or a rock. Again, I want everything—love, children, adventure, intimacy, work. (Can you make any sense out of this ramble? I am putting down one thing after another.) So I go from being half in love with you, & wanting you to be with me always, & know everything about me, to the extreme of wildness & aloofness. I sometimes think that if I married you, I could have everything—& then—is it the sexual side of it that comes between us? As I told you brutally the other day, I feel no physical attraction in you. There are moments—when you kissed me the other day was one—when I feel no more than a rock. And yet your caring for me as you do almost overwhelms me. It is so real, & so strange. Why should you? What am I really except a pleasant attractive creature? But its just because you care so much that I feel I've got to care before I marry you. I feel I must give you everything; & that if I cant, well, marriage would only be second-best for you as well as for me. If you can still go on, as before, letting me find my own way, that is what would please me best; & then we must both take the risks. But you have made me very happy too. We both of us want a marriage that is a tremendous living thing, always alive, always hot, not dead & easy in parts as most marriages are. We ask a great deal of life, dont we? Perhaps we shall get it; then how splendid! One doesn't get much said in a letter, does one?

But she had said enough; for all his doubts—and they must have been considerable—Leonard was now fixed in his determination not to return to Ceylon. His resignation was finally accepted on 7 May.

Now indeed his boats were really burnt and in fact she had not given him very much reason to hope. The best that she could say was that she was half in love with him, wanted to love him and to marry him if only she could. This, to be sure, was something quite different from her previous flirtations.

"No, I shan't float into a bloodless alliance with Lytton—though he is in some ways perfect as a friend, only he's a female friend." This she wrote in March 1912, and in the same letter:

I began life with a tremendous, absurd, ideal of marriage; then my bird's eye view of many marriages disgusted me, and I thought I must be asking what was not to be had. But that has passed too. Now I only ask for someone to make me vehement, and then I'll marry them!

But could Leonard make her "vehement"? Clearly she had the gravest doubts about it. It was something gained, however, that she was by this time anxious to give him every chance of doing so. When she returned again to Brunswick Square he was her neighbour. She began to know him thoroughly and could now understand how admirably his character suited hers. He had the intellectual eminence that she had found hitherto only in Lytton, and with it a reliable strength that Lytton did not possess. Leonard too was a writer, a novelist, and he had told her, after reading one of her manuscripts that one day she "might write something astonishingly good"; every morning at Brunswick Square each sat down to write 500 words—it was an agreed programme. And when their writing was done they were free; they might lunch together or wander out into the Square to sit quietly beneath the shade of the trees and find new pleasure in each other's company. The more she saw of him the better she liked him and the amenity of their intercourse may well have been increased by the fact that Vanessa, Clive and Roger were in Italy. It was an advantage to be out of sight of those quizzical spectators. From Italy Vanessa wrote: "I hope you aren't getting too much worried by the Leonard question. I should let it slide on & see what happens. Its sure to be all right in the end."

And it was all right. As their intimacy progressed Virginia's fears melted away, her confidence grew, her feeling for Leonard became more definite and at length, on 29 May, she was able to tell him that she loved him and would marry him. It was the wisest decision of her life.

APPENDIX A
Chronology

1878
26 March   Marriage of Leslie Stephen and Julia Prinsep Duckworth (*née* Jackson). They settle at 22 Hyde Park Gate, Kensington, where their four children are born

1879
30 May   Birth of Vanessa Stephen

1880
8 September   Birth of Julian Thoby Stephen

1881
September   Leslie Stephen buys the lease of Talland House, St Ives, where his family spend each summer from 1882 to 1894

1882
25 January   Birth of Adeline Virginia Stephen
November   Leslie Stephen begins work as the Editor of the *Dictionary of National Biography*

1883
27 October   Birth of Adrian Leslie Stephen

1888
April   The Stephen children all have whooping cough; in May they convalesce in Bath with their grandmother Mrs Jackson

1889/90
Winter   Margaret (Madge) Symonds, aged 20, stays at 22 Hyde Park Gate for some months

1891
January   Thoby goes to Evelyn's Preparatory School, Hillingdon
February   The *Hyde Park Gate News* begins publication
April   Leslie Stephen gives up the editorship of the *D.N.B.*

1892
January   Adrian goes to Evelyn's School
3 February   Death of J. K. Stephen
2 April   Death of Mrs Jackson at 22 Hyde Park Gate

VIRGINIA WOOLF

1894

February	Vanessa and Virginia go to stay with Mr and Mrs G. F. Watts at Limner's Lease, Guildford
11 March	Death of Sir James Fitzjames Stephen
September	Thoby goes to Clifton College, Bristol

1895

Mid-February	Mrs Leslie Stephen ill with influenza
11 April	George, Stella and Gerald Duckworth go abroad
5 May	Death of Mrs Leslie Stephen
Summer	Stephen family at Freshwater, Isle of Wight Virginia's first breakdown
November	Caroline Emelia Stephen settles in Cambridge; Vanessa and Virginia stay with her there fairly often, particularly after Thoby goes up to Cambridge in 1899 The lease of Talland House, St Ives, is sold

1896

	Vanessa begins to go to Drawing Classes
Summer	Stephen family at Hindhead House, Haslemere (let by Mrs John Tyndall)
22 August	Stella Duckworth accepts J. W. Hills, after two refusals
24 September	Adrian enters Westminster School
November	Virginia and Vanessa travel for a week in Northern France with George and Miss Duckworth (Aunt Minna)

1897

3 January	Virginia begins to keep a regular diary
8–13 February	Virginia goes to Bognor with Vanessa, Stella and Jack Hills
15 February	Virginia allowed to start lessons again
10 April	Marriage of Stella Duckworth to John Waller Hills at St Mary Abbots Church, Kensington
14–28 April	Stephen family at 9 St Aubyns, Hove; daily communication with the Fisher family
28 April	Return to 22 Hyde Park Gate to find Stella ill with peritonitis at her new home, 24 Hyde Park Gate
2 May	Stella pronounced "out of danger"
9 May	Virginia examined by Dr Seton; her lessons are stopped and she is prescribed milk and medicine
5 June	Stella again ill
22 June	Queen Victoria's Diamond Jubilee; Vanessa, Virginia and Thoby watch the procession from St Thomas's Hospital

APPENDIX A

1897

11 July	Virginia feverish and ill
19 July	Death of Stella
28 July– *23 September*	Stephen family at Painswick Vicarage, Gloucestershire
25 September– *2 October*	Vanessa and Virginia go with Jack Hills to visit his parents at Corby Castle, Carlisle
November	Virginia attends Greek and History classes at King's College, London

1898

1 January	Virginia concludes her diary
	Greek classes with Dr Warre at King's College
April	Stephen family spend Easter holidays at 9 St Aubyns, Hove
21/22 May	Vanessa and Virginia visit their aunts at Cambridge and Godmanchester
25 June	Vanessa and Virginia go to Clifton to see Thoby
9 July	Vanessa, Virginia and others go for the day to the Fens to hunt for moths
28 July	Marriage of William Wyamar Vaughan, Virginia's cousin, to Madge Symonds at All Saints, Ennismore Gardens; Vanessa a bridesmaid
August and *September*	Stephen family at the Manor House, Ringwood. Guests include Rezia, Guido and Nerino Rasponi, Charles and Cordelia Fisher, Susan Lushington, and Dermod O'Brien
21 September	Return to 22 Hyde Park Gate
17 October	Term begins at King's College; Virginia takes Latin with Miss Pater and Greek with Dr Warre

1899

12–28 April	Stephen family at 9 St Aubyns, Hove. Thoby has pneumonia
August and *September*	Stephen family at the Rectory, Warboys, Huntingdonshire. Guests include Emma and Margaret Vaughan, and Susan Lushington
21 September	Return to 22 Hyde Park Gate
3 October	Thoby enters Trinity College, Cambridge, together with Lytton Strachey, Saxon Sydney-Turner, Leonard Woolf and Clive Bell

1900

March	Virginia has measles
April	Easter(?) at 9 St Aubyns, Hove. Vanessa goes to Paris for a week on 18 April

1900

12(?) June Virginia goes to the Trinity May Ball with Thoby and Vanessa, the Maitlands, and Cordelia Fisher

Dictionary of National Biography completed in 63 volumes

6 July Vanessa and Virginia go to Henley with Jack Hills

7 July Vanessa and Virginia go with George Duckworth to Crabbet for the sale of Blunt's horses

August and September Stephen family at Fritham House, Lyndhurst, Hampshire. Guests include Margaret Booth and Austen Chamberlain. Leslie Stephen in poor health

17 September Return to 22 Hyde Park Gate

October Virginia attends classes at King's College

1901

4 April Stephen family spend a fortnight at Little Park, Lyme Regis; Madge and Will Vaughan near, staying with her mother, Mrs. A. J. A. Symonds

8–9 June Vanessa and Virginia at Cambridge

1 August– mid-September Stephen family go to Fritham House, Lyndhurst. Guests include Miss Pater, Filippo and Rezia Corsini (on their honeymoon), and Margery Snowden

September Vanessa enters the Royal Academy Schools

October Virginia takes up bookbinding

25–26 November Vanessa and Virginia accompany Leslie Stephen to Oxford, where he receives an Hon. D.Litt.

1902

(?) January Virginia starts private lessons in Greek with Miss Janet Case

1 April Leslie, Thoby, Virginia and Adrian Stephen go to Hindhead Copse, Haslemere (Sir Frederick Pollock's house); Vanessa and George Duckworth go to Rome and Florence for three weeks; visit cut short by Leslie Stephen's illness

26 June Leslie Stephen created K.C.B. in the Coronation Honours

31 July Stephen family to Fritham House, Lyndhurst. Guests include Theodore Llewelyn Davies, Emma Vaughan, Margery Snowden, Clive Bell, and Violet Dickinson, who now becomes, and for many years remains, Virginia's most intimate friend

19 September Return to 22 Hyde Park Gate. The Stephen family acquires a pianola

October Adrian enters Trinity College, Cambridge; Thoby returns there for a further year

APPENDIX A

1902

12 December   Leslie Stephen operated by Sir Frederick Treves in a nursing home in Duchess Street, W.1

1903

6 January   Leslie Stephen returns to 22 Hyde Park Gate

February   Owing to his ill health, Leslie Stephen receives his insignia at home

16–30 April   Stephen family at Blatchfield, Chilworth, Surrey

31 July   Stephen family go to Netherhampton House, Salisbury. Guests include Susan Lushington, Violet Dickinson, Ronald Norman, J. W. Hills. The Fisher family stay in The Close, Salisbury. Visits to Wilton, Stonehenge, Romsey Abbey &c

18 September   Return to 22 Hyde Park Gate. Sir Leslie slowly dying

October   Virginia resumes Greek lessons with Miss Case; Vanessa at the Royal Academy Schools; Thoby reading for the Bar

14 November   Sir Leslie dictates the last entry in the 'Mausoleum Book' to Virginia

1904

22 February   Death of Sir Leslie Stephen

27 February– c. 25 March   Vanessa, Thoby, Adrian and Virginia with George Duckworth at Manorbier, Pembrokeshire

1 April   Vanessa, Thoby, Virginia and Adrian go to Venice with Gerald Duckworth

13 April   Stephens to Florence, where they are joined by Violet Dickinson. Adrian returns to Cambridge on 20 April; Thoby departs on a walking tour. Vanessa, Virginia and Violet Dickinson visit Prato, Siena, Genoa

1 May   Vanessa and Virginia with Violet Dickinson rejoin Thoby in Paris, where they are entertained by Clive Bell and Gerald Kelly, and meet Lady Beatrice Thynne. Visits to Rodin's and Kelly's studios

9 May   Vanessa and Virginia, escorted by George Duckworth, return to 22 Hyde Park Gate

10 May   Beginning of Virginia's second serious breakdown; at first she is under the care of Dr Savage and three nurses; later with Nurse Traill she spends almost three months at Violet Dickinson's house, Burnham Wood, Welwyn; here she also has scarlet fever

2nd half of August   Stephens at The Manor House, Teversal, Nottinghamshire, for the summer holiday; Virginia with Nurse Traill rejoins her family there; she is convalescent and able to study a little and go for walks

VIRGINIA WOOLF

1904

September   Violet Dickinson stays at Teversal

10 September   Marriage of George Duckworth to Lady Margaret Herbert at Dulverton, Somerset. Vanessa, Thoby and Adrian attend

Late September   Margery Snowden and Clive Bell stay at Teversal

c. 8 October   Stephens return to London. Virginia and Vanessa stay with the Booths during the move from 22 Hyde Park Gate to 46 Gordon Square, Bloomsbury

c. 18 October   Virginia goes to Cambridge to stay with her aunt Caroline Emelia Stephen at The Porch; she is helping F. W. Maitland with his *Life* of her father

8–18 November   Virginia at 46 Gordon Square; begins to send articles to Mrs Lyttelton, editor of the Women's Supplement of *The Guardian*. Leonard Woolf dines with the Stephens on 17th before sailing for Ceylon

18–29 November   Virginia stays with Madge and Will Vaughan at Giggleswick; returns to 46 Gordon Square

3–10 December   Virginia at The Porch, Cambridge; returns to Gordon Square

14 December   Virginia's first publication, an unsigned review, printed in *The Guardian*

21 December   The Stephens go to Lane End, Bank, near Lyndhurst (lent by Miss Minna Duckworth), for a Christmas holiday

1905

4 January   Return to Gordon Square

14 January   Virginia 'discharged cured' by Dr Savage; she undertakes to give a weekly class at Morley College

16 February   Thoby Stephen starts 'Thursday Evenings' at 46 Gordon Square

1 March   Formal housewarming party at 46 Gordon Square

5 March   The 'Sultan of Zanzibar' hoax by Adrian, Horace Cole and others, at Cambridge

29 March   Virginia and Adrian sail from Liverpool to Oporto by Booth Line, landing 5 April; they visit Lisbon, Seville and Granada; on 20th, they embark at Lisbon on the SS *Madeirensa* and reach Liverpool on Easter Sunday, 23 April

24 April   Return to 46 Gordon Square

June and July   Virginia pays brief visits to Herbert and Lettice Fisher at Oxford; to Cambridge (Trinity College Ball); to the Freshfields at Forest Row Sussex; and to Sir George Young's family at Formosa Place, Cookham. Clive Bell proposes to Vanessa and is refused

APPENDIX A

1905

10 August Stephens go to Trevose View, Carbis Bay (near St Ives) for the summer holidays; they are visited there by Kitty and Leo Maxse, Gerald Duckworth, Imogen Booth, Sylvia Milman, Jack Hills and Saxon Sydney-Turner

5 October Return to 46 Gordon Square

1905/6

Autumn and Winter All four Stephens in residence at Gordon Square: Virginia writing, reviewing and teaching at Morley College, Thoby and Adrian studying Law. Vanessa organises the Friday Club. 'Thursday Evenings' continue

1906

12-25 April Virginia at Giggleswick, Yorkshire, lodging with Mrs Turner, near Madge and Will Vaughan; Vanessa joins her on 21st after painting Lord Robert Cecil's portrait at Chelwood Gate

June and July Virginia pays brief visits to her aunt at Cambridge; to Lady Robert Cecil at Chelwood Gate; to Violet Dickinson at Welwyn; and to Eton for the wedding of Desmond MacCarthy and Mary Warre Cornish on 10 July

3-31 August Vanessa and Virginia at Blo' Norton Hall, East Harling, Norfolk; Thoby and Adrian stay two days, then return to London and leave for Trieste on 10 August. Guests include George Duckworth, Hester Ritchie and Emma Vaughan

8 September Virginia, Vanessa and Violet Dickinson leave London for Greece; they meet Thoby and Adrian at Olympia on 13th. They all go *via* Corinth to Athens, thence to Nauplia by boat for Epidaurus, Tiryns and Mycenae; Vanessa ill at Corinth on return journey

1-5 October Virginia and her brothers visit the Noels at Achmetaga, Euboea; Vanessa goes with Violet Dickinson to Athens, where she is ill for two weeks

21 October Thoby returns to England; the others go to Constantinople, where Vanessa is again ill

29 October Vanessa, Virginia, Adrian, and Violet Dickinson return to England by Orient Express, reaching London on 1 November

November Thoby and Vanessa both ill in bed at 46 Gordon Square

20 November Thoby Stephen dies of typhoid fever

22 November Vanessa agrees to marry Clive Bell

VIRGINIA WOOLF

1906

December — Walter Headlam offers to criticise Virginia's writings, and asks to dedicate his translation of the *Agamemnon* to her

21 December — Virginia and Adrian go to Lane End, Bank, for Christmas. Vanessa is at Cleeve House, Seend, Wiltshire, with Clive Bell's family

31 December — Virginia and Adrian go to Cleeve House

1907

3 January — Virginia and Adrian return to 46 Gordon Square for a night, and then make a brief visit to the Booths at Gracedieu Manor, Leicestershire

7 February — Marriage of Vanessa Stephen to Clive Bell at St Pancras Registry Office

February — Virginia house-hunting. 16–18th she visits Caroline Emelia Stephen at Cambridge; she also stays with Violet Dickinson at Welwyn. Meetings and correspondence with Walter Headlam

23–25 March — Virginia and Adrian sleep at Violet Dickinson's house in Manchester Square while their move to 29 Fitzroy Square takes place

28 March — Virginia and Adrian go to Paris with Clive and Vanessa Bell; meetings with Duncan Grant

10 April — Virginia and Adrian return to London and take up residence in their new home, 29 Fitzroy Square, W.1

May-July — Virginia pays brief visits to Cambridge and to Cleeve House, Seend

8 August — Virginia and Adrian go to The Steps, Playden, Rye, for the summer holidays; Beatrice Thynne, Pernel Strachey and Katherine Stephen each stay a few days

26 August — Bells to Curfew Cottage, Rye; Margery Snowden, Walter Lamb, Lytton Strachey and Saxon Sydney-Turner stay at Playden or Rye

26 September — Virginia returns to 29 Fitzroy Square. She resumes teaching at Morley College; and agrees to sit to Francis Dodd for a portrait

October–December — Virginia works on her novel (*Melymbrosia*); she and Adrian begin 'Thursday Evenings' at Fitzroy Square; she stays with H. A. L. and Lettice Fisher at Oxford; and decides to give up teaching

21 December — Inception of the Play Reading Society at 46 Gordon Square: Vanessa and Clive Bell, Virginia and Adrian Stephen, Lytton Strachey and Saxon Sydney-Turner; nine subsequent meetings till 24 May 1908

APPENDIX A

1908

4 February	Birth of Julian Heward Bell at 46 Gordon Square
17 April	Virginia goes to Trevose House, St Ives; joined there by Adrian on 23rd and Bells on 24th
2 May	Virginia returns to 29 Fitzroy Square
Summer	Virginia and Adrian have German lessons with Miss Daniel
20 June	Death of Walter Headlam
July	Day visits by Virginia to her aunt Lady Stephen at Godmanchester, and to Violet Dickinson at Welwyn. Sits to Francis Dodd
1–17 August	Virginia (with two dogs) in lodgings in Wells; expeditions to Glastonbury and Cheddar; and twice to meet Clive and Vanessa Bell in Bath
18–31 August	Virginia lodges at Manorbier, Pembrokeshire; expedition to Tenby. 100 pages of *Melymbrosia* completed
3 September	Virginia goes with the Bells to Italy; they stay in Siena and Perugia; and visit Pavia and Assisi. On the 24th they return to Paris for a week
1 October	Return to London. 'Thursday Evenings' at Fitzroy Square begin again
27 October	Play Reading Society resumes its meetings after five months' break; five meetings during the winter
12(?)–17 November	Virginia and Adrian at The Lizard with Lytton Strachey
November	Virginia pays a brief visit to Lady Stephen at Godmanchester
Christmas	Virginia and Adrian at 29 Fitzroy Square

1909

15 January	Last meeting of the Play Reading Society until its revival on 29 October 1914
Late January– mid-March	Letter-writing game with Virginia, Vanessa and Clive Bell, Lytton Strachey, Walter Lamb, Saxon Sydney-Turner and Adrian Stephen
Early February	Seven chapters of *Melymbrosia* read and criticised by Clive Bell
13–15 February	Virginia stays with the H. A. L. Fishers at Oxford
17 February	Lytton Strachey proposes marriage to Virginia
End of February	Virginia's last visit to her aunt Caroline Emelia Stephen at Cambridge
2(?) March	Virginia goes with the Bells to The Lizard; she returns to Fitzroy Square on the 9th; the Bells remain until the 19th

1909

30 March	Virginia dines for the first time with Lady Ottoline Morrell
7 April	Death of Caroline Emelia Stephen; Virginia attends her cremation at Golders Green on 14th; is left a legacy of £2500
23 April	Virginia goes with Clive and Vanessa Bell to Florence
9 May	Virginia returns alone to 29 Fitzroy Square
15–17 May	Virginia goes to Cambridge to stay with the Verralls; Hilton Young's proposal(?)
22–24 May	Virginia and Adrian stay with the Freshfields at Forest Row
Summer	Lady Ottoline Morrell comes to 'Thursday Evenings' at 29 Fitzroy Square
6 June–16 July	Adrian keeps a diary
5 August	Virginia goes to Bayreuth with Adrian and Saxon Sydney-Turner for the Wagner Festival
22 August	They go on to Dresden
3(?) September	Virginia and Adrian return to 29 Fitzroy Square
10–13 September	Virginia meets the Bells in Salisbury; she returns to London, the Bells to Cleeve House
c. 16 September– 2 October	Virginia at Studland, where she rents a cottage near the Bells' lodgings; Adrian comes; and Walter Lamb stays with the Bells from 23rd September
10 November	*The Cornhill* rejects *Memoirs of a Novelist*
27–29 November	Virginia stays with the George Darwins at Cambridge; she attends a performance of *The Wasps*; lunches and spends the afternoon with Lytton Strachey before returning to London
24–28 December	Virginia alone at Lelant, Cornwall

1910

January	Virginia volunteers to work for Women's Suffrage
10 February	'The Dreadnought Hoax'
25 February	Roger Fry talks to The Friday Club
c. 5–10 March	Virginia with Clive and Vanessa Bell makes an unpremeditated excursion to Lelant, Cornwall; Virginia ill in bed after her return
26 March	Virginia goes with the Bells to lodgings at Harbour View, Studland, for three weeks' rest
16 April	Virginia returns to 29 Fitzroy Square; her health remains uncertain throughout the summer
Early June	Virginia with Adrian visits George and Margaret Duckworth for the day at Chalfont St Giles; also goes with Clive Bell for a day with the Youngs at Formosa Place, Cookham

APPENDIX A

1910

7 June
Virginia goes with the Bells, their child and domestic staff to The Moat House, Blean, near Canterbury

21 June
Vanessa returns to London and consults Dr Savage about Virginia's health

30 June–
c. 10 August
Virginia undergoes a rest cure at Miss Thomas's private Nursing Home, Burley Park, Twickenham

c. 16 August 1–
6 September
Virginia goes on a walking tour in Cornwall with Miss Jean Thomas

19 August
Birth of Claudian [Quentin] Bell at 46 Gordon Square

6 September
Virginia returns to London

10 September
Virginia goes to Studland with Saxon Sydney-Turner to join Clive and Julian Bell; Vanessa and baby arrive on 13th. Visitors include Desmond and Mary (Molly) MacCarthy, Sydney and Alice Waterlow, Marjorie Strachey, and H. T. J. Norton

10 October
Virginia returns to 29 Fitzroy Square

15–18 October
Virginia stays at Court Place, Iffley, Oxford, with Pearsall Smiths and Costelloes

8 November–
15 January
The first Post-Impressionist exhibition (*Manet and the Post-Impressionists*), organised by Roger Fry, shown at the Grafton Galleries, London

November–
December
Virginia resumes her activity on behalf of Women's Suffrage; she visits Miss Thomas at Twickenham; she spends a week-end with the Cornishes at Eton; and one with Violet Dickinson at Welwyn

24 December
Virginia and Adrian stay at The Pelham Arms, Lewes, for a week; she visits Saxon Sydney-Turner and his parents at Brighton; Miss Thomas joins her for a day; she finds a house to rent in Firle

1911

1 January
Virginia and Adrian return to 29 Fitzroy Square. During January she takes possession of, and starts to furnish, Little Talland House, Firle

19–23 January
Virginia stays at Court Place, Iffley, and Bagley Wood, near Oxford, with Rachel and Karin Costelloe and Marjorie Strachey; she meets Katherine (Ka) Cox

4–6 February
Virginia and Vanessa at Firle completing the furnishing of Little Talland House

April
Virginia at Firle with two servants; her guests include Rachel Costelloe, Ka Cox, Elinor Darwin. Eight chapters of *Melymbrosia* completed

c. 22 April
Virginia sets out for Broussa, Turkey, where Vanessa, travelling with Clive Bell, Roger Fry and H. T. J. Norton, has fallen ill

1911

29 April	Virginia with Bells and Roger Fry return by Orient Express to London
May–June	Virginia mostly at 29 Fitzroy Square, with visits to Firle, where Ka Cox stays with her; to Cambridge for the wedding of Jacques Raverat and Gwen Darwin on 27 May; and to Durbins, Guildford (Roger Fry's house)
3 July	Leonard Woolf, on leave from Ceylon, dines with the Bells at 46 Gordon Square; Virginia, Duncan Grant and Walter Lamb come in after dinner
July	Virginia and Adrian plan to give up 29 Fitzroy Square in favour of a new system of living; they consider sharing a house in Bedford Square with friends
20 July	Virginia and Walter Lamb make an excursion to Richmond Park; his 'declaration'
22–25 July	Virginia at Firle; Janet Case to stay for two days
27 July and 9 August	Virginia visits Vanessa at Millmead Cottage, Guildford, where she is convalescing
12–14 August	Virginia stays with Philip and Lady Ottoline Morrell at Peppard Common
14–19 August	Virginia stays at The Old Vicarage, Grantchester, with Rupert Brooke
19–26 August	Virginia at Firle with her servants, Sophia and Maud
c. 27–30 August	Virginia and Ka Cox go to camp near Clifford Bridge, Drewsteignton, Devon, with Rupert Brooke, Maynard Keynes and others
31 August	Virginia back at Firle
16–19 September	Leonard Woolf and Marjorie Strachey stay with Virginia at Firle
19–27 September	Virginia in lodgings at 2 Harmony Cottages, Studland, near the Bells; Lytton Strachey and Roger Fry with his family also at Studland
October	Virginia engages in negotiations over Asham House, Beddingham, and 38 Brunswick Square, Bloomsbury. She goes to the *Ring* cycle at Covent Garden; and sees Leonard Woolf frequently
4–6 November	Virginia goes to Cambridge to stay with Francis and Frances Cornford
11–14 November	Virginia with Vanessa and Adrian (and Duncan Grant?) go to Firle; they go to see and measure Asham House
14–19 November	Virginia sleeps at 46 Gordon Square during the establishment of her new home
20 November	Virginia starts living at 38 Brunswick Square, W.C.1, a house shared with Adrian, Maynard Keynes, Duncan Grant and, after 4 December, Leonard Woolf

APPENDIX A

1911

6 December Virginia writes to Sydney Waterlow to say that she cannot love him. To Firle for the week-end with Vanessa

Christmas Day Luncheon party at 46 Gordon Square: the Bells, Virginia, Leonard Woolf, Maynard Keynes and Duncan Grant. Adrian is in a Nursing Home

1912

11 January Leonard Woolf comes up from Somerset and proposes to Virginia at 38 Brunswick Square

13–15 January Virginia at Firle

16–19 January Virginia goes to Niton, Isle of Wight, to stay with Vanessa; on her return to London she falls ill

3–5 February Virginia's housewarming party at Asham, with Adrian, Marjorie Strachey and Leonard Woolf

9–12 February The Bells' housewarming party at Asham, with Virginia, Adrian, Duncan Grant, Roger Fry and Leonard Woolf

16 February Virginia enters Miss Thomas's Nursing Home at Twickenham for a rest cure

28 February Virginia goes to Asham for further rest and quiet

March Virginia spends three week-ends at Asham: one with Vanessa, one with Ka Cox, and on the 16th with Vanessa, Adrian, Leonard Woolf, Roger Fry and Marjorie Strachey

9 March Virginia sees a psychologist, Dr Wright

April Virginia mostly at Asham; her guests there include Leonard Woolf and Ka Cox

2 May Virginia returns to 38 Brunswick Square

7 May Leonard Woolf's resignation accepted by the Colonial Office

29 May Virginia Stephen agrees to marry Leonard Woolf

APPENDIX B

Report on Teaching at Morley College

This report, a heavily corrected draft in Virginia's handwriting, is headed:

July 1905

This is the season for another report upon that class of working women whom I have already mentioned.

It was to be a class of history this time; in spite of the fact that those in authority looked rather coldly on it; history they told me, was the least popular subject in the College; at the same time they could not confute me when I asserted that it was also one of the most important. My class it is true dropped instantly to half its previous size; I had four instead of a possible eight; but then those four were regular attendants, & they came with one serious desire in common. The change then, was to my liking.

I have already described those four working women; so that my remarks this time are merely a development of that tentative sketch. Only in one instance did I find that I must reconsider my judgment. That Miss Williams whom I described as the 'least interesting of my class' 'rather handsome & well dressed – with wits sharpened in the streets, inattentive & critical' came to the first history class, & to my surprise hardly missed a Wednesday throughout the term. One night, too, I so far cornered her as to make her reveal herself; she then told me that she was a reporter on the staff of a Religious paper – reported sermons in shorthand – did typewriting, & also wrote reviews of books; the germ of a literary lady in short! & a curious one. Here was literature stripped of the least glamour of art: words were handled by this woman as that other one manipulated the bottles of a patent mouth wash. She was a writing machine to be set in motion by the editor. For some reason, unconnected with the author, the notice was to be favourable or unfavourable; but to record this notice it was not necessary by any means to read the book; that indeed would be impossible, considering the number of reviews to be turned out; but with a little practise it was easy to get sufficient material to support your statements by a rapid turning of the pages with a keen eye; quotations picked up at random need only be linked together by a connecting word, & the column was filled out of someone else's pocket. But at the same time, as she made no pretence that her work was of any higher nature than this so there seemed to be no reason to condemn it; indeed she was certainly of a higher level of intelligence than the other women.

The three other girls have been described already: the two friends, &

one of the two sisters, who came last term. This sister, Burke was her name, had been as I found, writing that account of her own life which I had suggested before. It did not take up many pages, & only described certain memories of childhood; it was a curious little production, floundering among long words, & involved periods, with sudden ponderous moral sentiments thrown into the midst. But she could write grammatical sentences, which followed each other logically enough; & she had evidently some facility of expression; in other circumstances I suppose, she would have been a writer!

The faithful pair of friends sat receptive & open mouthed as usual. Meanwhile, I had to administer each week some semblance of English history. Each week I read through a reign or two in Freeman or Green; noting as I went. Each time I tried to include one good 'scene' upon which I hoped to concentrate their interest. I talked from notes, with as little actual reading as possible. I found it not difficult to skim along fluently—though superficially; & I tried to make the real interest of history—as it appears to me—visible to them. Then they were provided with a sheet of hard dates to take home with them; so that they might have something solid to cling to in the vagueness of my speech. So we made our way through Early British, & Romans, & Angles Saxons & Danes, & Normans, till we were on the more substantial ground of the Plantagenet Kings. I do not know how many of the phantoms that passed through that dreary school room left any image of themselves upon the women; I used to ask myself how is it *possible* to make them feel the flesh & blood in these shadows? So thin is the present to them; must not the past remain a spectre always? Of course it was not possible in the way I took to make them know anything accurately; my task, as I conceived it, was rather to prepare the soil for future sowers. Pictures I showed them, & I lent them books; sometimes they seemed to gape not in mere impotent wonder, but to be trying to piece together what they heard; to seek reasons; to connect ideas. On the whole they were possessed of more intelligence than I expected; though that intelligence was almost wholly uncultivated. But of this I am convinced; what it would not be hard to educate them sufficiently to give them a new interest in life; They have tentacles languidly stretching forth from their minds, feeling vaguely for substance, & easily applied by a guiding hand to something that [they] could really grasp.

But like all other educational establishments, Morley College has to effect compromises & to prefer the safeness of mediocrity to the possible dangers of a high ideal. That is one way of saying that they would rather that a great number should learn a less valuable subject, like English Composition, than that a few should be encouraged to the study of English History. Accordingly I am to stop at King John: & turn my mind next term to essay writing & the expression of ideas. Meanwhile, my four women can hear eight lectures on the French Revolution if they wish to continue their historical learning. And what,

I ask, will be the use of that? Eight lectures dropped into their minds, like meteors from another sphere impinging on this planet, & dissolving in dust again. Such disconnected fragments will these eight lectures be: to people who have absolutely no power of receiving them as part of a whole, & applying them to their proper ends.

(MH/A 22)

APPENDIX C
Virginia Woolf and the Authors of *Euphrosyne*

Euphrosyne was published in the summer of 1905. Virginia wrote the following commentary on its authors and dated it 21st May 1906. The manuscript contains a great many deletions and corrections (which I have not attempted to reproduce); it appears to be unfinished.

Among all the advantages of that sex which is soon, we read, to have no [dis]advantages,* there is much to be said surely for that respectable custom which allows the daughter to educate herself at home, while the son is educated by others abroad.

At least I am fain to think that system beneficial which preserves her from the omniscience, the early satiety, the melancholy self satis- faction which a training at either of our great universities produces in her brothers. You see a pink cheeked boy whose only talk is of cricket, & whose most ardent admiration is kept for some champion of the ball or bat, enter upon his first term at Oxbridge, & you predict in your mild maidenly way, all kinds of manly triumphs for him there, & assure him that this will be the happiest time in his life, that is the phrase which parents use, & Aunts, & elderly bachelors; & from this un- animous Chorus one would think that life was a very poor business save for those three or four years at College & that if he failed to enjoy those, you had not much to promise him in this world or the next— unless indeed there is some kind of university in the fields of Paradise.

But it must be either that this is one of those parental fictions, like the existence of the Good Santa Claus, with which it is thought fit to veil the dreary truth from the eyes of the young, or, times have changed very much since our parents & uncles & elderly bachelor friends were happy at Oxbridge.

For when those three years of happiness are over, the result is one that suggests that the word has taken on a new, & peculiar meaning. They come from their University, pale, preoccupied & silent; as though in their three years absence, some awful communication had been made them, & they went burdened with a secret too dreadful to impart. Such a one is S.T., & G.L.S. & C.B. & W.L.;† others I might name if I chose to continue the dismal catalogue. But they entered the College, young & ardent & conceited; pleased with themselves, but so well pleased with the world that their vanity might be forgiven them. They return not less impressed with their own abilities indeed, but that

* The text reads : ~~There is certainly one advantage in~~ Among all the ~~dis~~ advantages of that sex which is soon, we read, to have no advantages.
† i.e. Saxon Sydney-Turner, Lytton Strachey, Clive Bell and Walter Lamb.

VIRGINIA WOOLF

is the last illusion that is left to them. The things they once found pleasing, please them no longer; they neither play nor work. They fail to pass their Examinations, because they say, that success is failure & they despise success.

It is perhaps because they fear to fall a victim to its snares that they are generally silent, & express for the most part a serene & universal ignorance; which does not disqualify them however to pronounce the opinions of others absurd.

They admire, however, the works of minor French poets, & crown certain English authors with the epithets "supreme" & "astounding"; but if the public show signs of appreciating the same things [they dexterously transfer their praise to some more obscure head].*

But their most permanent & unqualified admiration is reserved for the works which, unprinted as yet, "unprintable" they proudly give you to understand, repose in the desks of their immediate friends. For it is characteristic of them, that they live closely in one 'set', & made but few acquaintances outside it. They met on Sundays, when it was pleasant to picture the respectable world on its knees, & read these astoundingly brilliant & immoral productions; or, with the help of a table cloth, acted the clergyman himself, & annihilated the Christian faith in the doctrines that fell from his lips.

Some few songs & sonnets that were embedded in these gigantic works, were graciously issued to the public some little time ago, carelessly, as though the Beast could hardly appreciate such fare, even when simplified & purified to suit his coarse but innocent palate, but ought perhaps to be allowed the chance of tasting it. The poets sang of Love & Death, & Cats, & Duchesses,† as other poets have sung before, & may, unless the race is extinct, sing yet again. [It was melodious/ But such sadness, they said had never been known before; & it was/ the work was/ it marked an era; a decadence that was beyond the decadence of Swinburne himself. its significance was something they only could understand/ so tremendous.‡] But when taxed with their melancholy the poets confessed that such sadness had never been known, & marked the last & lowest tide of decadence.

(MH/A 13b)

* This phrase is partly deleted in the text but seems necessary.
† The allusion is to Lytton Strachey's poem *The Cat*. Love and Death abound in the pages of *Euphrosyne*, and the *Song* by Walter Lamb is addressed to a Duchess.
‡ These phrases are deleted in the original text.

Clive Bell and the Writing of
The Voyage Out

Virginia Stephen to Clive Bell

29, Fitzroy Square, W. [n.d.]

My dear Clive,

Will you think me a great bore if I turn to the dreary subject again, & ask you whether you have anything to say about that unfortunate work? I have a feeling at this moment that it is all a mistake, & I believe you could tell me.

At any rate I put myself in your hands with great confidence: I dont really think you will be bored by my demands, & I believe you do speak the truth.

At the same time, I groan over my egoism that wont let me or anyone else think of better things.

yr aff^{nt} AVS

Dont bother to write at length–in fact, dont write if you had rather not

Clive Bell to Virginia Stephen

Sunday night.
[? October 1908]

46, Gordon Square,
Bloomsbury.

My dear Virginia,

I find it hard to believe that you really attach importance to my opinion of your work. But to relieve myself rather than you I send this note which will be of greater interest when you have recovered your manuscript.

To my apprehension, the wonderful thing that I looked for is there unmistakeably: one can always recognise it when one gets that glimpse of the thrilling real beneath the dull apparent. Surely there can't be the least doubt, even in your own mind, about Geranium's (sic) entry with his wife Lucila (or Helen), page 36, and the description on page seven, nor yet about the Daloways' first night on board and pages 76 & 77. So, in spite of the immaturity–crudity even–and some places jagged like saws, that make my sensitive parts feel very much what the Christian martyrs must have felt, I believe this first novel will become a work that counts. 'Become', I say, because seven chapters never are, or never ought to be, a work of any sort.

Of course there are things such as page, 23, spots in the Sir T.B. conversation, ('Death soft and dark as velvet'), page 33, and other simillar or smaller excrescences, which fill me with horror and some fear; and I don't know how far they can be mended.

To give a sense of matter need one make so much use of words like 'solid' and 'block'—they become irritating: imaginations too, must they glimmer & shimmer always or be quite so often 'shadowy'.

But the style, the general form, (in its extreme oddity the lucidity of which however I believe I can appreciate & which will, I fancy develope & unroll itself quite harmoniously) the presentation of your ideas, seem to me an immense improvement on all your other descriptive writing. The first 3 pages are so beautiful as almost to reconcile me with your most feverish prose.

There are a hundred things that I long to talk or ask about, but I have time for this only; your power (to which I think I have always done justice) of lifting the veil & showing inanimate things in the mystery & beauty of their reality appears once or twice to equal–to excel rather–well never mind–; it is all very exciting and delightful, but in a day or two I hope to feel more securely critical.

Yrs ever
CB.

Clive Bell to Virginia Stephen

Friday
[? 5 February 1909]

46, Gordon Square,
Bloomsbury.

My dear Virginia,

if you really expected me to be disappointed with Melymbrosia, it must have been, I suppose, that you thought I might be disappointed with the last volume, that I should feel you have compromised with the Conventional & fallen away from the high–transcendent almost,– task, that you set yourself at the beginning. I do not feel that, and presently I will tell you why. My quarrels are all, or nearly all, with Vol. 1. and that is still so far from being finished that one hesitates to criticise it. But I do think it will be a difficult matter to make it supple, and I don't know that I like the new draft as well as the old. We have often talked about the atmosphere that you want to give; that atmosphere can only be insinuated, it cannot be set down in so many words. In the old form it was insinuated throughout, in the new it is more definite, more obvious, &, to use a horrid expression–'less felt'–by the reader I mean.

APPENDIX D

To give an example; Rachel's day-dreams flood one's mind with an exquisitely delicate sense of Rachel on a ship, alone; the sea-gulls conjure up nothing but rather commonplace visions of sea-voyages for health & pleasure. The conversations, stiff though they were, created wonderful pictures of the speakers' surroundings; the conversations have for the most part gone, and that first difficult forenoon has gained in consequence; but the two letters from Helen, most interesting in themselves, are as stiff and unreal as the old conversations, and coming on the mind in the state which you have been able to produce, by what has gone before, they seem inappropriate. For the first volume, I suggest, less definition, and a reversion to the original plan of giving an atmosphere, which atmosphere you must remember has got to serve through chapters of incident & criticism which are coming later. In this part of your book I shouldn't bother much about the characters of your people; I think they tell their own story beautifully along with the ship, and the less one knows about their antecedents the better, perhaps. Then, I must tell you again that I think the first part too didactic, not to say priggish. Our views about men & women are doubtless quite different, and the difference does'nt matter much; but to draw such sharp & marked contrasts between the subtle, sensitive, tactful, gracious, delicately perceptive, & perspicacious women, & the obtuse, vulgar, blind, florid, rude, tactless, emphatic, indelicate, vain, tyrannical, stupid men, is not only rather absurd, but rather bad art, I think.

To sum up my animadversions, then;–I feel, in the first part, that to give more 'humanity' to your work, you have sacrificed the 'inhuman',–the super-natural–the magic which I thought as beautiful as anything that had been written these hundred years; in so far as the book is purely Virginia, Virginia's view of the world is perfectly artistic, but is'nt there some danger that she may forget that an artist, like God, should create without coming to conclusions; lastly, I think you should be careful not to wonder how some other novelist would have written your book,–as if he could have written it! If you can manage to extract all the meaning from this short paragraph (about 6 pages full) you will know all I have to say against Melymbrosia.

I can now say, with a clear conscience, what I really think about your novel–that it is wonderful. As I read it I was perhaps most struck by what I took for the improvement in its prose. It seemed to me that you gave your words a force that one expects to find only in the best poetry; they came as near the truth underlying them as it is possible for words to come I should think. This refers, of course, to particular passages; in some places the style was quite bald, but these I took to be mere notes; I don't think I need retract a word of my praise from any at all finished passage. Though Helen is by far the best character, the Dalloways enjoy the advantage of being more like the people whom the world knows. They are very amusing, and more than life-like; them you have stripped quite naked at all events, I am stunned & amazed by

VIRGINIA WOOLF

your insight, though you know I have always believed in it. Of Helen
I cannot trust myself to speak, but I suppose you will make Vanessa
believe in herself. Rachel is, of course, mysterious & remote, some
strange, wild, creature who has come to give up half her secret; but she
is quite convincing as one reads, and in no true sense of the word unreal.
I am not so sure about Valentine & Vinrace, though they are both
good characters & interesting. Now about the last part, it is of course,
at first sight, less startling – more customary. But the whole situation
is seen in such a new, such a curiously personal way, by Rachel, that I
think it is really the best part of the book. I cannot tell you how interested
I am in all the new old figures – the inmates of the hotel – seen so differently
by Rachel, as entities, and as combinations. At first I thought it a mistake
to put Rachel outside the hotel, later I saw the genius of it. And then the
pic-nic; that is why I say the novel has lost none of its early promise.
Honestly, I think it challenges comparison with Box Hill & holds its
own, & something more. Nothing could be more alive, or more subtle.
Nothing is said to show that it was just half a failure, but everybody
feels it, except Rachel who is thinking about better things. How on earth,
by telling us what it was like at noon, do you show us what it was like
at five, at sunset, and at night? Believe me the pic-nic is your master-
piece, it surpasses anything in the first volume. Now, how are you
going to finish it? Surely the Dalloways must appear again, & the
Mary Jane? Unless, indeed, you have invented some new, undream't
of form? Well, I shall see some day.

If parts of your novel are notes, what is to be said about this letter?
You must consider it the merest jotting down of stray ideas. It is sure to
be full of stupidities, and almost unintelligible I'm afraid in parts. I have
had no time to give it a semblance of form or even to find the right
word, I hope you will be able to make something of it, but besides
being rather unintelligible it is probably also illegible.

Yours affectionately
CB

Virginia Stephen to Clive Bell

29 Fitzroy
Sunday [? 7 February 1909]

My dear Clive,
You are really angelic to take so much pains to give reasons & advice.
They seem to me excellent; for you have laid your finger on spots
already suspected by me. I will only offer some explanation of the
wretched first volume. Those bare passages of biography were not
meant to remain in the text: they are notes, to solidify my own con-

APPENDIX D

ception of the peoples characters. I thought it a good plan to write them down; but having served their purpose, they shall go. Helens letter also was an experiment. When I read the thing over (one very grey evening) I thought it so flat & monotonous that I did not even feel 'the atmosphere': certainly there was no character in it. Next morning I proceeded to slash & rewrite, in the hope of animating it; & (as I suspect, for I have not re-read it) destroyed the one virtue it had–a kind of continuity: for I wrote it originally in a dream like state, which was at any rate, unbroken. My intention now is to write straight on, & finish the book; & then, if that day ever comes, to catch if possible the first imagination & go over the beginning again with broad touches, keeping much of the original draft, & trying to deepen the atmosphere–Giving the feel of running water, & not much else. I have kept all the pages I cut out; so the thing can be re-constructed precisely as it was. Your objection, that my prejudice against men makes me didactic 'not to say priggish', has not quite the same force with me; I don't remember what I said that suggests the remark; I daresay it came out, without my knowledge: but I will bear it in mind. I never meant to preach, & agree that like God, one should'nt. Possibly, for psychological reasons which seem to me very interesting, a man, in the present state of the world, is not a very good judge of his sex; and a 'creation' may seem to him 'didactic'. I admit the justice of your hint that sometimes I have had an inkling of the way the book might be written by other people. It is very difficult to fight against it; as difficult as to ignore the opinion of one's probable readers–I think I gather courage as I go on. The only possible reason for writing down all this, is that it represents roughly a view of one's own. My boldness terrifies me. I feel I have so few of the gifts that make novels amusing.

I expect your praise is immensely exaggerated: you (I guess) have so much more of the dramatic instinct than I have that you see it into my scenes. But I take praise very gratefully; long for some assurance that all my words are'nt vapour. They accumulate behind me in such masses– dreadful, if they are nothing but muddy water. I think myself that the last part is really the best; at least I have written it with far greater relish, & with the sense of having the thing before me. What vanity these sheets will seem, one of these days, when Melymbrosia is a dirty book on your shelves, which Julian tries to read, but can't! However, there are numbers of things that I should be interested to say about the book; & we need not always be thinking of posterity. I too write in haste, just before dressing to go out; I will only add that I have blind faith in my power of making sentences presentable, so that I leave bald patches gaily, to furbish up next winter.

I was a little afraid that you would accuse me of compromise; but I was also quite sure that, made as I am, that sequel was the only one possible. I want to bring out a stir of live men & women, against a background. I think I am quite right to attempt it, but it is immensely

211

difficult to do. Ah, how you encourage me! It makes all the difference. Are you really interested? I suppose so, since you say it; but you have no notion how pale & transparent it reads to me sometimes—though I write with heat enough. That will do, for one evening! ...

On 19 July 1917 Clive Bell wrote a very enthusiastic letter to Virginia praising '*The Mark on the Wall*'; he concluded by saying: "Shall I post this letter now and risk having said something terribly ridiculous, or shall I wait for the sober morning mood?"

Virginia Woolf to Clive Bell

Hogarth House, Paradise Road, Richmond, Surrey.
Tuesday [24 July 1917]

My dear Clive,
I've always thought it very fine – the way you run risks, though I don't see that there's much risk in sending such a letter to such a woman. You know you always told me I was notorious for vanity, & its still a fine plant, though growing old.

But please dont put it all down to vanity. I do like you to praise me, not only because of your gift for knowing whats what, but for what you would call sentimental reasons too—as for instance that you were the first person who ever thought I'd write well. We talked so much about writing too. ...

Clive Bell to Leonard Woolf

Charleston, Firle, Sussex.
24 August 1956.

... I have a notion that the earlier and less 'gossipy' letters—the letters in which Virginia talks about her writing and her difficulties as an artist—are the most interesting. I will confess that I very much hope you will print a letter dated "Tuesday, Hogarth House, and beginning "I've always thought it very fine etc". Vanity? Not exactly perhaps. But there is a sentence—"you were the first person who ever thought I'd write well", which seems to me the finest feather I shall ever be able to stick in my cap. ...

See also Clive Bell on Virginia Woolf in *Old Friends*, 1956, p. 93.

APPENDIX E
The Dreadnought Hoax

Hoax on Naval Authorities.

Colonel LOCKWOOD asked the First Lord of the Admiralty, whether a hoax has been played upon the naval authorities by the pretended visit of some Abyssinian princes; and, if so, whether he will take steps to prevent such conduct in future?

The FIRST LORD of the ADMIRALTY (Mr McKenna): I understand that a number of persons have put themselves to considerable trouble and expense in pretending to be a party of Abyssinians, and in this disguise visited one of His Majesty's ships. The question is being considered whether any breach of the law has been committed which can be brought home to the offenders.

Mr WILLIAM REDMOND: Will the right hon. Gentleman include in his inquiry an inquiry as to whether it is not a fact that these gentlemen conferred the Royal Abyssinian Order on the Admiral, who wrote to the King to know whether he could wear it, and will he wear it?

Mr McKENNA: I shall be relieved from the necessity of inquiring into that matter because I know it not to be true.

Colonel LOCKWOOD: Does the right hon. Gentleman think with me that the joke was a direct insult to His Majesty's flag?

Mr McKENNA: I think I have answered the question on the paper fully. The hon. and gallant Gentleman will not ask me to go further into a matter which is obviously the work of foolish persons.

Hansard, 24 February 1910

H.M.S. "Dreadnought" (Officers' Reception)

Captain FABER asked the First Lord of the Admiralty, if he would state what were the circumstances which led to the giving of an official reception by the commander-in-chief, Vice-Admiral Sir W. May, and the officers of H.M.S. "Dreadnought", to certain reputed Abyssinian princes and their staff; whether these reputed Abyssinians were received by the admiral and the officers of the ship with full naval honours; whether by the admiral's orders they were furnished with a special train on the return journey to London; and whether an inquiry had yet been held?

The FIRST LORD of the ADMIRALTY (Mr McKenna): With regard to the first part of the question, I would refer the hon. and gallant Gentleman to the reply given to the right hon. and gallant Gentleman the Member for Epping last Thursday. No flags were hoisted or salutes fired, and no special train was ordered by the Admiral.

Captain FABER: Is it not a fact that certain pairs of white kid gloves were actually purchased for the occasion, and can the right hon. Gentleman say who will pay the expense?

Mr McKENNA: I am afraid that the hon. and gallant Gentleman is better informed than I am, but if he will kindly give me notice of his question I will inquire into the matter.

Hansard, 2 March 1910

Virginia wrote an account of her part in this hoax in the form of a paper which she read to the Women's Institute in Rodmell during the summer of 1940. The Memoir Club heard it soon afterwards; E. M. Forster mentions it: 'an unpublished paper which she herself once wrote for a Women's Institute, leaving it helpless with laughter', in his Rede Lecture, *Virginia Woolf* (Cambridge, 1942, p. 7). Only three pages of erratic typescript have been found. These I give.

friends we were told that the best thing we could do was to go to Mr McKenna who was then First Lord of the Admiralty and make a clean breast of it. We were told by a friend of Mr McKenna's that if we took all the blame on ourselves they would not take any steps against the admiral or the other officers. The House of Commons would be told that we had apologised and there would be an end of it. So my brother

A. & D. go
to McKenna.

and Duncan Grant went to the Admiralty and were shown in to Mr McKenna. And there they had a very queer interview. They tried to explain that they didn't want to get the admiral into trouble; and Mr McKenna dismissed the idea that such foolish people could get so great a man into a scrape, and pointed out that one of them had committed a forgery and was liable to go to gaol. So they argued at loggerheads. The truth was I think that Mr McKenna was secretly a good deal amused, and liked the hoax, but didn't want it repeated. At any rate he treated them as if they were school

boys, and told them not to do it again. But we heard afterwards that
Rules made.
one result of our visit had been that the regulations were
tightened up; and that rules were made about telegrams
that make it almost impossible now to repeat the joke. I am glad to think
that I too have been of help to my country. With that interview with
W.W.s visit
on Sunday.
the First Lord of the Admiralty we hoped that the affair
was over. But no—there was still the navy to reckon with.
I was just getting out of bed one Sunday morning soon
afterwards when there was a ring at the bell; and then I heard a man's
voice downstairs. I seemed to recognise the voice. It was my cousins. It
was Willy Fisher. And though I could [not] hear what he said I could
tell that he was saying something very forcible. At last the voices ceased and
my brother appeared. He was in his dressing gown. He looked very upset.
W.F.'s rage
And he told me that Willy Fisher had been in a tower-
ing rage; had said he had found out who we were. And
he was horrified. Did we realise that all the little boys ran after Admiral
May in the street calling out Bunga Bunga? Did we realise that we
owed our lives to the British Navy? Did we realise that we were im-
pertinent, idiotic? Did we realise that we ought to be whipped through
the streets, did we realise that if we had been discovered we should have
been stripped naked and thrown into the sea? And so on and so on. My
brother thought he was going to whip a knife out of his sleeve and
proceed to blows. But no, Willy Fisher explained that since my brother's
mother was his own Aunt, the rules of the Navy forbade any actual
physical punishment. Then he asked: 'I know who the others were; and
A. gives
addresses.
now you've got to tell me their addresses.' This my
brother did. The next moment he realised his mistake.
But it was too late. And Willy Fisher dashed out of the
house brushing aside the hand which my brother—who was after all
his first cousin—held out to him. We hadn't long to wait before we
Officers
call on D.
heard what happened next. Three naval officers were
waiting outside in a taxi. They drove off to the address
in Hampstead where Duncan Grant lived. Duncan Grant
was just sitting down to breakfast with his father and mother. They
sent word that a friend was outside and wished to speak to him. Duncan
Grant got up and went down into the street. One of the young men
tipped him up and flung him head foremost into [the taxi.] Mrs
Grant, who was looking out of the window saw her son disappear head
foremost and turned back in alarm. "What on earth are we to do"
she asked her husband. "Someone's kidnapping Duncan." Major Grant
who had been in the army himself merely smiled and said "I expect
its his friends from the Dreadnought." Duncan Grant found that he
D.G. alone.
was sitting on the floor at the feet of three large men
who carried a bundle of canes. Duncan asked where they
were taking him?

"You'll see plenty of Dreadnoughts where you're going" said Willy

Fisher. At last they stopped somewhere in a lonely part of Hampstead Heath. They all got out. Duncan Grant stood there like a lamb. It was useless to fight. They were three against one. And this rather upset them. Won't fight. "I can't make this chap out" said one of the officers. He doesnt put up any fight. You can't cane a chap like that". My cousin however ordered them to proceed. He was too high in the service to lend a hand himself. And so, very reluctantly, one of the junior officers took a cane and gave Duncan Grant two ceremonial taps. Then they said the honour of the navy was avenged. There was Duncan Grant standing without a hat in his bedroom slippers. They at once conceived an affection for him and I am not surprised. They were really sorry for him. "You can't go home like that" they said. But Duncan Grant felt that he would much rather go home in the tube in his slippers than be driven back by the officers. And so he shuffled off; and the officers disappeared in their car.

(MH/A 27)

In 1937, when Admiral Sir William Wordsworth Fisher died, Virginia wrote to Ethel Smyth:

Yes, I'm sorry about William—our last meeting was on the deck of the Dreadnought in 1910, I think; but I wore a beard. And I'm afraid he took it to heart a good deal. . . . (28 June 1937).

INDEX

This is not an exhaustive index. For the sake of brevity I have used the following contractions: VB for Vanessa Bell, VW for Virginia Woolf, 'ref:' for referred to.

INDEX

INDEX

INDEX

mental deficiency, 12; ref: 22, 26, 35

— Leslie, education, 7; loss of faith, 8–9; first marriage, 10, 11; widowed, 12; remarries, 14; portrait of Julia, 17–18; educates his children, 26, 27, 27n, 50, 51; financial anxieties, 39n; reactions to Julia's death, 40–41; resents Stella's engagement, 46, 47, 48, 52, 53; reconciled, 54; anger with VB, 62, 63, 64; refuses to intervene in her love affair, 72; his day, 73, 74, 75; accepts K.C.B., 82; has cancer, 82; illness and death, 84, 85, 86; mourned by VW, 87; biography of, 91; ref: 6, 19, 21, 28, 29, 31, 33, 36, 39, 43, 55, 60, 62, 62n, 70, 72, 89, 90, 91, 94, 96, 104, 114, 115, 116, 123, 124, 131

— Mary (née Cunningham, wife of Fitzjames, 'Aunt Stephen'), 8, 59, 66, 70

— Minny, see Harriet Marian

— Sibella (née Milner), 1, 2

— Thoby, birth, 18; character as a child, 22, 23, 23n; intellectual influence on VW, 27, 68; contributions to *Hyde Park Gate News*, 28, 29; at Clifton, 37, 50; at Cambridge, 70; reproves VB, 72; his 'Thursday Evenings', 97–9; his friends 'unsuitable', 100, 101; visit to Greece, illness, death, 109–10; efforts to commemorate, 112; possible influence on Bloomsbury, 113; ref: 24, 26, 31, 33n, 53, 55n, 65, 71, 76, 82, 84, 89, 90, 94, 95, 97, 98, 102, 104, 105, 114, 115, 116, 117, 120, 130

— Vanessa, see Bell, Vanessa

— Virginia, see Woolf, Virginia

— William (son of James Stephen of Ardenbraught), 1, 3

Strachey (family), described, 102; ref: 20

— James, 146, 171 and n, 173n

— Lytton, Thoby's friend, 69; contribution to *Euphrosyne*, 98; pre-eminent among his friends, 102; his sympathy, 113; he inspires awe, 121; makes Bloomsbury bawdy, 124 and n; character 129–30; VW's feelings for, 131; proposal, 141, 142 and n; VW's continued regard, 144, 186; breaks with Clive Bell, 166; relationship with Leonard Woolf, 177 and n, 178–79; ref: 70, 101, 112, 116, 119, 123, 128, 132, 134, 135, 142 and n, 143, 146, 152, 154, 166, 171, 173, 176, 183, 205 and n

— Marjorie, 166, 173, 179, 182

— Pernel, 105n

— Rachel (neé Costelloe), 173

Studland, Dorset, 152, 162, 165, 170

Swift, Jonathan, 18n, 101

Swinburne, A. C. (poet), 123, 206

Sydney-Turner, Saxon, Thoby's friend, 69; a wit? 98; contributes to *Euphrosyne*, 98; his manners, 99; his intelligence and sterility, 101, 102; considered as a lover, 128 and n; bantered, 147; with VW at Bayreuth, 149–51; his character, 151–52; ref: 97, 100, 103, 105n, 112, 113, 121, 123, 130, 132, 134, 136, 139, 142n, 162, 163, 166, 172, 176, 177, 205 and n

Symonds, John Addington, 60

— Katherine, see Furse, Katherine

— Margaret, see Vaughan, Madge

Talland House, St Ives, 30, 31, 32, 37, 80, 104, 118

Thackeray, Anne, see Ritchie, Anne

— Harriet Marian, see Stephen, Harriet Marian

225